Practical Hadoop Security

Bhushan Lakhe

Practical Hadoop Security

ISBN-13 (pbk): 978-1-4302-6544-3

ISBN-13 (electronic): 978-1-4302-6545-0

Managing Director: Welmoed Spahr
Acquisitions Editor: Robert Hutchinson
Developmental Editor: Linda Laflamme
Technical Reviewer: Robert L. Geiger
Editorial Board: Steve Anglin, Mark Beckner, Gary Cornell, Louise Corrigan, James DeWolf, Jonathan Gennick, Robert Hutchinson, Michelle Lowman, James Markham, Matthew Moodie, Jeff Olson, Jeffrey Pepper, Douglas Pundick, Ben Renow-Clarke, Gwenan Spearing, Matt Wade, Steve Weiss
Coordinating Editor: Rita Fernando
Copy Editor: James Fraleigh
Compositor: SPi Global
Indexer: SPi Global
Cover Designer: Anna Ishchenko

Distributed to the book trade worldwide by Springer Science+Business Media New York, 233 Spring Street, 6th Floor, New York, NY 10013. Phone 1-800-SPRINGER, fax (201) 348-4505, e-mail orders-ny@springer-sbm.com, or visit www.springeronline.com. Apress Media, LLC is a California LLC and the sole member (owner) is Springer Science + Business Media Finance Inc (SSBM Finance Inc). SSBM Finance Inc is a Delaware corporation.

For information on translations, please e-mail rights@apress.com, or visit www.apress.com.

Apress and friends of ED books may be purchased in bulk for academic, corporate, or promotional use. eBook versions and licenses are also available for most titles. For more information, reference our Special Bulk Sales–eBook Licensing web page at www.apress.com/bulk-sales.

Any source code or other supplementary material referenced by the author in this text is available to readers at www.apress.com. For detailed information about how to locate your book's source code, go to www.apress.com/source-code/.

To my beloved father . . . you will always be a part of me!

Contents at a Glance

Contents

About the Author

Bhushan Lakhe is a database professional, technology evangelist, and avid blogger residing in the windy city of Chicago. After graduating in 1988 from one of India's leading universities (Birla Institute of Technology & Science, Pilani), he started his career with India's biggest software house, Tata Consultancy Services. Soon sent to the UK on a database assignment, he joined ICL, a British computer company, and worked with prestigious British clients on database assignments. Moving to Chicago in 1995, he worked as a consultant with such Fortune 50 companies as Leo Burnett, Blue Cross and Blue Shield of Illinois, CNA Insurance, ABN AMRO Bank, Abbott Laboratories, Motorola, JPMorgan Chase, and British Petroleum, often in a critical and pioneering role.

After a seven-year stint executing successful Big Data (as well as Data Warehouse) projects for IBM's clients (and receiving the company's prestigious Gerstner Award in 2012), Mr. Lakhe spent two years helping Unisys Corporation's clients with Data Warehouse and Big Data implementations. Mr. Lakhe is currently working as Senior Vice President of Information and Data Architecture at Ipsos, the world's third largest market research corporation, and is responsible for the company's Global Data Architecture and Big Data strategy. Mr. Lakhe is active in the Chicago Hadoop community and regularly answers queries on various Hadoop user forums. You can find Mr. Lakhe on LinkedIn at `https://www.linkedin.com/pub/bhushan-lakhe/0/455/475`.

About the Technical Reviewer

Robert L. Geiger leads product strategy for Data Driven Business Solutions and Hybrid-Transactional Processing at TransLattice, Inc. Previously, he was an architect and team lead at Pivotal, working in the areas of Big Data system security, as well as Hadoop and Big Data as a service. Mr. Geiger served as Vice President of Engineering for Mu Dynamics (formerly Mu Security). Previously, he was Senior Director of Engineering at Symantec where he led the engineering team building Symantec's award-winning SNS Intrusion Protection product, after the acquisition of Recourse Technologies. Mr. Geiger spent 10 years at Motorola Labs working on electromagnetic systems modeling using massively parallel supercomputers, wireless data systems development, mobile security software, and e-commerce solutions. He holds several patents in the areas of mobile data, wireless security, and e-commerce. Mr Geiger has a Masters of Electrical Engineering degree from the University of Illinois, Urbana, and a Bachelor of Science degree in Electrical Engineering from the State University of New York.

Acknowledgments

While writing this book, I received help (both directly and indirectly) from a lot of people, and I would like to thank them all. Thanks to the Hadoop community and the user forums, from whom I have learned a great deal. There are many selfless people in the Hadoop community, and I feel that's the biggest strength of the "Hadoop revolution." In particular, thanks to my friend Satya Kondapalli for introducing Hadoop to me, and to my friends Naveed Asem and Zafar Ahmed for keeping me motivated!

I would like to thank the Intel Technical team (Bala Subramanian, Sunjay Karan, Manjunatha Prabhu) in Chicago for their help with Intel's Hadoop distribution and encryption at rest, as well as Cloudera's Justin Kestelyn for providing information about Sentry. Last, I would like to thank my friend Milind Bhandarkar (of Pivotal) for his help and support.

I am grateful to my editors, Linda Laflamme and Rita Fernando, at Apress for their help in getting this book together. Linda and Rita have been there throughout to answer any questions that I have, to read and improve my first (and second and third . . .) drafts, and to keep me on schedule! I am also very thankful to Robert Geiger for taking time to review my book technically. Bob always had great suggestions for improving a topic, recommended additional details, and, of course, resolved technical shortcomings!

Last, writing this book has been a lot of work, and I couldn't have done it without the constant support from my family. My wife, Swati, and my kids, Anish and Riya, have been very understanding. I'm looking forward to spending lots more time with all of them!

Introduction

Last year, I was designing security for a client who was looking for a reference book that talked about security implementations in the Hadoop arena, simply so he could avoid known issues and pitfalls. To my chagrin, I couldn't locate a single book for him that covered the security aspect of Hadoop in detail or provided options for people who were planning to secure their clusters holding sensitive data! I was disappointed and surprised. Everyone planning to secure their Hadoop cluster must have been going through similar frustration. So I decided to put my security design experience to broader use and write the book myself.

As Hadoop gains more corporate support and usage by the day, we all need to recognize and focus on the security aspects of Hadoop. Corporate implementations also involve following regulations and laws for data protection and confidentiality, and such security issues are a driving force for making Hadoop "corporation ready."

Open-source software usually lacks organized documentation and consensus on performing a particular functional task uniquely, and Hadoop is no different in that regard. The various distributions that mushroomed in last few years vary in their implementation of various Hadoop functions, and some, such as authorization or encryption, are not even provided by all the vendor distributions. So, in this way, Hadoop is like Unix of the '80s or '90s: Open source development has led to a large number of variations and in some cases deviations from functionality. Because of these variations, devising a common strategy to secure your Hadoop installation is difficult. In this book, I have tried to provide a strategy and solution (an open source solution when possible) that will apply in most of the cases, but exceptions may exist, especially if you use a Hadoop distribution that's not well-known.

It's been a great and exciting journey developing this book, and I deliberately say "developing," because I believe that authoring a technical book is very similar to working on a software project. There are challenges, rewards, exciting developments, and of course, unforeseen obstacles—not to mention deadlines!

Who This Book Is For

This book is an excellent resource for IT managers planning a production Hadoop environment or Hadoop administrators who want to secure their environment. This book is also for Hadoop developers who wish to implement security in their environments, as well as students who wish to learn about Hadoop security. This book assumes a basic understanding of Hadoop (although the first chapter revisits many basic concepts), Kerberos, relational databases, and Hive, plus an intermediate-level understanding of Linux.

How This Book Is Structured

The book is divided in five parts: Part I, "Introducing Hadoop and Its Security," contains Chapters 1, 2, and 3; Part II, "Authenticating and Authorizing Within Your Hadoop Cluster," spans Chapters 4 and 5; Part III, "Audit Logging and Security Monitoring," houses Chapters 6 and 7; Part IV, "Encryption for Hadoop," contains Chapter 8; and Part V holds the four appendices.

Here's a preview of each chapter in more detail:

- Chapter 1, "Understanding Security Concepts," offers an overview of security, the security engineering framework, security protocols (including Kerberos), and possible security attacks. This chapter also explains how to secure a distributed system and discusses Microsoft SQL Server as an example of secure system.

- Chapter 2, "Introducing Hadoop," introduces the Hadoop architecture and Hadoop Distributed File System (HDFS), and explains the security issues inherent to HDFS and why it's easy to break into a HDFS installation. It also introduces Hadoop's MapReduce framework and discusses its security shortcomings. Last, it discusses the Hadoop Stack.

- Chapter 3, "Introducing Hadoop Security," serves as a roadmap to techniques for designing and implementing security for Hadoop. It introduces authentication (using Kerberos) for providing secure access, authorization to specify the level of access, and monitoring for unauthorized access or unforeseen malicious attacks (using tools like Ganglia or Nagios). You'll also learn the importance of logging all access to Hadoop daemons (using the Log4j logging system) and importance of data encryption (both in transit and at rest).

- Chapter 4, "Open Source Authentication in Hadoop," discusses how to secure your Hadoop cluster using open source solutions. It starts by securing a client using PuTTY, then describes the Kerberos architecture and details a Kerberos implementation for Hadoop step by step. In addition, you'll learn how to secure interprocess communication that uses the RPC (remote procedure call) protocol, how to encrypt HTTP communication, and how to secure the data communication that uses DTP (data transfer protocol).

- Chapter 5, "Implementing Granular Authorization," starts with ways to determine security needs (based on application) and then examines methods to design fine-grained authorization for applications. Directory- and file-level permissions are demonstrated using a real-world example, and then the same example is re-implemented using HDFS Access Control Lists and Apache Sentry with Hive.

- Chapter 6, "Hadoop Logs: Relating and Interpretation," discusses the use of logging for security. After a high-level discussion of the Log4j API and how to use it for audit logging, the chapter examines the Log4j logging levels and their purposes. You'll learn how to correlate Hadoop logs to implement security effectively, get a look at Hadoop analytics and a possible implementation using Splunk.

- Chapter 7, "Monitoring in Hadoop," discusses monitoring for security. It starts by discussing features that a monitoring system needs, with an emphasis on monitoring distributed clusters. Thereafter, it discusses the Hadoop metrics you can use for security purposes and examines the use of Ganglia and Nagios, the two most popular monitoring applications for Hadoop. It concludes by discussing some helpful plug-ins for Ganglia and Nagios that provide security-related functionality and also discusses Ganglia integration with Nagios.

- Chapter 8, "Encryption in Hadoop," begins with some data encryption basics, discusses popular encryption algorithms and their applications (certificates, keys, hash functions, digital signatures), defines what can be encrypted for a Hadoop cluster, and lists some of the popular vendor options for encryption. A detailed implementation of HDFS and Hive data at rest follows, showing Intel's distribution in action. The chapter concludes with a step-by-step implementation of encryption at rest using Elastic MapReduce VM (EMR) from Amazon Web Services.

Downloading the Code

The source code for this book is available in ZIP file format in the Downloads section of the Apress web site (`www.apress.com`).

Contacting the Author

You can reach Bhushan Lakhe at `blakhe@aol.com` or `bclakhe@gmail.com`.

## PART I

Introducing Hadoop and Its Security

■ ■ ■

## CHAPTER 1

Understanding Security Concepts

In today's technology-driven world, computers have penetrated all walks of our life, and more of our personal and corporate data is available electronically than ever. Unfortunately, the same technology that provides so many benefits can also be used for destructive purposes. In recent years, individual hackers, who previously worked mostly for personal gain, have organized into groups working for financial gain, making the threat of personal or corporate data being stolen for unlawful purposes much more serious and real. Malware infests our computers and redirects our browsers to specific advertising web sites depending on our browsing context. Phishing emails entice us to log into web sites that appear real but are designed to steal our passwords. Viruses or direct attacks breach our networks to steal passwords and data. As Big Data, analytics, and machine learning push into the modern enterprise, the opportunities for critical data to be exposed and harm to be done rise exponentially.

If you want to counter these attacks on your personal property (yes, your data is your personal property) or your corporate property, you have to understand thoroughly the threats as well as your own vulnerabilities. Only then can you work toward devising a strategy to secure your data, be it personal or corporate.

Think about a scenario where your bank's investment division uses Hadoop for analyzing terabytes of data and your bank's competitor has access to the results. Or how about a situation where your insurance company decides to stop offering homeowner's insurance based on Big Data analysis of millions of claims, and their competitor, who has access (by stealth) to this data, finds out that most of the claims used as a basis for analysis were fraudulent? Can you imagine how much these security breaches would cost the affected companies? Unfortunately, only the breaches highlight the importance of security. To its users, a good security setup—be it personal or corporate—is always transparent.

This chapter lays the foundation on which you can begin to build that security strategy. I first define a security engineering framework. Then I discuss some psychological aspects of security (the human factor) and introduce security protocols. Last, I present common potential threats to a program's security and explain how to counter those threats, offering a detailed example of a secure distributed system. So, to start with, let me introduce you to the concept of security engineering.

Introducing Security Engineering

Security engineering is about designing and implementing systems that do not leak private information and can reliably withstand malicious attacks, errors, or mishaps. As a science, it focuses on the tools, processes, and methods needed to design and implement complete systems and adapt existing systems.

Security engineering requires expertise that spans such dissimilar disciplines as cryptography, computer security, computer networking, economics, applied psychology, and law. Software engineering skills (ranging from business process analysis to implementation and testing) are also necessary, but are relevant mostly for countering error and "mishaps"—not for malicious attacks. Designing systems to counter malice requires specialized skills and, of course, specialized experience.

Security requirements vary from one system to another. Usually you need a balanced combination of user authentication, authorization, policy definition, auditing, integral transactions, fault tolerance, encryption, and isolation. A lot of systems fail because their designers focus on the wrong things, omit some of these factors, or focus on the right things but do so inadequately. Securing Big Data systems with many components and interfaces is particularly challenging. A traditional database has one catalog, and one interface: SQL connections. A Hadoop system has many "catalogs" and many interfaces (Hadoop Distributed File System or HDFS, Hive, HBase). This increased complexity, along with the varied and voluminous data in such a system, introduces many challenges for security engineers.

Securing a system thus depends on several types of processes. To start with, you need to determine your security requirements and then how to implement them. Also, you have to remember that secure systems have a very important component in addition to their technical components: the human factor! That's why you have to make sure that people who are in charge of protecting the system and maintaining it are properly motivated. In the next section, I define a framework for considering all these factors.

Security Engineering Framework

Good security engineering relies on the following five factors to be considered while conceptualizing a system:

- **Strategy:** Your strategy revolves around your objective. A specific objective is a good starting point to define authentication, authorization, integral transactions, fault tolerance, encryption, and isolation for your system. You also need to consider and account for possible error conditions or malicious attack scenarios.

- **Implementation:** Implementation of your strategy involves procuring the necessary hardware and software components, designing and developing a system that satisfies all your objectives, defining access controls, and thoroughly testing your system to match your strategy.

- **Reliability:** Reliability is the amount of reliance you have for each of your system components and your system as a whole. Reliability is measured against failure as well as malfunction.

- **Relevance:** Relevance decides the ability of a system to counter the latest threats. For it to remain relevant, especially for a security system, it is also extremely important to update it periodically to maintain its ability to counter new threats as they arise.

- **Motivation:** Motivation relates to the drive or dedication that the people responsible for managing and maintaining your system have for doing their job properly, and also refers to the lure for the attackers to try to defeat your strategy.

Figure 1-1 illustrates how these five factors interact.

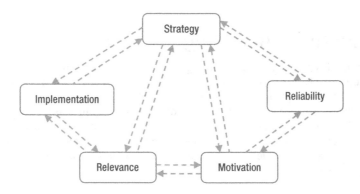

Figure 1-1. *Five factors to consider before designing a security framework*

CHAPTER 1 ■ UNDERSTANDING SECURITY CONCEPTS

Notice the relationships, such as strategy for relevance, implementation of a strategy, implementation of relevance, reliability of motivation, and so on.

Consider Figure 1-1's framework through the lens of a real-world example. Suppose I am designing a system to store the grades of high school students. How do these five key factors come into play?

With my objective in mind—create a student grading system—I first outline a *strategy* for the system. To begin, I must define levels of authentication and authorization needed for students, staff, and school administrators (the access policy). Clearly, students need to have only read permissions on their individual grades, staff needs to have read and write permissions on their students' grades, and school administrators need to have read permissions on all student records. Any data update needs to be an *integral transaction*, meaning either it should complete all the related changes or, if it aborts while in progress, then all the changes should be reverted. Because the data is sensitive, it should be encrypted—students should be able to see only their own grades. The grading system should be isolated within the school intranet using an internal firewall and should prompt for authentication when anyone tries to use it.

My strategy needs to be *implemented* by first procuring the necessary hardware (server, network cards) and software components (SQL Server, C#, .NET components, Java). Next is design and development of a system to meet the objectives by designing the process flow, data flow, logical data model, physical data model using SQL Server, and graphical user interface using Java. I also need to define the access controls that determine who can access the system and with what permissions (roles based on authorization needs). For example, I define the School_Admin role with read permissions on all grades, the Staff role with read and write permissions, and so on. Last, I need to do a security practices review of my hardware and software components before building the system.

While thoroughly testing the system, I can measure *reliability* by making sure that no one can access data they are not supposed to, and also by making sure all users can access the data they are permitted to access. Any deviation from this functionality makes the system unreliable. Also, the system needs to be available 24/7. If it's not, then that reduces the system's reliability, too. This system's *relevance* will depend on its impregnability. In other words, no student (or outside hacker) should be able to hack through it using any of the latest techniques.

The system administrators in charge of managing this system (hardware, database, etc.) should be reliable and *motivated* to have good professional integrity. Since they have access to all the sensitive data, they shouldn't disclose it to any unauthorized people (such as friends or relatives studying at the high school, any unscrupulous admissions staff, or even the media). Laws against any such disclosures can be a good motivation in this case; but professional integrity is just as important.

Psychological Aspects of Security Engineering

Why do you need to understand the psychological aspects of security engineering? The biggest threat to your online security is deception: malicious attacks that exploit psychology along with technology. We've all received *phishing* e-mails warning of some "problem" with a checking, credit card, or PayPal account and urging us to "fix" it by logging into a cleverly disguised site designed to capture our usernames, passwords, or account numbers for unlawful purposes. *Pretexting* is another common way for private investigators or con artists to steal information, be it personal or corporate. It involves phoning someone (the victim who has the information) under a false pretext and getting the confidential information (usually by pretending to be someone authorized to have that information). There have been so many instances where a developer or system administrator got a call from the "security administrator" and were asked for password information supposedly for verification or security purposes. You'd think it wouldn't work today, but these instances are very common even now! It's always best to ask for an e-mailed or written request for disclosure of any confidential or sensitive information.

Companies use many countermeasures to combat phishing:

- **Password Scramblers:** A number of browser plug-ins encrypt your password to a strong, domain-specific password by hashing it (using a secret key) and the domain name of the web site being accessed. Even if you always use the same password, each web site you visit will be provided with a different, unique password. Thus, if you mistakenly enter your Bank of America password into a phishing site, the hacker gets an unusable variation of your real password.

- **Client Certificates or Custom-Built Applications:** Some banks provide their own laptops and VPN access for using their custom applications to connect to their systems. They validate the client's use of their own hardware (e.g., through a media access control, or MAC address) and also use VPN credentials to authenticate the user before letting him or her connect to their systems. Some banks also provide client certificates to their users that are authenticated by their servers; because they reside on client PCs, they can't be accessed or used by hackers.

- **Two-Phase Authentication:** With this system, logon involves both a token password and a saved password. Security tokens generate a password (either for one-time use or time based) in response to a challenge sent by the system you want to access. For example, every few seconds a security token can display a new eight-digit password that's synchronized with the central server. After you enter the token password, the system then prompts for a saved password that you set up earlier. This makes it impossible for a hacker to use your password, because the token password changes too quickly for a hacker to use it. Two-phase authentication is still vulnerable to a real-time "man-in-the-middle" attack (see the "Man-in-the-Middle Attack" sidebar for more detail).

MAN-IN-THE-MIDDLE ATTACK

A man-in-the-middle attack works by a hacker becoming an invisible relay (the "man in the middle") between a legitimate user and authenticator to capture information for illegal use. The hacker (or "phisherman") captures the user responses and relays them to the authenticator. He or she then relays any challenges from the authenticator to the user, and any subsequent user responses to the authenticator. Because all responses pass through the hacker, he is authenticated as a user instead of the real user, and hence is free to perform any illegal activities while posing as a legitimate user!

For example, suppose a user wants to log in to his checking account and is enticed by a phishing scheme to log into a phishing site instead. The phishing site simultaneously opens a logon session with the user's bank. When the bank sends a challenge; the phisherman relays this to the user, who uses his device to respond to it; the phisherman relays this response to the bank, and is now authenticated to the bank as the user! After that, of course, he can perform any illegal activities on that checking account, such as transferring all the money to his own account.

Some banks counter this by using an authentication code based on last amount withdrawn, the payee account number, or a transaction sequence number as a response, instead of a simple response.

- **Trusted Computing:** This approach involves installing a TPM (trusted platform module) security chip on PC motherboards. TPM is a dedicated microprocessor that generates cryptographic keys and uses them for encryption/decryption. Because localized hardware is used for encryption, it is more secure than a software solution. To prevent any malicious code from acquiring and using the keys, you need to ensure that the whole process of encryption/decryption is done within TPM rather than TPM generating the keys and passing them to external programs. Having such hardware transaction support integrated into the PC will make it much more difficult for a hacker to break into the system. As an example, the recent Heartbleed bug in OpenSSL would have been defeated by a TPM as the keys would not be exposed in system memory and hence could not have been leaked.

- **Strong Password Protocols:** Steve Bellovin and Michael Merritt came up with a series of protocols for encrypted key exchange, whereby a key exchange is combined with a shared password in such a way that a man in the middle (phisherman) can't guess the password. Various other researchers came up with similar protocols, and this technology was a precursor to the "secure" (HTTPS) protocol we use today. Since use of HTTPS is more convenient, it was implemented widely instead of strong pass word protocol, which none of today's browsers implement.

- **Two-Channel Authentication:** This involves sending one-time access codes to users via a separate channel or a device (such as their mobile phone). This access code is used as an additional password, along with the regular user password. This authentication is similar to two-phase authentication and is also vulnerable to real-time man-in-the-middle attack.

Introduction to Security Protocols

A security system consists of components such as users, companies, and servers, which communicate using a number of channels including phones, satellite links, and networks, while also using physical devices such as laptops, portable USB drives, and so forth. *Security protocols* are the rules governing these communications and are designed to effectively counter malicious attacks.

Since it is practically impossible to design a protocol that will counter all kinds of threats (besides being expensive), protocols are designed to counter only certain types of threats. For example, the Kerberos protocol that's used for authentication assumes that the user is connecting to the correct server (and not a phishing web site) while entering a name and password.

Protocols are often evaluated by considering the possibility of occurrence of the threat they are designed to counter, and their effectiveness in negating that threat.

Multiple protocols often have to work together in a large and complex system; hence, you need to take care that the combination doesn't open any vulnerabilities. I will introduce you to some commonly used protocols in the following sections.

The Needham–Schroeder Symmetric Key Protocol

The *Needham–Schroeder Symmetric Key Protocol* establishes a *session key* between the requestor and authenticator and uses that key throughout the session to make sure that the communication is secure. Let me use a quick example to explain it.

A user needs to access a file from a secure file system. As a first step, the user requests a session key to the authenticating server by providing her *nonce* (a random number or a serial number used to guarantee the freshness of a message) and the name of the secure file system to which she needs access (step 1 in Figure 1-2). The server provides a session key, encrypted using the key shared between the server and the user. The session key also contains the user's nonce, just to confirm it's not a replay. Last, the server provides the user a copy of the session key encrypted using the key shared between the server and the secure file system (step 2). The user forwards the key to the secure file system, which can decrypt it using the key shared with the server, thus authenticating the session key (step 3). The secure file system sends the user a nonce encrypted using the session key to show that it has the key (step 4). The user performs a simple operation on the nonce, re-encrypts it, and sends it back, verifying that she is still alive and that she holds the key. Thus, secure communication is established between the user and the secure file system.

The problem with this protocol is that the secure file system has to assume that the key it receives from authenticating server (via the user) is fresh. This may not be true. Also, if a hacker gets hold of the user's key, he could use it to set up session keys with many other principals. Last, it's not possible for a user to revoke a session key in case she discovers impersonation or improper use through usage logs.

To summarize, the Needham–Schroeder protocol is vulnerable to replay attack, because it's not possible to determine if the session key is fresh or recent.

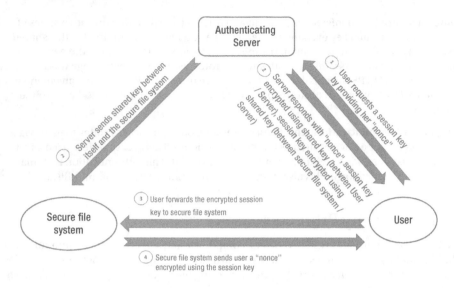

Figure 1-2. *Needham–Schroeder Symmetric Key Protocol*

Kerberos

A derivative of the Needham–Schroeder protocol, Kerberos originated at MIT and is now used as a standard authentication tool in Linux as well as Windows. Instead of a single trusted server, Kerberos uses two: an authentication server that authenticates users to log in; and a ticket-granting server that provides tickets, allowing access to various resources (e.g., files or secure processes). This provides more scalable access management.

What if a user needs to access a secure file system that uses Kerberos? First, the user logs on to the authentication server using a password. The client software on the user's PC fetches a ticket from this server that is encrypted under the user's password and that contains a session key (valid only for a predetermined duration like one hour or one day). Assuming the user is authenticated, he now uses the session key to get access to secure file system that's controlled by the ticket-granting server.

Next, the user requests access to the secure file system from the ticket-granting server. If the access is permissible (depending on user's rights), a ticket is created containing a suitable key and provided to the user. The user also gets a copy of the key encrypted under the session key. The user now verifies the ticket by sending a timestamp to the secure file system, which confirms it's alive by sending back the timestamp incremented by 1 (this shows it was able to decrypt the ticket correctly and extract the key). After that, the user can communicate with the secure file system.

Kerberos fixes the vulnerability of Needham–Schroeder by replacing random nonces with timestamps. Of course, there is now a new vulnerability based on timestamps, in which clocks on various clients and servers might be desynchronized deliberately as part of a more complex attack.

Kerberos is widely used and is incorporated into the Windows Active Directory server as its authentication mechanism. In practice, Kerberos is the most widely used security protocol, and other protocols only have a historical importance. You will learn more about Kerberos in later chapters, as it is the primary authentication used with Hadoop today.

Burrows–Abadi–Needham Logic

Burrows-Abadi-Needham (BAN) logic provides framework for defining and analyzing sensitive information. The underlying principle is that a message is authentic if it meets three criteria: it is encrypted with a relevant key, it's from a trusted source, and it is also fresh (that is, generated during the current run of the protocol). The verification steps followed typically are to

1. Check if origin is trusted,

2. Check if encryption key is valid, and

3. Check timestamp to make sure it's been generated recently.

Variants of BAN logic are used by some banks (e.g., the COPAC system used by Visa International). BAN logic is a very extensive protocol due to its multistep verification process; but that's also the precise reason it's not very popular. It is complex to implement and also vulnerable to timestamp manipulation (just like Kerberos).

Consider a practical implementation of BAN logic. Suppose Mindy buys an expensive purse from a web retailer and authorizes a payment of $400 to the retailer through her credit card. Mindy's credit card company must be able to verify and prove that the request really came from Mindy, if she should later disavow sending it. The credit card company also wants to know that the request is entirely Mindy's, that it has not been altered along the way. In addition, the company must be able to verify the encryption key (the three-digit security code from the credit card) Mindy entered. Last, the company wants to be sure that the message is new—not a reuse of a previous message. So, looking at the requirements, you can conclude that the credit card company needs to implement BAN logic.

Now, having reviewed the protocols and ways they can be used to counter malicious attacks, do you think using a strong security protocol (to secure a program) is enough to overcome any "flaws" in software (that can leave programs open to security attacks)? Or is it like using an expensive lock to secure the front door of a house while leaving the windows open? To answer that, you will first need to know what the flaws are or how they can cause security issues.

Securing a Program

Before you can secure a program, you need to understand what factors make a program insecure. To start with, using security protocols only guards the door, or access to the program. Once the program starts executing, it needs to have robust logic that will provide access to the necessary resources only, and not provide any way for malicious attacks to modify system resources or gain control of the system. So, is this how a program can be free of flaws? Well, I will discuss that briefly, but first let me define some important terms that will help you understand flaws and how to counter them.

Let's start with the term *program*. A program is any executable code. Even operating systems or database systems are programs. I consider a program to be secure if it exactly (and only) does what it is supposed to do—nothing else! An assessment of security may also be decided based on program's conformity to specifications—the code is secure if it meets security requirements. Why is this important? Because when a program is executing, it has capability to modify your environment, and you have to make sure it only modifies what you want it to.

So, you need to consider the factors that will prevent a program from meeting the security requirements. These factors can potentially be termed *flaws* in your program. A flaw can either be fault or a failure.

A *fault* is an anomaly introduced in a system due to human error. A fault can be introduced at the design stage due to the designer misinterpreting an analyst's requirements, or at the implementation stage by a programmer not understanding the designer's intent and coding incorrectly. A single error can generate many faults. To summarize, a fault is a logical issue or contradiction noticed by the designers or developers of the system after it is developed.

A *failure* is a deviation from required functionality for a system. A failure can be discovered during any phase of the software development life cycle (SDLC), such as testing or operation. A single fault may result in multiple failures (e.g., a design fault that causes a program to exit if no input is entered). If the functional requirements document contains faults, a failure would indicate that the system is not performing as required (even though it may be performing as specified). Thus, a failure is an apparent effect of a fault: an issue visible to the user(s).

Fortunately, not every fault results in a failure. For example, if the faulty part of the code is never executed or the faulty part of logic is never entered, then the fault will never cause the code to fail—although you can never be sure when a failure will expose that fault!

Broadly, the flaws can be categorized as:

- Non-malicious (buffer overruns, validation errors etc.) and

- Malicious (virus/worm attacks, malware etc.).

In the next sections, take a closer look at these flaws, the kinds of security breaches they may produce, and how to devise a strategy to better secure your software to protect against such breaches.

Non-Malicious Flaws

Non-malicious flaws result from unintentional, inadvertent human errors. Most of these flaws only result in program malfunctions. A few categories, however, have caused many security breaches in the recent past.

Buffer Overflows

A *buffer* (or *array* or *string*) is an allotted amount of memory (or RAM) where data is held temporarily for processing. If the program data written to a buffer exceeds a buffer's previously defined maximum size, that program data essentially overflows the buffer area. Some compilers detect the buffer overrun and stop the program, while others simply presume the overrun to be additional instructions and continue execution. If execution continues, the program data may overwrite system data (because all program and data elements share the memory space with the operating system and other code during execution). A hacker may spot the overrun and insert code in the system space to gain control of the operating system with higher privileges.[1]

Several programming techniques are used to protect from buffer overruns, such as

- Forced checks for buffer overrun;

- Separation of system stack areas and user code areas;

- Making memory pages either writable or executable, but not both; and

- Monitors to alert if system stack is overwritten.

Incomplete Mediation

Incomplete mediation occurs when a program accepts user data without validation or verification. Programs are expected to check if the user data is within a specified range or that it follows a predefined format. When that is not done, then a hacker can manipulate the data for unlawful purposes. For example, if a web store doesn't mediate user data, a hacker may turn off any client JavaScript (used for validation) or just write a script to interact with the web server (instead of using a web browser) and send arbitrary (unmediated) values to the server to manipulate a sale. In some cases vulnerabilities of this nature are due to failure to check default configuration on components; a web server that by default enables shell escape for XML data is a good example.

Another example of incomplete mediation is SQL Injection, where an attacker is able to insert (and submit) a database SQL command (instead of or along with a parameter value) that is executed by a web application, manipulating the back-end database. A SQL injection attack can occur when a web application accepts user-supplied

---

[1]Please refer to the IEEE paper "Beyond Stack Smashing: Recent Advances in Exploiting Buffer Overruns" by Jonathan Pincus and Brandon Baker for more details on these kind of attacks. A PDF of the article is available at http://classes.soe.ucsc.edu/cmps223/Spring09/Pincus%2004.pdf.

input data without thorough validation. The cleverly formatted user data tricks the application into executing unintended commands or modifying permissions to sensitive data. A hacker can get access to sensitive information such as Social Security numbers, credit card numbers, or other financial data.

An example of SQL injection would be a web application that accepts the login name as input data and displays all the information for a user, but doesn't validate the input. Suppose the web application uses the following query:

```
"SELECT * FROM logins WHERE name ='" + LoginName + "';"
```

A malicious user can use a LoginName value of "' or '1'='1" which will result in the web application returning login information for all the users (with passwords) to the malicious user.

If user input is validated against a set of defined rules for length, type, and syntax, SQL injection can be prevented. Also, it is important to ensure that user permissions (for database access) should be limited to least possible privileges (within the concerned database only), and system administrator accounts, like sa, should never be used for web applications. Stored procedures that are not used should be removed, as they are easy targets for data manipulation.

Two key steps should be taken as a defense:

- Server-based mediation must be performed. All client input needs to be validated by the program (located on the server) before it is processed.

- Client input needs to be checked for range validity (e.g., month is between January and December) as well as allowed size (number of characters for text data or value for numbers for numeric data, etc.).

Time-of-Check to Time-of-Use Errors

Time-of-Check to Time-of-Use errors occur when a system's state (or user-controlled data) changes between the check for authorization for a particular task and execution of that task. That is, there is lack of synchronization or serialization between the authorization and execution of tasks. For example, a user may request modification rights to an innocuous log file and, between the check for authorization (for this operation) and the actual granting of modification rights, may switch the log file for a critical system file (for example, /etc/password for Linux operating system).

There are several ways to counter these errors:

- Make a copy of the requested user data (for a request) to the system area, making modifications impossible.

- Lock the request data until the requested action is complete.

- Perform checksum (using validation routine) on the requested data to detect modification.

Malicious Flaws

Malicious flaws produce unanticipated or undesired effects in programs and are the result of code deliberately designed to cause damage (corruption of data, system crash, etc.). Malicious flaws are caused by viruses, worms, rabbits, Trojan horses, trap doors, and malware:

- A *virus* is a self-replicating program that can modify uninfected programs by attaching a copy of its malicious code to them. The infected programs turn into viruses themselves and replicate further to infect the whole system. A *transient virus* depends on its host program (the executable program of which it is part) and runs when its host executes, spreading itself and performing the malicious activities for which it was designed. A *resident virus* resides in a system's memory and can execute as a stand-alone program, even after its host program completes execution.

- A *worm*, unlike the virus that uses other programs as mediums to spread itself, is a stand-alone program that replicates through a network.

- A *rabbit* is a virus or worm that self-replicates without limit and exhausts a computing resource. For example, a rabbit might replicate itself to a disk unlimited times and fill up the disk.

- A *Trojan horse* is code with a hidden malicious purpose in addition to its primary purpose.

- A *logic trigger* is malicious code that executes when a particular condition occurs (e.g., when a file is accessed). A *time trigger* is a logic trigger with a specific time or date as its activating condition.

- A *trap door* is a secret entry point into a program that can allow someone to bypass normal authentication and gain access. Trap doors have always been used by programmers for legitimate purposes such as troubleshooting, debugging, or testing programs; but they become threats when unscrupulous programmers use them to gain unauthorized access or perform malicious activities. *Malware* can install malicious programs or trap doors on Internet-connected computers. Once installed, trap doors can open an Internet port and enable anonymous, malicious data collection, promote products (adware), or perform any other destructive tasks as designed by their creator.

How do we prevent infections from malicious code?

- Install only commercial software acquired from reliable, well-known vendors.

- Track the versions and vulnerabilities of all installed open source components, and maintain an open source component-security patching strategy.

- Carefully check all default configurations for any installed software; do not assume the defaults are set for secure operation.

- Test any new software in isolation.

- Open only "safe" attachments from known sources. Also, avoid opening attachments from known sources that contain a strange or peculiar message.

- Maintain a recoverable system image on a daily or weekly basis (as required).

- Make and retain backup copies of executable system files as well as important personal data that might contain "infectable" code.

- Use antivirus programs and schedule daily or weekly scans as appropriate. Don't forget to update the virus definition files, as a lot of new viruses get created each day!

Securing a Distributed System

So far, we have examined potential threats to a *program's* security, but remember—a distributed system is also a program. Not only are all the threats and resolutions discussed in the previous section applicable to distributed systems, but the special nature of these programs makes them vulnerable in other ways as well. That leads to a need to have multilevel security for distributed systems.

When I think about a secure distributed system, ERP (enterprise resource) systems such as SAP or PeopleSoft come to mind. Also, relational database systems such as Oracle, Microsoft SQL Server, or Sybase are good examples of secure systems. All these systems are equipped with multiple layers of security and have been functional for a long time. Subsequently, they have seen a number of malicious attacks on stored data and have devised effective countermeasures. To better understand what makes these systems safe, I will discuss how Microsoft SQL Server secures sensitive employee salary data.

For a secure distributed system, data is hidden behind multiple layers of defenses (Figure 1-3). There are levels such as authentication (using login name/password), authorization (roles with set of permissions), encryption (scrambling data using keys), and so on. For SQL Server, the first layer is a user authentication layer. Second is an authorization check to ensure that the user has necessary authorization for accessing a database through database role(s). Specifically, any connection to a SQL Server is authenticated by the server against the stored credentials. If the authentication is successful, the server passes the connection through. When connected, the client inherits authorization assigned to connected login by the system administrator. That authorization includes access to any of the system or user databases with assigned roles (for each database). That is, a user can only access the databases he is authorized to access—and is only assigned tables with assigned permissions. At the database level, security is further compartmentalized into table- and column-level security. When necessary, views are designed to further segregate data and provide a more detailed level of security. Database roles are used to group security settings for a group of tables.

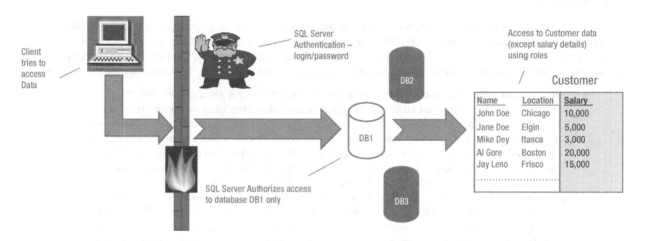

Figure 1-3. *SQL Server secures data with multiple levels of security*

In Figure 1-3, the user who was authenticated and allowed to connect has been authorized to view employee data in database DB1, except for the salary data (since he doesn't belong to role HR and only users from Human Resources have the HR role allocated to them). Access to sensitive data can thus be easily limited using roles in SQL Server. Although the figure doesn't illustrate them, more layers of security are possible, as you'll learn in the next few sections.

Authentication

The first layer of security is authentication. SQL Server uses a login/password pair for authentication against stored credential metadata. You can also use integrated security with Windows, and you can use a Windows login to connect to SQL Server (assuming the system administrator has provided access to that login). Last, a certificate or pair of asymmetric keys can be used for authentication. Useful features such as password policy enforcement (strong password), date validity for a login, ability to block a login, and so forth are provided for added convenience.

Authorization

The second layer is authorization. It is implemented by creating users corresponding to logins in the first layer within various databases (on a server) as required. If a user doesn't exist within a database, he or she doesn't have access to it.

Within a database, there are various objects such as tables (which hold the data), views (definitions for filtered database access that may spread over a number of tables), stored procedures (scripts using the database scripting language), and triggers (scripts that execute when an event occurs, such as an update of a column for a table or inserting of a row of data for a table), and a user may have either read, modify, or execute permissions for these objects. Also, in case of tables or views, it is possible to give partial data access (to some columns only) to users. This provides flexibility and a very high level of granularity while configuring access.

Encryption

The third security layer is encryption. SQL Server provides two ways to encrypt your data: symmetric keys/certificates and Transparent Database Encryption (TDE). Both these methods encrypt data "at rest" while it's stored within a database. SQL Server also has the capability to encrypt data in transit from client to server, by configuring corresponding public and private certificates on the server and client to use an encrypted connection. Take a closer look:

- **Encryption using symmetric keys/certificate:** A *symmetric key* is a sequence of binary or hexadecimal characters that's used along with an encryption algorithm to encrypt the data. The server and client must use the same key for encryption as well as decryption. To enhance the security further, a *certificate* containing a public and private key pair can be required. The client application must have this pair available for decryption. The real advantage of using certificates and symmetric keys for encryption is the granularity it provides. For example, you can encrypt only a single column from a single table (Figure 1-4)—no need to encrypt the whole table or database (as with TDE). Encryption and decryption are CPU-intensive operations and take up valuable processing resources. That also makes retrieval of encrypted data slower as compared to unencrypted data. Last, encrypted data needs more storage. Thus it makes sense to use this option if only a small part of your database contains sensitive data.

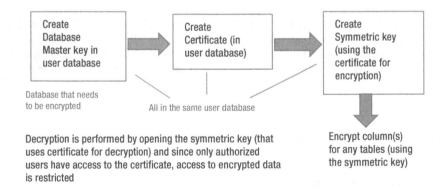

Figure 1-4. *Creating column-level encryption using symmetric keys and certificates*

- **TDE:** TDE is the mechanism SQL Server provides to encrypt a database completely using symmetric keys and certificates. Once database encryption is enabled, all the data within a database is encrypted while it is stored on the disk. This encryption is transparent to any clients requesting the data, because data is automatically decrypted when it is transferred from disk to the buffers. Figure 1-5 details the steps for implementing TDE for a database.

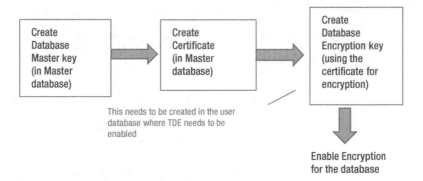

Figure 1-5. *Process for implementing TDE for a SQL Server database*

- **Using encrypted connections:** This option involves encrypting client connections to a SQL Server and ensures that the data in transit is encrypted. On the server side, you must configure the server to accept encrypted connections, create a certificate, and export it to the client that needs to use encryption. The client's user must then install the exported certificate on the client, configure the client to request an encrypted connection, and open up an encrypted connection to the server.

Figure 1-6 maps the various levels of SQL Server security. As you can see, data can be filtered (as required) at every stage of access, providing granularity for user authorization.

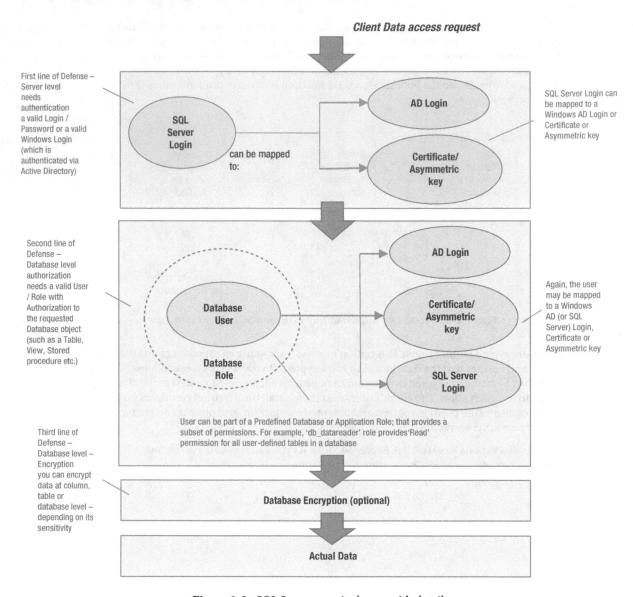

Figure 1-6. *SQL Server security layers with details*

Hadoop is also is a distributed system and can benefit from many of the principles you learned here. In the next two chapters, I will introduce Hadoop and give an overview of Hadoop's security architecture (or the lack of it).

Summary

This chapter introduced general security concepts to help you better understand and appreciate the various techniques you will use to secure Hadoop. Remember, however, that the psychological aspects of security are as important to understand as the technology. No security protocol can help you if you readily provide your password to a hacker!

Securing a program requires knowledge of potential flaws so that you can counter them. Non-malicious flaws can be reduced or eliminated using quality control at each phase of the SDLC and extensive testing during the implementation phase. Specialized antivirus software and procedural discipline is the only solution for malicious flaws.

A distributed system needs multilevel security due to its architecture, which spreads data on multiple hosts and modifies it through numerous processes that execute at a number of locations. So it's important to design security that will work at multiple levels and to secure various hosts within a system depending on their role (e.g., security required for the central or master host will be different compared to other hosts). Most of the times, these levels are authentication, authorization and encryption.

Last, the computing world is changing rapidly and new threats evolve on a daily basis. It is important to design a secure system, but it is equally important to keep it up to date. A security system that was best until yesterday is not good enough. It has to be the best today—and possibly tomorrow!

CHAPTER 2

■ ■ ■

Introducing Hadoop

I was at a data warehousing conference and talking with a top executive from a leading bank about Hadoop. As I was telling him about the technology, he interjected, "But does it have any use for us? We don't have any Internet usage to analyze!" Well, he was just voicing a common misconception. Hadoop is not a technology meant for analyzing web usage or log files only; it has a genuine use in the world of petabytes (of 1,000 terabytes apiece). It is a super-clever technology that can help you manage very large volumes of data efficiently and quickly—without spending a fortune on hardware.

Hadoop may have started in laboratories with some really smart people using it to analyze data for behavioral purposes, but it is increasingly finding support today in the corporate world. There are some changes it needs to undergo to survive in this new environment (such as added security), but with those additions, more and more companies are realizing the benefits it offers for managing and processing very large data volumes.

For example, the Ford Motor Company uses Big Data technology to process the large amount of data generated by their hybrid cars (about 25GB per hour), analyzing, summarizing, and presenting it to the driver via a mobile app that provides information about the car's performance, the nearest charging station, and so on. Using Big Data solutions, Ford also analyzes the data available on social media through consumer feedback and comments about their cars. It wouldn't be possible to use conventional data management and analysis tools to analyze such large volumes of diverse data.

The social networking site LinkedIn uses Hadoop along with custom-developed distributed databases, called Voldemort and Espresso, to power its voluminous amount of data, enabling it to provide popular features such as "People you might know" lists or the LinkedIn social graph at great speed in response to a single click. This wouldn't have been possible with conventional databases or storage.

Hadoop's use of low-cost commodity hardware and built-in redundancy are major factors that make it attractive to most companies using it for storage or archiving. In addition, features such as distributed processing that multiplies your processing power by the number of nodes, capability of handling petabytes of data at ease; expanding capacity without downtime; and a high amount of fault tolerance make Hadoop an attractive proposition for an increasing number of corporate users.

In the next few sections, you will learn about Hadoop architecture, the Hadoop stack, and also about the security issues that Hadoop architecture inherently creates. Please note that I will only discuss these security issues briefly in this chapter; Chapter 4 contains a more detailed discussion about these issues, as well as possible solutions.

Hadoop Architecture

The hadoop.apache.org web site defines Hadoop as "a framework that allows for the distributed processing of large data sets across clusters of computers using simple programming models." Quite simply, that's the philosophy: to provide a framework that's simple to use, can be scaled easily, and provides fault tolerance and high availability for production usage.

The idea is to use existing low-cost hardware to build a powerful system that can process petabytes of data very efficiently and quickly. Hadoop achieves this by storing the data locally on its *DataNodes* and processing it locally as well. All this is managed efficiently by the *NameNode*, which is the brain of the Hadoop system. All client applications read/write data through NameNode as you can see in Figure 2-1's simplistic Hadoop cluster.

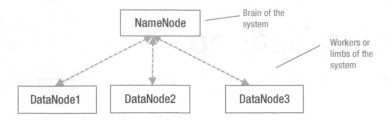

Figure 2-1. *Simple Hadoop cluster with NameNode (the brain) and DataNodes for data storage*

Hadoop has two main components: the Hadoop Distributed File System (HDFS) and a framework for processing large amounts of data in parallel using the MapReduce paradigm. Let me introduce you to HDFS first.

HDFS

HDFS is a distributed file system layer that sits on top of the native file system for an operating system. For example, HDFS can be installed on top of ext3, ext4, or XFS file systems for the Ubuntu operating system. It provides redundant storage for massive amounts of data using cheap, unreliable hardware. At load time, data is distributed across all the nodes. That helps in efficient MapReduce processing. HDFS performs better with a few large files (multi-gigabytes) as compared to a large number of small files, due to the way it is designed.

Files are "write once, read multiple times." Append support is now available for files with the new version, but HDFS is meant for large, streaming reads—not random access. High sustained throughput is favored over low latency.

Files in HDFS are stored as *blocks* and replicated for redundancy or reliability. By default, blocks are replicated thrice across DataNodes; so three copies of every file are maintained. Also, the block size is much larger than other file systems. For example, NTFS (for Windows) has a maximum block size of 4KB and Linux ext3 has a default of 4KB. Compare that with the default block size of 64MB that HDFS uses!

NameNode

NameNode (or the "brain") stores metadata and coordinates access to HDFS. Metadata is stored in NameNode's RAM for speedy retrieval and reduces the response time (for NameNode) while providing addresses of data blocks. This configuration provides simple, centralized management—and also a single point of failure (SPOF) for HDFS. In previous versions, a Secondary NameNode provided recovery from NameNode failure; but current version provides capability to cluster a Hot Standby (where the standby node takes over all the functions of NameNode without any user intervention) node in Active/Passive configuration to eliminate the SPOF with NameNode and provides NameNode redundancy.

Since the metadata is stored in NameNode's RAM and each entry for a file (with its block locations) takes some space, a large number of small files will result in a lot of entries and take up more RAM than a small number of entries for large files. Also, files smaller than the block size (smallest block size is 64 MB) will still be mapped to a single block, reserving space they don't need; that's the reason it's preferable to use HDFS for large files instead of small files.

Figure 2-2 illustrates the relationship between the components of an HDFS cluster.

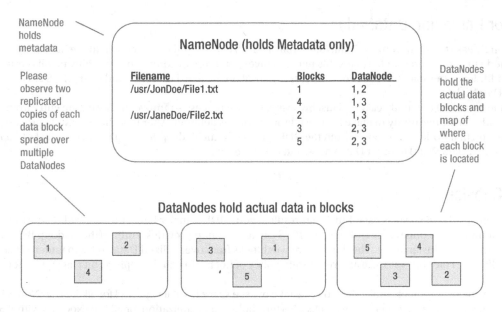

NameNode holds metadata

Please observe two replicated copies of each data block spread over multiple DataNodes

DataNodes hold the actual data blocks and map of where each block is located

Figure 2-2. *HDFS cluster with its components*

HDFS File Storage and Block Replication

The HDFS file storage and replication system is significant for its built-in intelligence of block placement, which offers a better recovery from node failures. When NameNode processes a file storage request (from a client), it stores the first copy of a block locally on the client—if it's part of the cluster. If not, then NameNode stores it on a DataNode that's not too full or busy. It stores the second copy of the block on a different DataNode residing on the same rack (yes, HDFS considers rack usage for DataNodes while deciding block placement) and third on a DataNode residing on a different rack, just to reduce risk of complete data loss due to a rack failure. Figure 2-2 illustrates how two replicas (of each block) for the two files are spread over available DataNodes.

DataNodes send heartbeats to NameNode, and if a DataNode doesn't send heartbeats for a particular duration, it is assumed to be "lost." NameNode finds other DataNodes (with a copy of the blocks located on that DataNode) and instructs them to make a fresh copy of the lost blocks to another DataNode. This way, the total number of replicas for all the blocks would always match the configured *replication factor* (which decides how many copies of a file will be maintained).

Adding or Removing DataNodes

It is surprisingly easy to add or remove DataNodes from a HDFS cluster. You just need to add the hostname for the new DataNode to a configuration file (a text file named slaves) and run an administrative utility to tell NameNode about this addition. After that, the DataNode process is started on the new DataNode and your HDFS cluster has an additional DataNode.

DataNode removal is equally easy and just involves a reverse process—remove the hostname entry from slaves and run the administrative utility to make NameNode aware of this deletion. After this, the DataNode process can be shut down on that node and removed from the HDFS cluster. NameNode quietly replicates the blocks (from decommissioned DataNode) to other DataNodes, and life moves on.

Cluster Rebalancing

Adding or removing DataNodes is easy, but it may result in your HDFS cluster being unbalanced. There are other activities that may create unbalance within your HDFS cluster. Hadoop provides a utility (the Hadoop Balancer) that will balance your cluster again. The Balancer moves blocks from overutilized DataNodes to underutilized ones, while still following Hadoop's storage and replication policy of not having all the replicas on DataNodes located on a single rack.

Block movement continues until utilization (the ratio of used space to total capacity) for all the DataNodes is within a threshold percentage of each other. For example, a 5% threshold means utilization for all DataNodes is within 5%. The balancer runs in the background with a low bandwidth without taxing the cluster.

Disk Storage

HDFS uses local storage for NameNode, Secondary NameNode, and DataNodes, so it's important to use the correct storage type. NameNode, being the brain of the cluster, needs to have redundant and fault-tolerant storage. Using RAID 10 (striping and mirroring your data across at least two disks) is highly recommended. Secondary NameNode needs to have RAID 10 storage. As far as the DataNodes are concerned, they can use local JBOD (just a bunch of disks) storage. Remember, data on these nodes is already replicated thrice (or whatever the replication factor is), so there is no real need for using RAID drives.

Secondary NameNode

Let's now consider how Secondary NameNode maintains a standby copy of NameNode metadata. The NameNode uses an image file called `fsimage` to store the current state of HDFS (a map of all files stored within the file system and locations of their corresponding blocks) and a file called `edits` to store modifications to HDFS. With time, the `edits` file can grow very large; as a result, the `fsimage` wouldn't have an up-to-date image that correctly reflects the state of HDFS. In such a situation, if the NameNode crashes, the current state of HDFS will be lost and the data unusable.

To avoid this, the Secondary NameNode performs a checkpoint (every hour by default), merges the `fsimage` and `edits` files from NameNode locally, and copies the result back to the NameNode. So, in a worst-case scenario, only the edits or modifications made to HDFS will be lost—since the Secondary NameNode stores the latest copy of `fsimage` locally. Figure 2-3 provides more insight into this process.

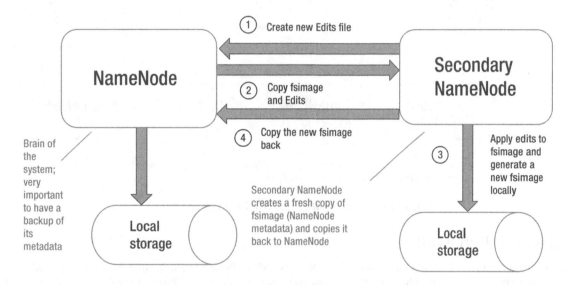

Figure 2-3. *Checkpoint performed by Secondary NameNode*

What does all this mean for your data? Consider how HDFS processes a request. Figure 2-4 shows how a data request is addressed by NameNode and data is retrieved from corresponding DataNodes.

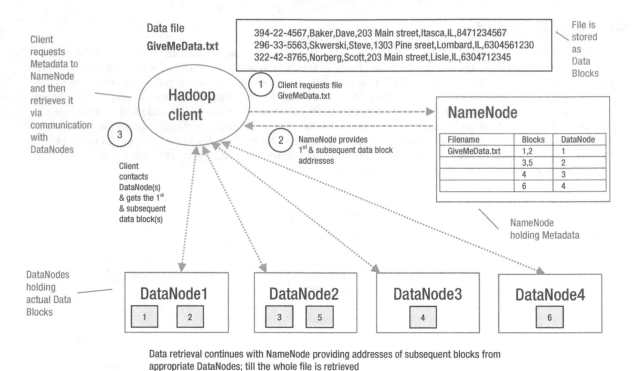

Figure 2-4. *Anatomy of a Hadoop data access request*

NameNode High Availability

As you remember from the Name Node section, NameNode is a SPOF. But if a Hadoop cluster is used as a production system, there needs to be a way to eliminate this dependency and make sure that the cluster will work normally even in case of NameNode failure. One of the ways to counter NameNode failure is using *NameNode high availability* (or *HA*), where a cluster is deployed with an active/passive pair of NameNodes. The edits write-ahead log needs to be available for both NameNodes (active/passive) and hence is located on a shared NFS directory. The active NameNode writes to the edits log and the standby NameNode replays the same transactions to ensure it is up to date (to be ready to take over in case of a failure). DataNodes send block reports to both the nodes.

You can configure an HA NameNode pair for manual or automatic failover (active and passive nodes interchanging roles). For manual failover, a command needs to be executed to have the Standby NameNode take over as Primary or active NameNode. For automatic failover, each NameNode needs to run an additional process called a *failover controller* for monitoring the NameNode processes and coordinate the state transition as required. The application ZooKeeper is often used to manage failovers.

In case of a failover, it's not possible to determine if an active NameNode is not available or if it's inaccessible from the standby NameNode. If both NameNode processes run parallel, they can both write to the shared state and corrupt the file system metadata. This constitutes a *split-brain* scenario, and to avoid this situation, you need to ensure that the failed NameNode is stopped or "fenced." Increasingly severe techniques are used to implement fencing; starting with a stop request via RPC (remote procedure call) to a *STONITH* (or "shoot the other node in the head") implemented by issuing a reboot remotely or (programmatically) cutting power to a machine for a short duration.

When using HA, since the standby NameNode takes over the role of the Secondary NameNode, no separate Secondary NameNode process is necessary.

Inherent Security Issues with HDFS Architecture

After reviewing HDFS architecture, you can see that this is not the traditional client/server model of processing data we are all used to. There is no server to process the data, authenticate the users, or manage locking. There was no security gateway or authentication mechanism in the original Hadoop design. Although Hadoop now has strong authentication built in (as you shall see later), complexity of integration with existing corporate systems and role-based authorization still presents challenges.

Any user with access to the server running NameNode processes and having execute permissions to the Hadoop binaries can potentially request data from NameNode and request deletion of that data, too! Access is limited only by Hadoop directory and file permissions; but it's easy to impersonate another user (in this case a Hadoop superuser) and access everything. Moreover, Hadoop doesn't enable you to provide role-based access or object-level access, or offer enough granularity for attribute-level access (for a particular object). For example, it doesn't offer special roles with ability to run specific Hadoop daemons (or services). There is an all-powerful Hadoop superuser in the admin role, but everyone else is a mere mortal. Users simply have access to connect to HDFS and access all files, unless file access permissions are specified for specific owners or groups.

Therefore, the flexibility that Hadoop architecture provides also creates vulnerabilities due to lack of a central authentication mechanism. Because data is spread across a large number of DataNodes, along with the advantages of distributed storage and processing, the DataNodes also serve as potential entry points for attacks and need to be secured well.

Hadoop clients perform metadata operations such as *create file* and *open file* at the NameNode using *RPC protocol* and read/write the data of a file directly from DataNodes using a streaming socket protocol called the *data-transfer protocol*. It is possible to encrypt communication done via RPC protocol easily through Hadoop configuration files, but encrypting the data traffic between DataNodes and client requires use of Kerberos or SASL (Simple Authentication and Security Layer) framework.

The HTTP communication between web consoles and Hadoop daemons (NameNode, Secondary NameNode, DataNode, etc.) is unencrypted and unsecured (it allows access without any form of authentication by default), as seen in Figure 2-5. So, it's very easy to access all the cluster metadata. To summarize, the following threats exist for HDFS due to its architecture:

- An unauthorized client may access an HDFS file or cluster metadata via the RPC or HTTP protocols (since the communication is unencrypted and unsecured by default).

- An unauthorized client may read/write a data block of a file at a DataNode via the pipeline streaming data-transfer protocol (again, unencrypted communication).

- A task or node may masquerade as a Hadoop service component (such as DataNode) and modify the metadata or perform destructive activities.

- A malicious user with network access could intercept unencrypted internode communications.

- Data on failed disks in a large Hadoop cluster can leak private information if not handled properly.

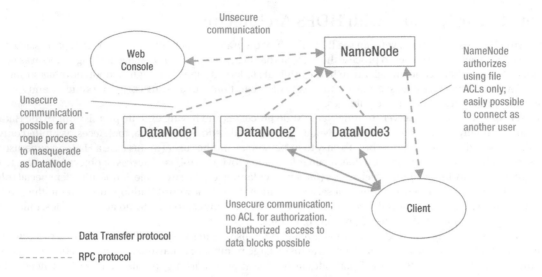

Figure 2-5. *Hadoop communication protocols and vulnerabilities*

When Hadoop daemons (or services) communicate with each other, they don't verify that the other service is really what it claims to be. So, it's easily possible to start a rogue TaskTracker to get access to data blocks. There are ways to have Hadoop services perform mutual authentication; but Hadoop doesn't implement them by default and they need configuration changes as well as some additional components to be installed. Figure 2-5 summarizes these threats.

We will revisit the security issues in greater detail (with pertinent solutions) in Chapters 4 and 5 (which cover authentication and authorization) and Chapter 8 (which focuses on encryption). For now, turn your attention to the other major Hadoop component: the framework for processing large amounts of data in parallel using MapReduce paradigm.

Hadoop's Job Framework using MapReduce

In earlier sections, we reviewed one aspect of Hadoop: HDFS, which is responsible for distributing (and storing) data across multiple DataNodes. The other aspect is distributed processing of that data; this is handled by Hadoop's job framework, which uses MapReduce.

MapReduce is a method for distributing a task across multiple nodes. Each node processes data stored on that node (where possible). It consists of two phases: Map and Reduce. The Map task works on a *split* or part of input data (a key-value pair), transforms it, and outputs the transformed intermediate data. Then there is a data exchange between nodes in a *shuffle* (sorting) process, and intermediate data of the same key goes to the same *Reducer*.

When a *Reducer* receives output from various mappers, it sorts the incoming data using the key (of the key-value pair) and groups together all values for the same key. The reduce method is then invoked (by the Reducer). It generates a (possibly empty) list of key-value pairs by iterating over the values associated with a given key and writes output to an output file.

The MapReduce framework utilizes two Hadoop daemons (JobTracker and TaskTracker) to schedule and process MapReduce jobs. The *JobTracker* runs on the master node (usually the same node that's running NameNode) and manages all jobs submitted for a Hadoop cluster. A JobTracker uses a number of *TaskTrackers* on slave nodes (DataNodes) to process parts of a job as required.

A *task attempt* is an instance of a task running on a slave (TaskTracker) node. Task attempts can fail, in which case they will be restarted. Thus there will be at least as many task attempts as there are tasks that need to be performed.

Subsequently, a MapReduce program results in the following steps:

1. The client program submits a job (data request) to Hadoop.

2. The job consists of a mapper, a reducer, and a list of inputs.

3. The job is sent to the JobTracker process on the master node.

4. Each slave node runs a process called the TaskTracker.

5. The JobTracker instructs TaskTrackers to run and monitor tasks (a Map or Reduce task for input data).

Figure 2-6 illustrates Hadoop's MapReduce framework and how it processes a job.

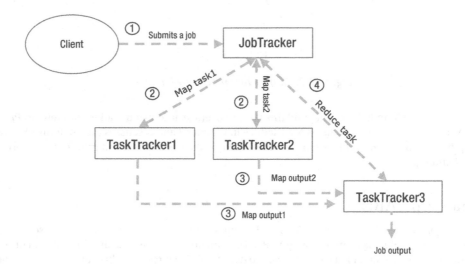

Figure 2-6. *MapReduce framework and job processing*

Task processes send heartbeats to the TaskTracker. TaskTrackers send heartbeats to the JobTracker. Any task that fails to report in 10 minutes is assumed to have failed and is killed by the TaskTracker. Also, any task that throws an exception is said to have failed.

Failed tasks are reported to the JobTracker by the TaskTracker. The JobTracker reschedules any failed tasks and tries to avoid rescheduling the task on the same TaskTracker where it previously failed. If a task fails more than four times, the whole job fails. Any TaskTracker that fails to report in 10 minutes is assumed to have crashed and all assigned tasks restart on another TaskTracker node.

Any TaskTracker reporting a high number of failed tasks is blacklisted (to prevent the node from blocking the entire job). There is also a *global blacklist* for TaskTrackers that fail on multiple jobs. The JobTracker manages the state of each job and partial results of failed tasks are ignored.

Figure 2-7 shows how the MapReduce paradigm works for input key-value pairs and results in a reduced output.

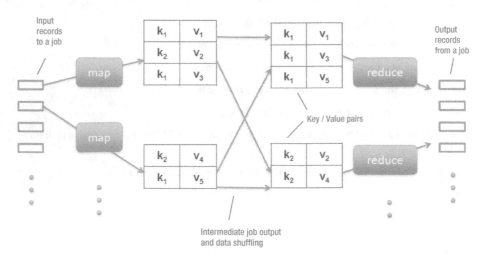

Figure 2-7. *MapReduce processing for a job*

A detailed coverage of MapReduce is beyond this book's coverage; interested readers can refer to *Pro Hadoop* by Jason Venner (Apress, 2009). Jason introduces MapReduce in Chapter 2 and discusses the anatomy of a MapReduce program at length in Chapter 5. Each of the components of MapReduce is discussed in great detail, offering an in-depth understanding.

Apache Hadoop YARN

The MapReduce algorithm used by earlier versions of Hadoop wasn't sufficient in many cases for scenarios where customized resource handling was required. With YARN, Hadoop now has a generic distributed data processing framework (with a built-in scheduler) that can be used to define your own resource handling. Hadoop MapReduce is now just one of the distributed data processing applications that can be used with YARN.

YARN allocates the two major functionalities of the JobTracker (resource management and job scheduling/ monitoring) to separate daemons: a global ResourceManager and a per-application ApplicationMaster. The ResourceManager and NodeManager (which runs on each "slave" node) form a generic distributed data processing system in conjunction with the ApplicationMaster.

ResourceManager is the overall authority that allocates resources for all the distributed data processing applications within a cluster. ResourceManager uses a pluggable *Scheduler* (of your choice—e.g., Fair or first-in, first-out [FIFO] scheduler) that is responsible for allocating resources to various applications based on their need. This Scheduler doesn't perform monitoring, track status, or restart failed tasks.

The per-application ApplicationMaster negotiates resources from the ResourceManager, works with the NodeManager(s) to execute the component tasks, tracks their status, and monitors their progress. This functionality was performed earlier by TaskTracker (plus the scheduling, of course).

The NodeManager is responsible for launching the applications' containers, monitoring their resource usage (CPU, memory, disk, network), and reporting it to the ResourceManager.

So, what are the differences between MapReduce and YARN? As cited earlier, YARN splits the JobTracker functionalities to ResourceManager (scheduling) and Application Master (resource management). Interestingly, that also moves all the application-framework-specific code to ApplicationMaster, generalizing the system so that multiple distributed processing frameworks such as MapReduce, MPI (Message Passing Interface, a message-passing system for parallel computers, used in development of many scalable large-scale parallel applications) and Graph Processing can be supported.

Inherent Security Issues with Hadoop's Job Framework

The security issues with the MapReduce framework revolve around the lack of authentication within Hadoop, the communication between Hadoop daemons being unsecured, and the fact that Hadoop daemons do not authenticate each other. The main security concerns are as follows:

- An unauthorized user may submit a job to a queue or delete or change priority of the job (since Hadoop doesn't authenticate or authorize and it's easy to impersonate a user).

- An unauthorized client may access the intermediate data of a Map job via its TaskTracker's HTTP shuffle protocol (which is unencrypted and unsecured).

- An executing task may use the host operating system interfaces to access other tasks and local data, which includes intermediate Map output or the local storage of the DataNode that runs on the same physical node (data at rest is unencrypted).

- A task or node may masquerade as a Hadoop service component such as a DataNode, NameNode, JobTracker, TaskTracker, etc. (no host process authentication).

- A user may submit a workflow (using a workflow package like Oozie) as another user (it's easy to impersonate a user).

As you remember, Figure 2-6 illustrated how the MapReduce framework processes a job. Comparing Figure 2-6 with Figure 2-8 will give you a better insight into the security issues with the MapReduce framework. Figure 2-8 details the security issues in the same context: job execution.

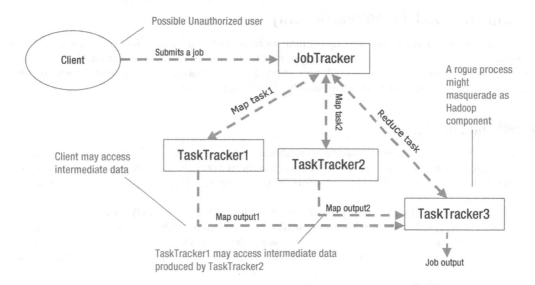

Figure 2-8. *MapReduce framework vulnerabilities*

Hadoop's Operational Security Woes

The security issues discussed so far stem from Hadoop's architecture and are not operational issues that we have to deal with on a daily basis. Some issues arise from Hadoop's relative newness and origins in isolated laboratories with insulated, secure environments. There was a time when Hadoop was "secured" by severely restricting network access to Hadoop clusters. Any access request had to be accompanied by several waivers from security departments and the requestor's own management hierarchy!

Also, some existing technologies have not had time to build interfaces or provide gateways to integrate with Hadoop. For example, a few features that are missing right now may even have been added by the time you read this. Like Unix of yesteryear, Hadoop is still a work in progress and new features as well as new technologies are added on a daily basis. With that in mind, consider some operational security challenges that Hadoop currently has.

Inability to Use Existing User Credentials and Policies

Suppose your organization uses single sign-on or active directory domain accounts for connecting to the various applications used. How can you use them with Hadoop? Well, Hadoop does offer LDAP (Lightweight Directory Access Protocol) integration, but configuring it is not easy, as this interface is still in a nascent stage and documentation is extremely sketchy (in some cases there is no documentation). The situation is compounded by Hadoop being used on a variety of Linux flavors, and issues vary by operating system used and its versions. Hence, allocating selective Hadoop resources to active directory users is not always possible.

Also, how can you enforce existing access control policies such as read access for application users, read/write for developers, and so forth? The answer is that you can't. The easiest way is to create separate credentials for Hadoop access and reestablish access control manually, following the organizational policies. Hadoop follows its own model for security, which is similar (in appearance) to Linux and confuses a lot of people. Hadoop and the Hadoop ecosystem combine many components with different configuration endpoints and varied authorization methods (POSIX file-based, SQL database-like), and this can present a big challenge in developing and maintaining security authorization policy. The community has projects to address these issues (e.g., Apache Sentry and Argus), but as of this writing no comprehensive solution exists.

Difficult to Integrate with Enterprise Security

Most of the organizations use an enterprise security solution for achieving a variety of objectives. Sometimes it is to mitigate the risk of cyberattacks, for security compliance, or for simply establishing customer trust. Hadoop, however, can't integrate with any of these security solutions. It may be possible to write a custom plug-in to accommodate Hadoop; but it may not be possible to have Hadoop comply with all the security policies.

Unencrypted Data in Transit

Hadoop is a distributed system and hence consists of several nodes (such as NameNode and a number of DataNodes) with data communication between them. That means data is transmitted over the network, but it is not encrypted. This may be sensitive financial data such as account information or personal data (such as a Social Security number), and it is open to attacks.

Internode communication in Hadoop uses protocols such as RPC, TCP/IP, and HTTP. Currently, only RPC communication can be encrypted easily (that's communication between NameNode, JobTracker, DataNodes, and Hadoop clients), leaving the actual read/write of file data between clients and DataNodes (TCP/IP) and HTTP communication (web consoles, communication between NameNode/Secondary NameNode and MapReduce shuffle data) open to attacks.

It is possible to encrypt TCP/IP or HTTP communication; but that needs use of Kerberos or SASL (Simple Authentication and Security Layer) frameworks. Also, Hadoop's built-in encryption has a very negative impact on performance and is not widely used.

No Data Encryption at Rest

At rest, data is stored on disk. Hadoop doesn't encrypt data that's stored on disk and that can expose sensitive data to malevolent attacks. Currently, no codec or framework is provided for this purpose. This is especially a big issue due to the nature of Hadoop architecture, which spreads data across a large number of nodes, exposing the data blocks at all those unsecured entry points.

There are a number of choices for implementing encryption at rest with Hadoop; but they are offered by different vendors and rely on their distributions for implementing encryption. Most notable was the Intel Hadoop distribution that provided encryption for data stored on disk and used Apache as well as custom codecs for encrypting data. Some of that functionality is proposed to be available through Project Rhino (an Apache open source project).

You have to understand that since Hadoop usually deals with large volumes of data and encryption/decryption takes time, it is important that the framework used performs the encryption/decryption fast enough, so that it doesn't impact performance. The Intel distribution claimed to perform these operations with great speed—provided Intel CPUs were used along with Intel disk drives and all the other related hardware.

Hadoop Doesn't Track Data Provenance

There are situations where a multistep MapReduce job fails at an intermediate step, and since the execution is often batch oriented, it is very difficult to debug the failure because the output data set is all that's available.

Data provenance is a process that captures how data is processed through the workflow and aids debugging by enabling *backward tracing*—finding the input data that resulted in output for any given step. If the output is unusual (or not what was expected), backward tracing can be used to determine the input that was processed.

Hadoop doesn't provide any facilities for data provenance (or backward tracing); you need to use a third-party tool such as RAMP if you require data provenance. That makes troubleshooting job failures really hard and time consuming.

This concludes our discussion of Hadoop architecture and the related security issues. We will discuss the Hadoop Stack next.

The Hadoop Stack

Hadoop core modules and main components are referred to as the *Hadoop Stack*. Together, the Hadoop *core modules* provide the basic working functionality for a Hadoop cluster. The *Hadoop Common module* provides the shared libraries, and HDFS offers the distributed storage and functionality of a fault-tolerant file system. MapReduce or YARN provides the distributed data processing functionality. So, without all the bells and whistles, that's a functional Hadoop cluster. You can configure a node to be the NameNode and add a couple of DataNodes for a basic, functioning Hadoop cluster.

Here's a brief introduction to each of the core modules:

- **Hadoop Common**: These are the common libraries or utilities that support functioning of other Hadoop modules. Since the other modules use these libraries heavily, this is the backbone of Hadoop and is absolutely necessary for its working.

- **Hadoop Distributed File System (HDFS)**: HDFS is at the heart of a Hadoop cluster. It is a distributed file system that is fault tolerant, easily scalable, and provides high throughput using local processing and local data storage at the data nodes. (I have already discussed HDFS in great detail in the "HDFS" section).

- **Hadoop YARN**: YARN is a framework for job scheduling and cluster resource management. It uses a global resource manager process to effectively manage data processing resources for a Hadoop cluster in conjunction with Node Manager on each data node.

  The resource manager also has a pluggable scheduler (any scheduler can be used such as the FIFO or Fair scheduler) that can schedule jobs and works with the Application Master Process on DataNodes. It uses MapReduce as a distributed data processing algorithm by default, but can also use any other distributed processing application as required.

- **Hadoop MapReduce**: A YARN-based system for parallel processing of large data sets. MapReduce is the algorithm that takes "processing to data." All the data nodes can process maps (transformations of input to desired output) and reduce (sorting and merging of output) locally, independently and in parallel, to provide the high throughput that's required for very large datasets. I have discussed MapReduce in detail earlier in the "Hadoop's Job Framework using MapReduce" section.

So, you now know what the Hadoop core modules are, but how do they relate to each other to form a cohesive system with the expected functionality? Figure 2-9 illustrates the interconnections.

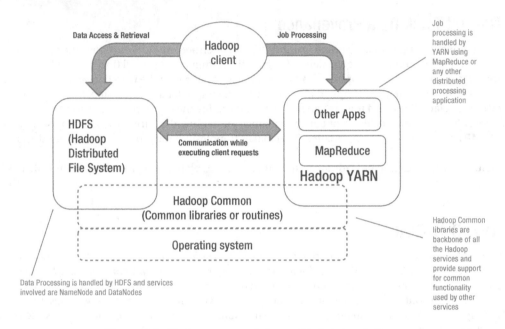

Figure 2-9. *Hadoop core modules and their interrelations*

As you can see, the two major aspects of Hadoop are distributed storage and distributed data processing. You can also see clearly the dependency of both these aspects on Hadoop Common libraries and the operating system. Hadoop is like any other application that runs in the context of the operating system. But then what happens to the security? Is it inherited from the operating system? Well, that's where the problem is. Security is not inherited from the operating system and Hadoop's security, while improving, is still immature and difficult to configure. You therefore have to find ways to authenticate, authorize, and encrypt data within your Hadoop cluster. You will learn about those techniques in Chapters 4, 5, 8, and 9.

Lastly, please note that in the real world, it is very common to have NameNode (which manages HDFS processing) and JobTracker (which manages job processing) running on the same node. So, Figure 2-9 only indicates a logical division of processing; it may not necessarily be true in case of physical implementation.

Main Hadoop Components

As you saw in the last section, Hadoop core modules provide basic Hadoop cluster functionality, but the main components are not limited to core modules. After all, a basic Hadoop cluster can't be used as a production environment. Additional functionality such as ETL and bulk-load capability from other (non-Hadoop) data sources, scheduling, fast key-based retrieval, and query capability (for data) are required for any data storage and management system. Hadoop's main components provide these missing capabilities as well.

For example, the Pig component provides a data flow language useful for designing ETL. Sqoop provides a way to transfer data between HDFS and relational databases. Hive provides query capability with an SQL-like language. Oozie provides scheduling functionality, and HBase adds columnar storage for massive data storage and fast key-based retrieval. Table 2-1 lists some popular components along with their usage.

Table 2-1. *Popular Hadoop Components*

Component	Description	Notes
HBase	HBase is an open source, distributed, versioned, column-oriented data store.	It can be used to store large volumes of structured and unstructured data. It provides key-based access to data and hence can retrieve data very quickly. It is highly scalable and uses HDFS for data storage. Real strengths of HBase are its ability to store unstructured schema-less data and retrieve it really fast using the row keys.
Hive	Hive provides a SQL-like query language (HiveQL) that can be used to query HDFS data.	Hive converts the queries to MapReduce jobs, runs them, and displays the results. Hive "tables" are actually files within HDFS. Hive is suited for data warehouse use, as it doesn't support row-level inserts, updates, or deletes. Over 95% of Facebook's Hadoop jobs are now driven by a Hive front end.
Pig	Pig is a data flow language that can effectively be used as an ETL system for warehousing environments.	Like actual pigs, which eat almost anything, the Pig programming language is designed to handle any kind of data—hence the name. Using Pig, you can load HDFS data you want to manipulate, run the data through a set of transformations (which, behind the scenes, are translated into MapReduce tasks), and display the results on screen or write them to a file.
Sqoop	Sqoop provides connectivity with relational databases (Microsoft SQL Server, Oracle, MySQL, etc.), data warehouses, as well as NoSQL databases (Cassandra, HBase, MongoDB, etc.).	It is easy to transfer data between HDFS (or Hive/HBase tables) and any of these data sources using Sqoop "connectors." Sqoop integrates with Oozie to schedule data transfer tasks. Sqoop's first version was a command-line client; but Sqoop2 has a GUI front end and a server that can be used with multiple Sqoop clients.

(*continued*)

Table 2-1. *(continued)*

Component	Description	Notes
Oozie	Oozie is a workflow scheduler, meaning it runs jobs based on workflow. In this context, *workflow* is a collection of actions arranged in a control dependency DAG (Direct Acyclic Graph).	Control dependency between actions simply defines the sequence of actions; for example, the second action can't start until the first action is completed. DAG refers to a loopless graph that has a starting point and an end point and proceeds in one direction without ever reversing.

To summarize, Oozie simply executes actions or jobs (considering the dependencies) in a predefined sequence. A following step in the sequence is not started unless Oozie receives a completion response from the remote system executing the current step or job. Oozie is commonly used to schedule Pig or Sqoop workflows and integrates well with them. |
| Flume | Flume is a distributed system for moving large amounts of data from multiple sources (while transforming or aggregating it as needed) to a centralized destination or a data store. | Flume has sources, decorators, and sinks. *Sources* are data sources such as log files, output of processes, traffic at a TCP/IP port, etc., and Flume has many predefined sources for ease of use. *Decorators* are operations on the source stream (e.g. compress or un-compress data, adding or removing certain characters from data stream, grouping and averaging numeric data etc.). *Sinks* are targets such as text files, console displays, or HDFS files. A popular use of Flume is to move diagnostic or job log files to a central location and analyze using keywords (e.g., "error" or "failure"). |
| Mahout | Mahout is a machine learning tool | Remember how Amazon or Netflix recommends products when you visit their sites based on your browsing history or prior purchases? That's Mahout or a similar machine-learning tool in action, coming up with the recommendations using what's termed *collaborative filtering*—one of the machine-learning tasks Mahout uses that generates recommendations based on a user's clicks, ratings, or past purchases.

Mahout uses several other techniques to "learn" or make sense of data, and it provides excellent means to develop machine-learning or data-mining libraries that are highly scalable (i.e., they can be still be used in case data volumes change astronomically). |

You might have observed that no component is dedicated to providing security. You will need to use open source products, such as Kerberos and Sentry, to supplement this functionality. You'll learn more about these in Chapters 4 and 5.

It is important to have this brief introduction to the main components, as I am assuming usage of an "extended" Hadoop cluster (core modules and main components) throughout the book while discussing security implementation as well as use of monitoring (Chapter 7), logging (Chapter 6), or encryption (Chapters 8 and 9).

Summary

This chapter introduced Hadoop's architecture, core modules, main components, and inherent security issues.

Hadoop is not a perfectly secure system, but what is? And how does Hadoop compare with it? What modifications will you need to make to Hadoop in order to make it a secure system? Chapter 1 briefly outlined a model secure system (SQL Server), and I will discuss how to secure Hadoop in Chapters 4 to 8 using various techniques.

In later chapters, you will also learn how a Hadoop cluster uses the Hadoop Stack (Hadoop core modules and main components together) presented here. Understanding the workings of the Hadoop Stack will also make it easier for you to understand the solutions I am proposing to supplement security. The next chapter provides an overview of the solutions I will discuss throughout the book. Chapter 3 will also help you decide which specific solutions you want to focus on and direct you to the chapter where you can find the details you need.

CHAPTER 3

■ ■ ■

Introducing Hadoop Security

We live in a very insecure world. Starting with the key to your home's front door to those all-important virtual keys, your passwords, everything needs to be secured—and well. In the world of Big Data where humungous amounts of data are processed, transformed, and stored, it's all the more important to secure your data.

A few years back, the London Police arrested a group of young people for fraud and theft of digital assets worth $30 million. Their 20-year-old leader used Zeus Trojan, software designed to steal banking information, from his laptop to commit the crime. Incidents like these are commonplace because of the large amount of information and myriad systems involved even while conducting simple business transactions. In the past, there were probably only thousands who could potentially access your data to commit a crime against you; now, with the advent of the Internet, there are potentially billions! Likewise, before Big Data existed, only direct access to specific data on specific systems was a danger; now, Big Data multiplies the places such information is stored and hence provides more ways to compromise your privacy or worse. Everything in the new technology-driven, Internet-powered world has been scaled up and scaled out—crime and the potential for crime included.

Imagine if your company spent a couple of million dollars installing a Hadoop cluster to gather and analyze your customers' spending habits for a product category using a Big Data solution. Because that solution was not secure, your competitor got access to that data and your sales dropped 20% for that product category. How did the system allow unauthorized access to data? Wasn't there any authentication mechanism in place? Why were there no alerts? This scenario should make you think about the importance of security, especially where sensitive data is involved.

Although Hadoop does have inherent security concerns due to its distributed architecture (as you saw in Chapter 2), the situation described is extremely unlikely to occur on a Hadoop installation that's managed securely. A Hadoop installation that has clearly defined user roles and multiple levels of authentication (and encryption) for sensitive data will not let any unauthorized access go through.

This chapter serves as a roadmap for the rest of the book. It provides a brief overview of each of the techniques you need to implement to secure your Hadoop installation; later chapters will then cover the topics in more detail. The purpose is to provide a quick overview of the security options and also help you locate relevant techniques quickly as needed. I start with authentication (using Kerberos), move on to authorization (using Hadoop ACLs and Apache Sentry), and then discuss secure administration (audit logging and monitoring). Last, the chapter examines encryption for Hadoop and available options. I have used open source software wherever possible, so you can easily build your own Hadoop cluster to try out some of the techniques described in this book.

As the foundation for all that, however, you need to understand the way Hadoop was developed and also a little about the Hadoop architecture. Armed with this background information, you will better understand the authentication and authorization techniques discussed later in the chapter.

Starting with Hadoop Security

When talking about Hadoop security, you have to consider how Hadoop was conceptualized. When Doug Cutting and Mike Cafarella started developing Hadoop, security was not exactly the priority. I am certain it was not even considered as part of the initial design. Hadoop was meant to process large amounts of web data in the public domain, and hence security was not the focus of development. That's why it lacked a security model and only provided basic authentication for HDFS—which was not very useful, since it was extremely easy to impersonate another user.

Another issue is that Hadoop was not designed and developed as a cohesive system with predefined modules, but was rather developed as a collage of modules that either correspond to various open source projects or a set of (proprietary) extensions developed by various vendors to supplement functionality lacking within the Hadoop ecosystem.

Therefore, Hadoop assumes the isolation of (or a cocoon of) a trusted environment for its cluster to operate without any security violations—and that's lacking most of the time. Right now, Hadoop is transitioning from an experimental or emerging technology stage to enterprise-level and corporate use. These new users need a way to secure sensitive business data.

Currently, the standard community-supported way of securing a Hadoop cluster is to use Kerberos security. Hadoop and its major components now fully support Kerberos authentication. That merely adds a level of authentication, though. With just Kerberos added there is still no consistent built-in way to define user roles for finer control across components, no way to secure access to Hadoop processes (or daemons) or encrypt data in transit (or even at rest). A secure system needs to address all these issues and also offer more features and ways to customize security for specific needs. Throughout the book, you will learn how to use these techniques with Hadoop. For now, let's start with a brief look at a popular solution to address Hadoop's authentication issue.

Introducing Authentication and Authorization for HDFS

The first and most important consideration for security is authentication. A user needs to be authenticated before he is allowed to access the Hadoop cluster. Since Hadoop doesn't do any secure authentication, Kerberos is often used with Hadoop to provide authentication.

When Kerberos is implemented for security, a client (who is trying to access Hadoop cluster) contacts the KDC (the central Kerberos server that hosts the credential database) and requests access. If the provided credentials are valid, KDC provides requested access. We can divide the Kerberos authentication process into three main steps:

1. **TGT generation**, where Authentication Server (AS) grants the client a Ticket Granting Ticket (TGT) as an authentication token. A client can use the same TGT for multiple TGS requests (until the TGT expires).

2. **TGS session ticket generation**, where the client uses credentials to decrypt TGT and then uses TGT to get a service ticket from the Ticket Granting Server (TGS) that is granting server access to a Hadoop cluster.

3. **Service access**, where the client uses the service ticket to authenticate and access a Hadoop cluster.

Chapter 4 discusses the details of Kerberos architecture and also how Kerberos can be configured to be used with Hadoop. In addition, you'll find a step-by-step tutorial that will help you in setting up Kerberos to provide authentication for your Hadoop cluster.

Authorization

When implementing security, your next step is authorization. Specifically, how can you implement fine-grained authorization and roles in Hadoop? The biggest issue is that all information is stored in files, just like on a Linux host (HDFS is, after all, a file system). There is no concept of a table (like relational databases) and that makes it harder to authorize a user for partial access to the stored data.

Whether you call it defining details of authorization, designing fine-grained authorization, or "fine tuning" security, it's a multistep process. The steps are:

1. Analyze your environment,

2. Classify data for access,

3. Determine who needs access to what data,

4. Determine the level of necessary access, and

5. Implement your designed security model.

However, you have to remember that Hadoop (and its distributed file system) stores all its data in files, and hence there are limitations to the granularity of security you can design. Like Unix or Linux, Hadoop has a permissions model very similar to the POSIX-based (portable operating system interface) model—and it's easy to confuse those permissions for Linux permissions—so the permission granularity is limited to read or write permissions to files or directories. You might say, "What's the problem? My Oracle or PostgreSQL database stores data on disk in files, why is Hadoop different?" Well, with the traditional database security model, all access is managed through clearly defined roles and channeled through a central server process. In contrast, with data files stored within HDFS, there is no such central process and multiple services like Hive or HBase can directly access HDFS files.

To give you a detailed understanding of the authorization possible using file/directory-based permissions, Chapter 5 discusses the concepts, explains the logical process, and also provides a detailed real-world example. For now, another real-world example, this one of authorization, will help you understand the concept better.

Real-World Example for Designing Hadoop Authorization

Suppose you are designing security for an insurance company's claims management system, and you have to assign roles and design fine-grained access for all the departments accessing this data. For this example, consider the functional requirements of two departments: the call center and claims adjustors.

Call center representatives answer calls from customers and then file or record claims if they satisfy all the stipulated conditions (e.g. damages resulting from "acts of God" do not qualify for claims and hence a claim can't be filed for them).

A claims adjustor looks at the filed claims and rejects those that violate any regulatory conditions. That adjustor then submits the rest of the claims for investigation, assigning them to specialist adjustors. These adjustors evaluate the claims based on company regulations and their specific functional knowledge to decide the final outcome.

Automated reporting programs pick up claims tagged with a final status "adjusted" and generate appropriate letters to be mailed to the customers, informing them of the claim outcome. Figure 3-1 summarizes the system.

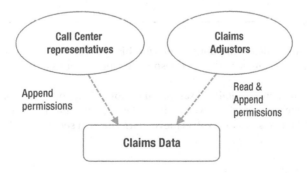

Figure 3-1. *Claims data and access needed by various departments*

As you can see, call center representatives will need to append claim data and adjustors will need to modify data. Since HDFS doesn't have a provision for updates or deletes, adjustors will simply need to append a new record or row (for a claim and its data) with updated data and a new version number. A scheduled process will need to generate a report to look for adjusted claims and mail the final claim outcome to the customers. That process, therefore, will need read access to the claims data.

In Hadoop, remember, data is stored in files. For this example, data is stored in file called Claims. Daily data is stored temporarily in file called Claims_today and appended to the Claims file on a nightly basis. The call center folks use the group ccenter, while the claims adjustors use the group claims, meaning the HDFS permissions on Claims and Claims_today look like those shown in Figure 3-2.

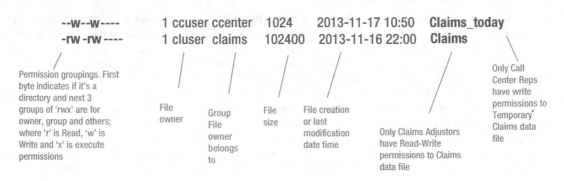

Figure 3-2. *HDFS file permissions*

The first file, Claims_today, has write permissions for owner and the group ccuser. So, all the representatives belonging to this group can write or append to this file.

The second file, Claims, has read and write permissions for owner and the group claims. So, all the claims adjustors can read Claims data and append new rows for the claims that they have completed their work on, and for which they are providing a final outcome. Also, notice that you will need to create a user named Reports within the group claims for accessing the data for reporting.

■ **Note** The permissions discussed in the example are HDFS permissions and not the operating system permissions. Hadoop follows a separate permissions model that appears to be the same as Linux, but the preceding permissions exist within HDFS—not Linux.

So, do these permissions satisfy all the functional needs for this system? You can verify easily that they do. Of course the user Reports has write permissions that he doesn't need; but other than that, all functional requirements are satisfied.

We will discuss this topic with a more detailed example in Chapter 5. As you have observed, the permissions you assigned were limited to complete data files. However, in the real world, you may need your permissions granular enough to access only parts of data files. How do you achieve that? The next section previews how.

Fine-Grained Authorization for Hadoop

Sometimes the necessary permissions for data don't match the existing group structure for an organization. For example, a bank may need a backup supervisor to have the same set of permissions as a supervisor, just in case the supervisor is on vacation or out sick. Because the backup supervisor might only need a subset of the supervisor's permissions, it is not practical to design a new group for him or her. Also, consider another situation where corporate accounts are being moved to a different department, and the group that's responsible for migration needs temporary access.

New versions of HDFS support ACL (Access Control List) functionality, and this will be very useful in such situations. With ACLs you can specify read/write permissions for specific users or groups as needed. In the bank example, if the backup supervisor needs write permission to a specific "personal accounts" file, then the HDFS ACL feature can be used to provide the necessary write permission without making any other changes to file permissions. For the migration scenario, the group that's performing migration can be assigned read/write permissions using HDFS ACL. In case you are familiar with POSIX ACLs, HDFS ACLs work exactly the same way. Chapter 5 discusses Hadoop ACLs again in detail in the "Access Control Lists for HDFS" section.

Last, how do you configure permissions only for part of a data file or certain part of data? Maybe a user needs to have access to nonsensitive information only. The only way you can configure further granularity (for authorization) is by using a NoSQL database such as Hive and specialized software such as Apache Sentry. You can define parts of file data as *tables* within Hive and then use Sentry to configure permissions. Sentry works with *users* and groups of users (called *groups*) and lets you define *rules* (possible actions on tables such as read or write) and *roles* (a group of rules). A user or group can have one or multiple roles assigned to them. Chapter 5 provides a real-world example using Hive and Sentry that explains how fine-tuned authorization can be defined for Hadoop. "Role-Based Authorization with Apache Sentry" in Chapter 5 also has architectural details for Apache Sentry.

Securely Administering HDFS

Chapters 4 and 5 will walk you through various techniques of authentication and authorization, which help secure your system but are not a total solution. What if authorized users access resources that they are not authorized to use, or unauthorized users access resources on a Hadoop cluster using unforeseen methods (read: hacking)? Secure administration helps you deal with these scenarios by monitoring or *auditing* all access to your cluster. If you can't stop this type of access, you at least need to know it occurred! Hadoop offers extensive logging for all its processes (also called *daemons*), and several open source tools can assist in monitoring a cluster. (Chapters 6 and 7 discuss audit logging and monitoring in detail.)

Securely administering HDFS presents a number of challenges, due to the design of HDFS and the way it is structured. Monitoring can help with security by alerting you of unauthorized access to any Hadoop cluster resources. You then can design countermeasures for malicious attacks based on the severity of these alerts. Although Hadoop provides metrics for this monitoring, they are cumbersome to use. Monitoring is much easier when you use specialized software such as Nagios or Ganglia. Also, standard Hadoop distributions by Cloudera and Hortonworks provide their own monitoring modules. Last, you can capture and monitor MapReduce counters.

Audit logs supplement the security by recording all access that flows through to your Hadoop cluster. You can decide the level of logging (such as only errors, or errors and warnings, etc.), and advanced log management provided by modules like Log4j provides a lot of control and flexibility for the logging process. Chapter 6 provides a detailed overview (with an example) of the audit logging available with Hadoop. As a preview, the next section offers a brief overview of Hadoop logging.

Using Hadoop Logging for Security

When a security issue occurs, having extensive activity logs available can help you investigate the problem. Before a breach occurs, therefore, you should enable audit logging to track all access to your system. You can always filter out information that's not needed. Even if you have enabled authentication and authorization, auditing cluster activity still has benefits. After all, even authorized users may perform tasks they are not authorized to do; for example, a user with update permissions could update an entry without appropriate approvals. You have to remember, however, that Hadoop logs are raw output. So, to make them useful to a security administrator, tools to ingest and process these logs are required (note that some installations use Hadoop itself to analyze the audit logs, so you can use Hadoop to protect Hadoop!).

Just capturing the auditing data is not enough. You need to capture Hadoop daemon data as well. Businesses subject to federal oversight laws like the Health Information Portability and Accountability Act (HIPAA) and the Sarbanes-Oxley Act (SOX) are examples of this need. For example, US law requires that all businesses covered by HIPAA prevent unauthorized access to "Protected Health Information" (patients' names, addresses, and all information pertaining to the patients' health and payment records) or applications that audit it. Businesses that must comply with SOX (a 2002 US federal law that requires the top management of any US public company to individually certify the accuracy of their firm's financial information), must audit all access to any data object (e.g., table) within an application. They also must monitor who submitted, managed, or viewed a job that can change any data within an audited application. For business cases like these, you need to capture:

- HDFS audit logs (to record all HDFS access activity within Hadoop),

- MapReduce audit logs (record all submitted job activity), and

- Hadoop daemon log files for NameNode, DataNode, JobTracker and TaskTracker.

The Log4j API is at the heart of Hadoop logging, be it audit logs or Hadoop daemon logs. The Log4j module provides extensive logging capabilities and contains several logging levels that you can use to limit the outputting of messages by category as well as limiting (or suppressing) the messages by their category. For example, if Log4j logging level is defined as INFO for NameNode logging, then an event will be written to NameNode log for any file access request that the NameNode receives (i.e. all the informational messages will be written to NameNode log file).

You can easily change the logging level for a Hadoop daemon at its URL. For example, `http://jobtracker-host:50030/logLevel` will change the logging level while this daemon is running, but it will be reset when it is restarted. If you encounter a problem, you can temporarily change the logging level for the appropriate daemon to facilitate debugging. When the problem is resolved, you can reset the logging level. For a permanent change to log level for a daemon, you need to change the corresponding property in the Log4j configuration file (`log4j.properties`).

The Log4j architecture uses a *logger* (a named channel for log events such as NameNode, JobTracker, etc.), an *Appender* (to which a log event is forwarded and which is responsible for writing it to console or a file), and a *layout* (a formatter for log events). The logging levels—FATAL, ERROR, WARN, INFO, DEBUG, and TRACE—indicate the severity of events in descending order. The minimum log level is used as a filter; log events with a log level greater than or equal to that which is specified are accepted, while less severe events are simply discarded.

Figure 3-3 demonstrates how level filtering works. The columns show the logging levels, while the rows show the level associated with the appropriate Logger Configuration. The intersection identifies whether the Event would be allowed to pass for further processing (YES) or discarded (NO). Using Figure 3-3 you can easily determine what category of events will be included in the logs, depending on the logging level configured. For example, if logging level for NameNode is set at INFO, then all the messages belonging to the categories INFO, WARN, ERROR and FATAL will be written to the NameNode log file. You can easily identify this, looking at the column INFO and observing the event levels that are marked as YES. The levels TRACE and DEBUG are marked as NO and will be filtered out. If logging level for JobTracker is set to FATAL, then only FATAL errors will be logged, as is obvious from the values in column FATAL.

Row data shows possible logging levels that can be used with Hadoop daemons or services (such as NameNode, JobTracker etc.)

Column data shows what levels of messages you will actually get in in your log files for that configured log level for a Hadoop service

Event	Logger Configuration level					
Level	TRACE	DEBUG	INFO	WARN	ERROR	FATAL
TRACE	YES	NO	NO	NO	NO	NO
DEBUG	YES	YES	NO	NO	NO	NO
INFO	YES	YES	YES	NO	NO	NO
WARN	YES	YES	YES	YES	NO	NO
ERROR	YES	YES	YES	YES	YES	NO
FATAL	YES	YES	YES	YES	YES	YES

Figure 3-3. Log4j logging levels and inclusions based on event levels

Chapter 6 will cover Hadoop logging (as well as its use in investigating security issues) comprehensively. You'll get to know the main features of monitoring in the next section.

Monitoring for Security

When you think of monitoring, you probably think about possible performance issues that need troubleshooting or, perhaps, alerts that can be generated if a system resource (such as CPU, memory, disk space) hits a threshold value. You can, however, use monitoring for security purposes as well. For example, you can generate alerts if a user tries to access cluster metadata or reads/writes a file that contains sensitive data, or if a job tries to access data it shouldn't. More importantly, you can monitor a number of metrics to gain useful security information.

It is more challenging to monitor a distributed system like Hadoop because the monitoring software has to monitor individual hosts and then consolidate that data in the context of the whole system. For example, CPU consumption on a DataNode is not as important as the CPU consumption on the NameNode. So, how will the system process CPU consumption alerts, or be capable of identifying separate threshold levels for hosts with different roles within the distributed system? Chapter 7 answers these questions in detail, but for now let's have a look at the Hadoop metrics that you can use for security purposes:

- Activity statistics on the NameNode
- Activity statistics for a DataNode
- Detailed RPC information for a service
- Health monitoring for sudden change in system resources

Tools of the Trade

The leading monitoring tools are Ganglia (http://ganglia.sourceforge.net) and Nagios (www.nagios.org). These popular open source tools complement each other, and each has different strengths. Ganglia focuses on gathering metrics and tracking them over a time period, while Nagios focuses more on being an alerting mechanism. Because gathering metrics and alerting both are essential aspects of monitoring, they work best in conjunction. Both Ganglia and Nagios have agents running on all hosts for a cluster and gather information.

Ganglia

Conceptualized at the University of California, Berkeley, Ganglia is an open source monitoring project meant to be used with large distributed systems. Each host that's part of the cluster runs a daemon process called *gmond* that collects and sends the metrics (like CPU usage, memory usage, etc.) from the operating system to a central host. After receiving all the metrics, the central host can display, aggregate, or summarize them for further use.

Ganglia is designed to integrate easily with other applications and gather statistics about their operations. For example, Ganglia can easily receive output data from Hadoop metrics and use it effectively. Gmond (which Ganglia has running on every host) has a very small footprint and hence can easily be run on every machine in the cluster without affecting user performance.

Ganglia's web interface (Figure 3-4) shows you the hardware used for the cluster, cluster load in the last hour, CPU and memory resource consumption, and so on. You can have a look at the summary usage for last hour, day, week, or month as you need. Also, you can get details of any of these resource usages as necessary. Chapter 7 will discuss Ganglia in greater detail.

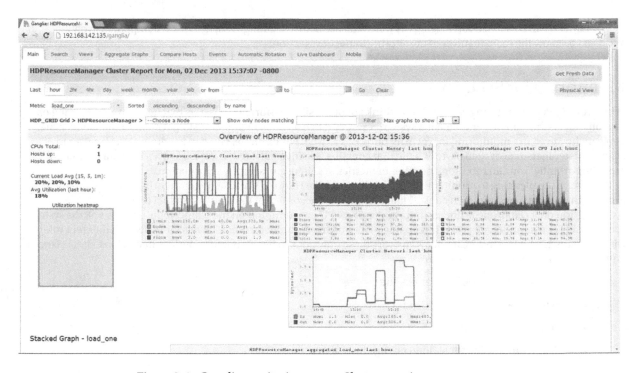

Figure 3-4. *Ganglia monitoring system: Cluster overview*

Nagios

Nagios provides a very good alerting mechanism and can use metrics gathered by Ganglia. Earlier versions of Nagios polled information from its target hosts but currently it uses plug-ins that run agents on hosts (that are part of the cluster). Nagios has an excellent built-in notification system and can be used to deliver alerts via pages or e-mails for certain events (e.g., NameNode failure or disk full). Nagios can monitor applications, services, servers, and network infrastructure. Figure 3-5 shows the Nagios web interface, which can easily manage status (of monitored resources), alerts (defined on resources), notifications, history, and so forth.

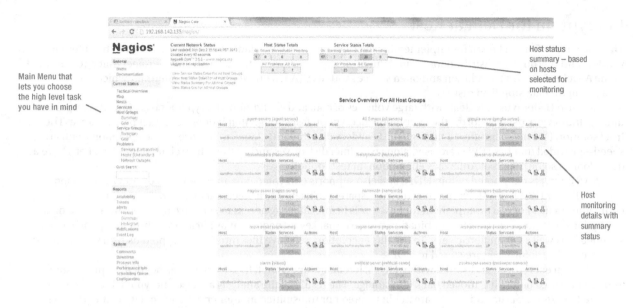

Main Menu that lets you choose the high level task you have in mind

Host status summary – based on hosts selected for monitoring

Host monitoring details with summary status

Figure 3-5. *Nagios web interface for monitoring*

The real strength of Nagios is the hundreds of user-developed plug-ins that are freely available to use. Plug-ins are available in all categories. For example, the System Metrics category contains the subcategory Users, which contains plug-ins such as Show Users that can alert you when certain users either log in or don't. Using these plug-ins can cut down valuable customization time, which is a major issue for all open source (and non–open source) software. Chapter 7 discusses the details of setting up Nagios.

Encryption: Relevance and Implementation for Hadoop

Being a distributed system, Hadoop has data spread across a large number of hosts and stored locally. There is a large amount of data communication between these hosts; hence data is vulnerable in transit as well as when at rest and stored on local storage. Hadoop started as a data store for collecting web usage data as well as other forms of nonsensitive large-volume data. That's why Hadoop doesn't have any built-in provision for encrypting data.

Today, the situation is changing and Hadoop is increasingly being used to store sensitive warehoused data in the corporate world. This has created a need for the data to be encrypted in transit and at rest. Now there are a number of alternatives available to help you encrypt your data.

Encryption for Data in Transit

Internode communication in Hadoop uses protocols such as RPC, TCP/IP, and HTTP. RPC communication can be encrypted using a simple Hadoop configuration option and is used for communication between NameNode, JobTracker, DataNodes, and Hadoop clients. That leaves the actual read/write of file data between clients and DataNodes (TCP/IP) and HTTP communication (web consoles, communication between NameNode/Secondary NameNode, and MapReduce shuffle data) unencrypted.

It is possible to encrypt TCP/IP or HTTP communication, but that requires use of Kerberos or SASL frameworks. The current version of Hadoop allows network encryption (in conjunction with Kerberos) by setting explicit values in the configuration files `core-site.xml` and `hdfs-site.xml`. Chapter 4 will revisit this detailed setup and discuss network encryption at length.

Encryption for Data at Rest

There are a number of choices for implementing encryption at rest with Hadoop, but they are offered by different vendors and rely on their distributions to implement encryption. Most notable are the Intel Project Rhino (committed to the Apache Software Foundation and open source) and AWS (Amazon Web Services) offerings, which provide encryption for data stored on disk.

Because Hadoop usually deals with large volumes of data and encryption/decryption takes time, it is important that the framework used performs the encryption/decryption fast enough that it doesn't impact performance. The Intel solution (shortly to be offered through the Cloudera distribution) claims to perform these operations with great speed—provided that Intel CPUs are used along with Intel disk drives and all the other related hardware. Let's have a quick look at some details of Amazon's encryption "at rest" option.

AWS encrypts data stored within HDFS and also supports encrypted data manipulation by other components such as Hive or HBase. This encryption can be transparent to users (if the necessary passwords are stored in configuration files) or can prompt them for passwords before allowing access to sensitive data, can be applied on a file-by-file basis, and can work in combination with external key management applications. This encryption can use symmetric as well as asymmetric keys. To use this encryption, sensitive files must be encrypted using a symmetric or asymmetric key before they are stored in HDFS.

When an encrypted file is stored within HDFS, it remains encrypted. It is decrypted as needed for processing and re-encrypted before it is moved back into storage. The results of the analysis are also encrypted, including intermediate results. Data and results are neither stored nor transmitted in unencrypted form. Figure 3-6 provides an overview of the process. Data stored in HDFS is encrypted using symmetric keys, while MapReduce jobs use symmetric keys (with certificates) for transferring encrypted data.

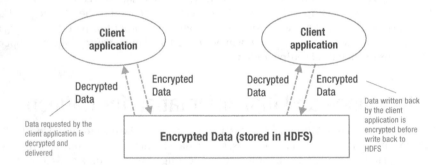

Figure 3-6. *Details of at-rest encryption provided by Intel's Hadoop distribution (now Project Rhino)*

Chapter 8 will cover encryption in greater detail. It provides an overview of encryption concepts and protocols and then briefly discusses two options for implementing encryption: using Intel's distribution (now available as Project Rhino) and using AWS to provide transparent encryption.

Summary

With a roadmap in hand, finding where you want to go and planning how to get there is much easier. This chapter has been your roadmap to techniques for designing and implementing security for Hadoop. After an overview of Hadoop architecture, you investigated authentication using Kerberos to provide secure access. You then learned how authorization is used to specify the level of access, and that you need to follow a multistep process of analyzing data and needs to define an effective authorization strategy.

To supplement your security through authentication and authorization, you need to monitor for unauthorized access or unforeseen malicious attacks continuously; tools like Ganglia or Nagios can help. You also learned the importance of logging all access to Hadoop daemons using the Log4j logging system and Hadoop daemon logs as well as audit logs.

Last, you learned about encryption of data in transit (as well as at rest) and why it is important as an additional level of security—because it is the only way to stop unauthorized access for hackers that have bypassed authentication and authorization layers. To implement encryption for Hadoop, you can use solutions from AWS (Amazon web services) or Intel's Project Rhino.

For the remainder of the book, you'll follow this roadmap, digging deeper into each of the topics presented in this chapter. We'll start in Chapter 4 with authentication.

## PART II

Authenticating and Authorizing Within Your Hadoop Cluster

CHAPTER 4

■ ■ ■

Open Source Authentication in Hadoop

In previous chapters, you learned what a secure system is and what Hadoop security is missing in comparison to what the industry considers a secure system—Microsoft SQL Server (a relational database system). This chapter will focus on implementing some of the features of a secure system to secure your Hadoop cluster from all the Big Bad Wolves out there. Fine-tuning security is more art than a science. There are no rules as to what is "just right" for an environment, but you can rely on some basic conventions to help you get closer—if not "just right." For example, because Hadoop is a distributed system and is mostly accessed using client software on a Windows PC, it makes sense to start by securing the client. Next, you can think about securing the Hadoop cluster by adding strong authentication, and so on.

Before you can measure success, however, you need a yardstick. In this case, you need a vision of the ideal Hadoop security setup. You'll find the details in the next section.

Pieces of the Security Puzzle

Figure 4-1 diagrams an example of an extensive security setup for Hadoop. It starts with a secure client. The SSH protocol secures the client using key pairs; the server uses a public key, and the client uses a private key. This is to counter *spoofing* (intercepting and redirecting a connection to an attacker's system) and also a hacked or compromised password. You'll delve deeper into the details of secure client setup in the upcoming "Establishing Secure Client Access" section. Before the Hadoop system allows access, it authenticates a client using Kerberos (an open-source application used for authentication). You'll learn how to set up Kerberos and make it work with Hadoop in the section "Building Secure User Authentication."

Once a user is connected, the focus is on limiting permissions as per the user's role. The user in Figure 4-1 has access to all user data except sensitive salary data. You can easily implement this by splitting the data into multiple files and assigning appropriate permissions to them. Chapter 5 focuses on these authorization issues and more.

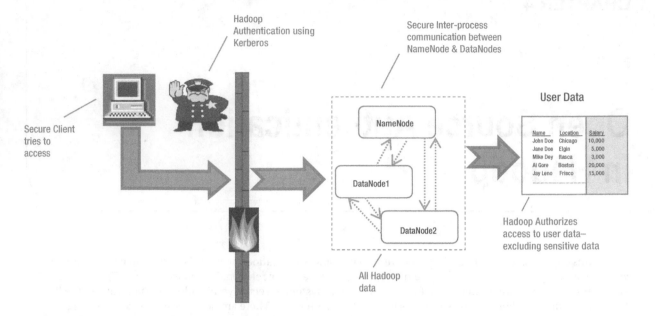

Figure 4-1. Ideal Hadoop Security, with all the required pieces in place

You will also observe that inter-process communication between various Hadoop processes (e.g., between NameNode and DataNodes) is secure, which is essential for a distributed computing environment. Such an environment involves a lot of communication between various hosts, and unsecured data is open to various types of malicious attacks. The final section of this chapter explores how to secure or encrypt the inter-process traffic in Hadoop.

These are the main pieces of the Hadoop security puzzle. One piece that's missing is encryption for data at rest, but you'll learn more about that in Chapter 8.

Establishing Secure Client Access

Access to a Hadoop cluster starts at the client you use, so start by securing the client. Unsecured data is open to malicious attacks that can result in data being destroyed or stolen for unlawful use. This danger is greater for distributed systems (such as Hadoop) that have data blocks spread over a large number of nodes. A client is like a gateway to the actual data. You need to secure the gate before you can think about securing the house.

OpenSSH or SSH protocol is commonly used to secure a client by using a login/password or keys for access. Keys are preferable because a password can be compromised, hacked, or spoofed. For both Windows-based and Linux-based clients, PuTTY (www.chiark.greenend.org.uk/~sgtatham/putty) is an excellent open-source client that supports the SSH protocol. Besides being free, a major advantage to PuTTY is its ability to allow access using keys and a passphrase instead of password (more on the benefits of this coming up). Assistance in countering spoofing is a less obvious, yet equally important additional benefit of PuTTY that deserves your attention.

Countering Spoofing with PuTTY's Host Keys

Spoofing, as you remember, is a technique used to extract your personal information (such as a password) for possible misuse, by redirecting your connection to the attacker's computer (instead of the one you think you are connected to), so that you send your password to the attacker's machine. Using this technique, attackers get access to your password, log in, and use your account for their own malicious purposes.

To counter spoofing, a unique code (called a *host key*) is allocated to each server. The way these keys are created, it's not possible for a server to forge another server's key. So if you connect to a server and it sends you a different host key (compared to what you were expecting), SSH (or a secure client like PuTTY that is using SSH) can warn you that you are connected to a different server—which could mean a spoofing attack is in progress!

PuTTY stores the host key (for servers you successfully connect to) via entries in the Windows Registry. Then, the next time you connect to a server to which you previously connected, PuTTY compares the host key presented by the server with the one stored in the registry from the last time. If it does not match, you will see a warning and then have a chance to abandon your connection before you provide a password or any other private information.

However, when you connect to a server for the first time, PuTTY has no way of checking if the host key is the right one or not. So it issues a warning that asks whether you want to trust this host key or not:

```
The server's host key is not cached in the registry. You
have no guarantee that the server is the computer you
think it is.
The server's rsa2 key fingerprint is:
ssh-rsa 1024 5c:d4:6f:b7:f8:e9:57:32:3d:a3:3f:cf:6b:47:2c:2a
If you trust this host, hit Yes to add the key to
PuTTY's cache and carry on connecting.
If you want to carry on connecting just once, without
adding the key to the cache, hit No.
If you do not trust this host, hit Cancel to abandon the
connection.
```

If the host is not known to you or you have any doubts about whether the host is the one you want to connect to, you can cancel the connection and avoid being a victim of spoofing.

Key-Based Authentication Using PuTTY

Suppose a super hacker gets into your network and gains access to the communication from your client to the server you wish to connect to. Suppose also that this hacker captures the host authentication string that the real host sends to your client and returns it as his own to get you to connect to his server instead of the real one. Now he can easily get your password and can use that to access sensitive data.

How can you stop such an attack? The answer is to use *key-based authentication* instead of a password. Without the public key, the hacker won't be able to get access!

One way to implement keys for authentication is to use SSH, which is a protocol used for communicating securely over a public channel or a public, unsecured network. The security of communication relies on a key pair used for encryption and decryption of data. SSH can be used (or implemented) in several ways. You can automatically generate a public/private key pair to encrypt a network connection and then use password authentication to log on. Another way to use SSH is to generate a public/private key pair manually to perform the authentication, which will allow users or programs to log in without specifying a password.

For Windows-based clients, you can generate the key pair using PuTTYgen, which is open source and freely available. Key pairs consist of a public key, which is copied to the server, and a private key, which is located on the secure client.

The private key can be used to generate a new signature. A signature generated with a private key cannot be forged by anyone who does not have that key. However, someone who has the corresponding public key can check if a particular signature is genuine.

When using a key pair for authentication, PuTTY can generate a signature using your private key (specified using a key file). The server can check if the signature is genuine (using your public key) and allow you to log in. If your client is being spoofed, all that the attacker intercepts is a signature that can't be reused, but your private key or password is not compromised. Figure 4-2 illustrates the authentication process.

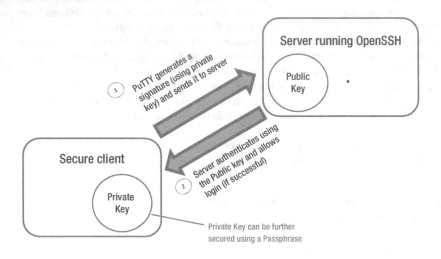

Figure 4-2. *Key-based authentication using PuTTY*

To set up key-based authentication using PuTTY, you must first select the type of key you want. For the example, I'll use RSA and set up a key pair that you can use with a Hadoop cluster. To set up a key pair, open the PuTTY Key Generator (PuTTYgen.exe). At the bottom of the window, select the parameters before generating the keys. For example, to generate an RSA key for use with the SSH-2 protocol, select **SSH-2 RSA** under **Type of key to generate**. The value for **Number of bits in a generated key** determines the size or strength of the key. For this example, 1024 is sufficient, but in a real-world scenario, you might need a longer key such as 2048 for better security. One important thing to remember is that a longer key is more secure, but the encryption/decryption processing time increases with the key length. Enter a key passphrase (to encrypt your private key for protection) and make a note of it since you will need to use it later for decryption.

■ **Note** The most common public-key algorithms available for use with PuTTY are RSA and DSA. PuTTY developers *strongly* recommend you use RSA; DSA (also known as DSS, the United States' federal Digital Signature Standard) has an intrinsic weakness that enables easy creation of a signature containing enough information to give away the *private* key. (To better understand why RSA is almost impossible to break, see Chapter 8.)

Next, click the **Generate** button. In response, PuTTYgen asks you to move the mouse around to generate randomness (that's the PuTTYgen developers having fun with us!). Move the mouse in circles over the blank area in the Key window; the progress bar will gradually fill as PuTTYgen collects enough randomness and keys are generated as shown in Figure 4-3.

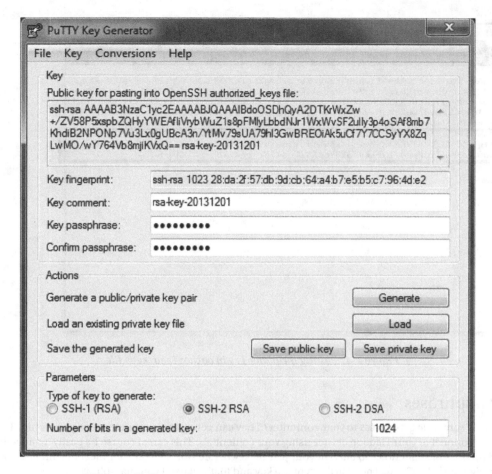

Figure 4-3. Generating a key pair for implementing secure client

Once the keys are generated, click the **Save public key** and **Save private key** buttons to save the keys.

Next, you need to copy the public key to the file `authorized_keys` located in the `.ssh` directory under your home directory on the server you are trying to connect to. For that purpose, please refer to the section **Public key for pasting into Open SSH authorized_keys file** in Figure 4-3. Move your cursor to that section and copy all the text (as shown). Then, open a PuTTY session and connect using your login and password. Change to directory `.ssh` and open the `authorized_keys` file using editor of your choice. Paste the text of the public key that you created with PuTTYgen into the file, and save the file (Figure 4-4).

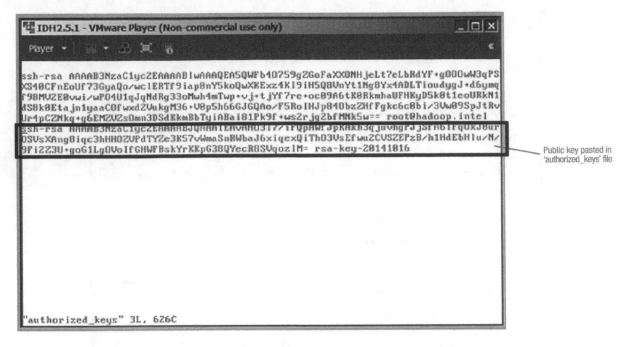

Figure 4-4. Pasting the public key in authorized_keys *file*

Using Passphrases

What happens if someone gets access to your computer? They can generate signatures just as you would. Then, they can easily connect to your Hadoop cluster using your credentials! This can of course be easily avoided by using the *passphrase* of your choice to encrypt your private key before storing it on your local machine. Then, for generating a signature, PuTTY will need to decrypt the key and that will need your passphrase, thereby preventing any unauthorized access.

Now, the need to type a passphrase whenever you log in can be inconvenient. So, Putty provides Pageant, which is an *authentication agent* that stores decrypted private keys and uses them to generate signatures as requested. All you need to do is start Pageant and enter your private key along with your passphrase. Then you can invoke PuTTY any number of times; Pageant will automatically generate the signatures. This arrangement will work until you restart your Windows client. Another nice feature of Pageant is that when it shuts down, it will never store your decrypted private key on your local disk.

So, as a last step, configure your PuTTY client to use the private key file instead of a password for authentication (Figure 4-5). Click the + next to option **SSH** to open the drill-down and then click option **Auth** (authorization) under that. Browse and select the private key file you saved earlier (generated through PuTTYgen). Click **Open** to open a new session.

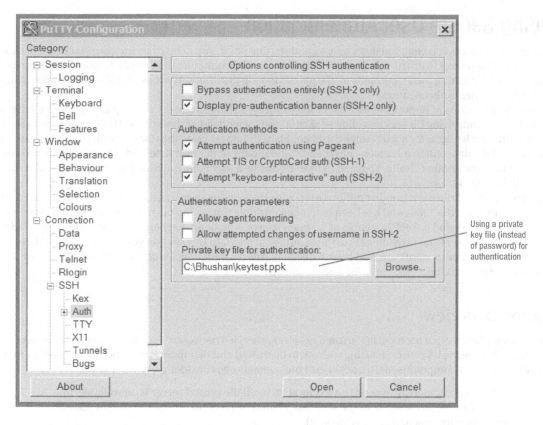

Figure 4-5. *Configuration options for private key authentication with PuTTY*

Now you are ready to be authenticated by the server using login and passphrase as shown in Figure 4-6. Enter the login name at the login prompt (root in this case) and enter the passphrase to connect!

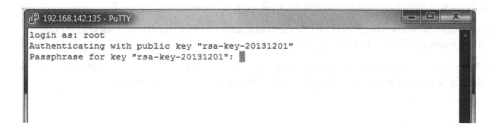

Figure 4-6. *Secure authentication using login and a passphrase*

In some situations (e.g., scheduled batch processing), it will be impossible to type the passphrase; at those times, you can start Pageant and load your private key into it by typing your passphrase once. Please refer to Appendix A for an example of Pageant use and implementation and Appendix B for PuTTY implementation for Linux-based clients.

Building Secure User Authentication

A secure client connection is vital, but that's only a good starting point. You need to secure your Hadoop cluster when this secure client connects to it. The user security process starts with authenticating a user. Although Hadoop itself has no means of authenticating a user, currently all the major Hadoop distributions are available with Kerberos installed, and Kerberos provides authentication.

With earlier versions of Hadoop, when a user tried to access a Hadoop cluster, Hadoop simply checked the ACL to ensure that the underlying OS user was allowed access, and then provided this access. This was not a very secure option, nor did it limit access for a user (since a user could easily impersonate the Hadoop superuser). The user then had access to all the data within a Hadoop cluster and could modify or delete it if desired. Therefore, you need to configure Kerberos or another similar application to authenticate a user before allowing access to data—and then, of course, limit that access, too!

Kerberos is one of the most popular options used with Hadoop for authentication. Developed by MIT, Kerberos has been around since the 1980s and has been enhanced multiple times. The current version, Kerberos version 5 was designed in 1993 and is freely available as an open source download. Kerberos is most commonly used for securing Hadoop clusters and providing secure user authentication. In this section you'll learn how Kerberos works, what its main components are, and how to install it. After installation, I will discuss a simple Kerberos implementation for Hadoop.

Kerberos Overview

Kerberos is an authentication protocol for "trusted hosts on untrusted networks." It simply means that Kerberos assumes that all the hosts it's communicating with are to be trusted and that there is no spoofing involved or that the secret key it uses is not compromised. To use Keberos more effectively, consider a few other key facts:

- Kerberos continuously depends on a central server. If the central server is unavailable, no one can log in. It is possible to use multiple "central" servers (to reduce the risk) or additional authentication mechanisms (as fallback).

- Kerberos is heavily time dependent, and thus the clocks of all the governed hosts must be synchronized within configured limits (5 minutes by default). Most of the times, Network Time Protocol daemons help to keep the clocks of the governed hosts synchronized.

- Kerberos offers a single sign-on approach. A client needs to provide a password only once per session and then can transparently access all authorized services.

- Passwords should not be saved on clients or any intermediate application servers. Kerberos stores them centrally without any redundancy.

Figure 4-7 provides an overview of Kerberos authentication architecture. As shown, the Authentication Server and Ticket Granting Server are major components of the Kerberos key distribution center.

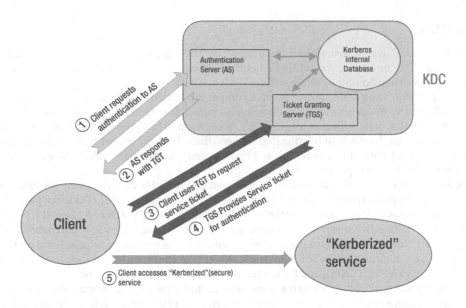

Figure 4-7. *Kerberos key distribution center with its main components (TGT = Ticket Granting Ticket)*

A client requests access to a Kerberos-enabled service using Kerberos client libraries. The Kerberos client contacts the Kerberos Distribution Center, or KDC (the central Kerberos server that hosts the credential database) and requests access. If the provided credentials are valid, KDC provides requested access. The KDC uses an internal database for storing credentials, along with two main components: the Authentication Server (AS) and the Ticket Granting Server (TGS).

Authentication

The Kerberos authentication process contains three main steps:

1.   The AS grants the user (and host) a Ticket Granting Ticket (TGT) as an authentication token. A TGT is valid for a specific time only (validity is configured by Administrator through the configuration file). In case of services principles (logins used to run services or background processes) requesting TGT, credentials are supplied to the AS through special files called *keytabs*.

2.   The client uses credentials to decrypt the TGT and then uses the TGT to get service ticket from the Ticket Granting Server to access a "kerberized" service. A client can use the same TGT for multiple TGS requests (till the TGT expires).

3.   The user (and host) uses the service ticket to authenticate and access a specific Kerberos-enabled service.

Important Terms

To fully understand Kerberos, you need to speak its language of realms, principals, tickets, and databases. For an example of a Kerberos implementation, you are implementing Kerberos on a single node cluster called pract_hdp_sec, and you are using a virtual domain or realm called EXAMPLE.COM.

The term *realm* indicates an administrative domain (similar to a Windows domain) used for authentication. Its purpose is to establish the virtual boundary for use by an AS to authenticate a user, host, or service. This does not mean that the authentication between a user and a service forces them to be in the same realm! If the two objects belong to different realms but have a trust relationship between them, then the authentication can still proceed (called *cross-authentication*). For our implementation, I have created a single realm called EXAMPLE.COM (note that by convention a realm typically uses capital letters).

A *principal* is a user, host, or service associated with a realm and stored as an entry in the AS database typically located on KDC. A principal in Kerberos 5 is defined using the following format: Name[/Instance]@REALM. Common usage for users is *username@REALM* or *username/role@REALM* (e.g., alex/admin@REALM and alex@REALM are two different principals that might be defined). For service principals, the common format is *service/hostname@REALM* (e.g., hdfs/host1.myco.com). Note that Hadoop expects a specific format for its service principals. For our implementation, I have defined principles, such as hdfs/pract_hdp_sec@EXAMPLE.COM (hdfs for NameNode and DataNode), mapred/pract_hdp_sec@EXAMPLE.COM (mapred for JobTracker and TaskTracker), and so on.

A *ticket* is a token generated by the AS when a client requests authentication. Information in a ticket includes: the requesting user's principal (generally the username), the principal of the service it is intended for, the client's IP address, validity date and time (in timestamp format), ticket's maximum lifetime, and session key (this has a fundamental role). Each ticket expires, generally after 24 hours, though this is configurable for a given Kerberos installation.

In addition, tickets may be renewed by user request until a configurable time period from issuance (e.g., 7 days from issue). Users either explicitly use the Kerberos client to obtain a ticket or are provided one automatically if the system administrator has configured the login client (e.g., SSH) to obtain the ticket automatically on login. Services typically use a keytab file (a protected file having the services' password contained within) to run background threads that obtain and renew the TGT for the service as needed. All Hadoop services will need a keytab file placed on their respective hosts, with the location of this file being defined in the service site XML.

Kerberos uses an encrypted *database* to store all the principal entries associated with users and services. Each entry contains the following information: principal name, encryption key, maximum validity for a ticket associated with a principal, maximum renewal time for a ticket associated with a principal, password expiration date, and expiration date of the principal (after which no tickets will be issued).

There are further details associated with Kerberos architecture, but because this chapter focuses on installing and configuring Kerberos for Hadoop, basic understanding of Kerberos architecture will suffice for our purposes. So let's start with Kerberos installation.

Installing and Configuring Kerberos

The first step for installing Kerberos is to install all the Kerberos services for your new KDC. For Red Hat Enterprise Linux (RHEL) or CentOS operating systems, use this command:

```
yum install krb5-server krb5-libs krb5-auth-dialog krb5-workstation
```

When the server is installed, you must edit the two main configuration files, located by default in the following directories (if not, use Linux utility "find" to locate them):

- /etc/krb5.conf
- /var/kerberos/krb5kdc/kdc.conf

The next phase is to specify your realm (EXAMPLE.COM for the example) and to change the KDC value to the name of the fully qualified Kerberos server host (here, pract_hdp_sec). You must also copy the updated version of /etc/krb5.conf to every node in your cluster. Here is /etc/krb5.conf for our example:

```
[logging]
 default = FILE:/var/log/krb5libs.log
 kdc = FILE:/var/log/krb5kdc.log
 admin_server = FILE:/var/log/kadmind.log

[libdefaults]
 default_realm = EXAMPLE.COM
 dns_lookup_realm = false
 dns_lookup_kdc = false
 ticket_lifetime = 24h
 renew_lifetime = 7d
 forwardable = true

[kdc]
profile = /var/kerberos/krb5kdc/kdc.conf

[realms]
 EXAMPLE.COM = {
  kdc = pract_hdp_sec
  admin_server = pract_hdp_sec
 }

[domain_realm]
 .example.com = EXAMPLE.COM
 example.com = EXAMPLE.COM
```

Please observe the changed values for the realm name and KDC name. The example tickets will be valid for up to 24 hours after creation, so ticket_lifetime is set to 24h. After 7 days those tickets can be renewed, because renew_lifetime is set to 7d. Following is the /var/kerberos/krb5kdc/kdc.conf I am using:

```
[kdcdefaults]
 kdc_ports = 88
 kdc_tcp_ports = 88

[realms]
 EXAMPLE.COM = {
  profile = /etc/krb5.conf
  supported_enctypes = aes128-cts:normal des3-hmac-sha1:normal
arcfour-hmac:normal des-hmac-sha1:normal des-cbc-md5:normal des-cbc-crc:normal
allow-null-ticket-addresses = true
database_name = /var/Kerberos/krb5kdc/principal
#master_key_type = aes256-cts
  acl_file = /var/kerberos/krb5kdc/kadm5.acl
  admin_keytab = /var/kerberos/krb5kdc/kadm5.keytab
  dict_file = /usr/share/dict/words
  max_life = 2d 0h 0m 0s
  max_renewable_life = 7d 0h 0m 0s
```

```
admin_database_lockfile = /var/kerberos/krb5kdc/kadm5_adb.lock
key_stash_file = /var/kerberos/krb5kdc/.k5stash
kdc_ports = 88
kadmind_port = 749
default_principle_flags = +renewable
}
```

Included in the settings for realm EXAMPLE.COM, the acl_file parameter specifies the ACL (file /var/kerberos/krb5kdc/kadm5.acl in RHEL or CentOS) used to define the principals that have admin (modifying) access to the Kerberos database. The file can be as simple as a single entry:

```
*/admin@EXAMPLE.COM *
```

This entry specifies all principals with the /admin *instance* extension have full access to the database. Kerberos service kadmin needs to be restarted for the change to take effect.

Also, observe that the max_life (maximum ticket life) setting is 2d (2 days) for the realm EXAMPLE.COM. You can override configuration settings for specific realms. You can also specify these values for a principal.

Note in the [realms] section of the preceding code that I have disabled 256-bit encryption. If you want to use 256-bit encryption, you must download the Java Cryptography Extension (JCE) and follow the instructions to install it on any node running Java processes using Kerberos (for Hadoop, all cluster nodes). If you want to skip this and just use 128-bit encryption, remove the line #master_key_type = aes256-cts and remove the references to aes-256 before the generation of your KDC master key, as described in the section "Creating a Database."

This concludes installing and setting up Kerberos. Please note that it's not possible to cover all the possible options (operating systems, versions, etc.) and nuances of Kerberos installation in a single section. For a more extensive discussion of Kerberos installation, please refer to MIT's Kerberos installation guide at http://web.mit.edu/kerberos/krb5-1.6/krb5-1.6/doc/krb5-install.html. O'Reilly's *Kerberos: The Definitive Guide* is also a good reference.

Getting back to Kerberos implementation, let me create a database and set up principals (for use with Hadoop).

Preparing for Kerberos Implementation

Kerberos uses an internal database (stored as a file) to save details of principals that are set up for use. This database contains users (principals) and their private keys. Principals include internal users that Kerberos uses as well as those you define. The database file is stored at location defined in configuration file kdc.conf file; for this example, /var/kerberos/krb5kdc/principal.

Creating a Database

To set up a database, use the utility kdb5_util:

```
kdb5_util create -r EXAMPLE.COM -s
```

You will see a response like:

```
Loading random data
Initializing database '/var/kerberos/krb5kdc/principal' for realm 'EXAMPLE.COM',
master key name 'K/M@EXAMPLE.COM'
You will be prompted for the database Master Password.
It is important that you NOT FORGET this password.
Enter KDC database master key:
Re-enter KDC database master key to verify:
```

Please make a note of the master key. Also, please note that -s option allows you to save the master server key for the database in a *stash* file (defined using parameter key_stash_file in kdc.conf). If the stash file doesn't exist, you need to log into the KDC with the master password (specified during installation) each time it starts. This will automatically regenerate the master server key.

Now that the database is created, create the first user principal. This must be done on the KDC server itself, while you are logged in as root:

```
/usr/sbin/kadmin.local -q "addprinc root/admin"
```

You will be prompted for a password. Please make a note of the password for principal root/admin@EXAMPLE.COM. You can create other principals later; now, it's time to start Kerberos. To do so for RHEL or CentOS operating systems, issue the following commands to start Kerberos services (for other operating systems, please refer to appropriate command reference):

```
/sbin/service kadmin start
/sbin/service krb5kdc start
```

Creating Service Principals

Next, I will create service principals for use with Hadoop using the kadmin utility. Principal name hdfs will be used for HDFS; mapred will be used for MapReduce, HTTP for HTTP, and yarn for YARN-related services (in this code, kadmin: is the prompt; commands are in bold):

```
[root@pract_hdp_sec]# kadmin
Authenticating as principal root/admin@EXAMPLE.COM with password.
Password for root/admin@EXAMPLE.COM:
kadmin:  addprinc -randkey hdfs/pract_hdp_sec@EXAMPLE.COM
Principal "hdfs/pract_hdp_sec@EXAMPLE.COM" created.
kadmin:  addprinc -randkey mapred/pract_hdp_sec@EXAMPLE.COM
Principal "mapred/pract_hdp_sec@EXAMPLE.COM" created.
kadmin:  addprinc -randkey HTTP/pract_hdp_sec@EXAMPLE.COM
Principal "HTTP/pract_hdp_sec@EXAMPLE.COM" created.
kadmin:  addprinc -randkey yarn/pract_hdp_sec@EXAMPLE.COM
Principal "yarn/pract_hdp_sec@EXAMPLE.COM" created.
kadmin:
```

Creating Keytab Files

Keytab files are used for authenticating services non-interactively. Because you may schedule the services to run remotely or at specific time, you need to save the authentication information in a file so that it can be compared with the Kerberos internal database. Keytab files are used for this purpose.

Getting back to file creation, extract the related keytab file (using kadmin) and place it in the keytab directory (/etc/security/keytabs) of the respective components (kadmin: is the prompt; commands are in bold):

```
[root@pract_hdp_sec]# kadmin
Authenticating as principal root/admin@EXAMPLE.COM with password.
Password for root/admin@EXAMPLE.COM:
kadmin: xst -k mapred.keytab hdfs/pract_hdp_sec@EXAMPLE.COM HTTP/pract_hdp_sec@EXAMPLE.COM
Entry for principal hdfs/pract_hdp_sec@EXAMPLE.COM with kvno 5, encryption type aes128-cts-hmac-
sha1-96 added to keytab WRFILE:mapred.keytab.
```

```
Entry for principal hdfs/pract_hdp_sec@EXAMPLE.COM with kvno 5, encryption type des3-cbc-sha1
added to keytab WRFILE:mapred.keytab.
Entry for principal hdfs/pract_hdp_sec@EXAMPLE.COM with kvno 5, encryption type arcfour-hmac
added to keytab WRFILE:mapred.keytab.
Entry for principal hdfs/pract_hdp_sec@EXAMPLE.COM with kvno 5, encryption type des-hmac-sha1
added to keytab WRFILE:mapred.keytab.
Entry for principal hdfs/pract_hdp_sec@EXAMPLE.COM with kvno 5, encryption type des-cbc-md5
added to keytab WRFILE:mapred.keytab.
Entry for principal HTTP/pract_hdp_sec@EXAMPLE.COM with kvno 4, encryption type aes128-cts-hmac-
sha1-96 added to keytab WRFILE:mapred.keytab.
Entry for principal HTTP/pract_hdp_sec@EXAMPLE.COM with kvno 4, encryption type des3-cbc-sha1
added to keytab WRFILE:mapred.keytab.
Entry for principal HTTP/pract_hdp_sec@EXAMPLE.COM with kvno 4, encryption type arcfour-hmac
added to keytab WRFILE:mapred.keytab.
Entry for principal HTTP/pract_hdp_sec@EXAMPLE.COM with kvno 4, encryption type des-hmac-sha1
added to keytab WRFILE:mapred.keytab.
Entry for principal HTTP/pract_hdp_sec@EXAMPLE.COM with kvno 4, encryption type des-cbc-md5
added to keytab WRFILE:mapred.keytab.
```

Please observe that key entries for all types of supported encryption (defined in configuration file kdc.conf as parameter supported_enctypes) are added to the keytab file for the principals.

Getting back to keytab creation, create keytab files for the other principals (at the kadmin prompt) as follows:

```
kadmin:xst -k mapred.keytab hdfs/pract_hdp_sec@EXAMPLE.COM http/pract_hdp_sec@EXAMPLE.COM
kadmin:xst -k yarn.keytab hdfs/pract_hdp_sec@EXAMPLE.COM http/pract_hdp_sec@EXAMPLE.COM
```

You can verify that the correct keytab files and principals are associated with the correct service using the klist command. For example, on the NameNode:

```
[root@pract_hdp_sec]# klist -kt mapred.keytab
Keytab name: FILE:mapred.keytab
KVNO Timestamp         Principal
---- ---------------- --------------------------------------------------------
   5 10/18/14 12:42:21 hdfs/pract_hdp_sec@EXAMPLE.COM
   5 10/18/14 12:42:21 hdfs/pract_hdp_sec@EXAMPLE.COM
   5 10/18/14 12:42:21 hdfs/pract_hdp_sec@EXAMPLE.COM
   5 10/18/14 12:42:21 hdfs/pract_hdp_sec@EXAMPLE.COM
   5 10/18/14 12:42:21 hdfs/pract_hdp_sec@EXAMPLE.COM
   4 10/18/14 12:42:21 HTTP/pract_hdp_sec@EXAMPLE.COM
   4 10/18/14 12:42:21 HTTP/pract_hdp_sec@EXAMPLE.COM
   4 10/18/14 12:42:21 HTTP/pract_hdp_sec@EXAMPLE.COM
   4 10/18/14 12:42:21 HTTP/pract_hdp_sec@EXAMPLE.COM
   4 10/18/14 12:42:21 HTTP/pract_hdp_sec@EXAMPLE.COM
```

So far, you have defined principals and extracted keytab files for HDFS, MapReduce, and YARN-related principals only. You will need to follow the same process and define principals for any other component services running on your Hadoop cluster such as Hive, HBase, Oozie, and so on. Note that the principals for web communication *must* be named HTTP as web-based protocol implementations for using Kerberos require this naming.

For deploying the keytab files to slave nodes, please copy (or move if newly created) the keytab files to the /etc/hadoop/conf folder. You need to secure the keytab files (only the owner can see this file). So, you need to change the owner to the service username accessing the keytab (e.g., if the HDFS process runs as user hdfs, then user hdfs should own the keytab file) and set file permission 400. Please remember, the service principals for hdfs, mapred, and http have a FQDN (fully qualified domain name) associated with the username. Also, service principals are host specific and unique for each node.

```
[root@pract_hdp_sec]# sudo mv hdfs.keytab mapred.keytab /etc/hadoop/conf/
[root@pract_hdp_sec]# sudo chown hdfs:hadoop /etc/hadoop/conf/hdfs.keytab
[root@pract_hdp_sec]# sudo chown mapred:hadoop /etc/hadoop/conf/mapred.keytab
[root@pract_hdp_sec]# sudo chmod 400 /etc/hadoop/conf/hdfs.keytab
[root@pract_hdp_sec]# sudo chmod 400 /etc/hadoop/conf/mapred.keytab
```

Implementing Kerberos for Hadoop

So far, I have installed and configured Kerberos and also created the database, principals, and keytab files. So, what's the next step for using this authentication for Hadoop? Well, I need to add the Kerberos setup information to relevant Hadoop configuration files and also map the Kerberos principals set up earlier to operating systems users (since operating system users will be used to actually run the Hadoop services). I will also need to assume that a Hadoop cluster in a non-secured mode is configured and available. To summarize, configuring Hadoop for Kerberos will be achieved in two stages:

- Mapping service principals to their OS usernames
- Adding information to various Hadoop configuration files

Mapping Service Principals to Their OS Usernames

Rules are used to map service principals to their respective OS usernames. These rules are specified in the Hadoop configuration file core-site.xml as the value for the optional key hadoop.security.auth_to_local.

The default rule is simply named DEFAULT. It translates all principals in your default domain to their first component. For example, hdfs@EXAMPLE.COM and hdfs/admin@EXAMPLE.COM both become hdfs, assuming your default domain or realm is EXAMPLE.COM. So if the service principal and the OS username are the same, the default rule is sufficient. If the two names are not identical, you have to create rules to do the mapping.

Each rule is divided into three parts: base, filter, and substitution. The *base* begins by specifying the number of components in the principal name (excluding the realm), followed by a colon, and the pattern for building the username from the sections of the principal name. In the pattern section $0 translates to the realm, $1 translates to the first component, and $2 to the second component. So, for example, [2:$1] translates hdfs/admin@EXAMPLE.COM to hdfs.

The filter consists of a regular expression in parentheses that must match the generated string for the rule to apply. For example, (.*@EXAMPLE.COM) matches any string that ends in @EXAMPLE.COM.

The substitution is a sed (popular Linux stream editor) rule that translates a regular expression into a fixed string. For example: s/@[A-Z]*\.COM// removes the first instance of @ followed by an uppercase alphabetic name, followed by .COM.

In my case, I am using the OS user hdfs to run the NameNode and DataNode services. So, if I had created Kerberos principals nn/pract_hdp_sec@EXAMPLE.COM and dn/pract_hdp_sec@EXAMPLE.COM for use with Hadoop, then I would need to map these principals to the OS user hdfs. The rule for this purpose would be:

```
RULE: [2:$1@$0] ([nd]n@.*EXAMPLE.COM) s/.*/hdfs/
```

Adding Information to Various Hadoop Configuration Files

To enable Kerberos to work with HDFS, you need to modify two configuration files:

- `core-site.xml`
- `hdfs-site.xml`

Table 4-1 shows modifications to properties within `core-site.xml`. Please remember to propagate these changes to all the hosts in your cluster.

Table 4-1. *Modifications to Properties in Hadoop Configuration File* `core-site.xml`

Property Name	Property Value	Description
`hadoop.security.authentication`	`kerberos`	Set Authentication type for the cluster. Valid values are `simple` (default) or Kerberos.
`hadoop.security.authorization`	`true`	Enable authorization for different protocols
`hadoop.security.auth_to_local`	`[2:$1]` `DEFAULT`	The mapping from Kerberos principal names to local OS user names using the mapping rules
`hadoop.rpc.protection`	`privacy`	Possible values are `authentication`, `integrity`, and `privacy`.
		`authentication` = mutual client/server authentication
		`integrity` = authentication and integrity; guarantees the integrity of data exchanged between client and server as well as authentication
		`privacy` = authentication, integrity, and confidentiality; encrypts data exchanged between client and server

The `hdfs-site.xml` configuration file specifies the keytab locations as well as principal names for various HDFS daemons. Please remember, `hdfs` and `http` principals are specific to a particular node.

A Hadoop cluster may contain a large number of DataNodes, and it may be virtually impossible to configure the principals manually for each of them. Therefore, Hadoop provides a _HOST variable that resolves to a fully qualified domain name at runtime. This variable allows site XML to remain consistent throughout the cluster. However, please note that _HOST variable can't be used with all the Hadoop configuration files. For example, the `jaas.conf` file used by Zookeeper (which provides resource synchronization across cluster nodes and can be used by applications to ensure that tasks across the cluster are serialized or synchronized) and Hive doesn't support the _HOST variable. Table 4-2 shows modifications to properties within `hdfs-site.xml`, some of which use the _HOST variable. Please remember to propagate these changes to all the hosts in your cluster.

Table 4-2. *Modified Properties for Hadoop Confguration File* `hdfs-site.xml`

Property Name	Property Value	Description
dfs.block.access.token.enable	True	If true, access tokens are used for accessing DataNodes
dfs.namenode.kerberos.principal	hdfs/_HOST@*EXAMPLE.COM*	Kerberos principal name for the NameNode
dfs.secondary.namenode.kerberos.principal	hdfs/_HOST @*EXAMPLE.COM*	Address of secondary NameNode webserver
*dfs.secondary.https.port	50490	The https port to which the secondary NameNode binds
dfs.web.authentication.kerberos.principal	HTTP/_HOST @*EXAMPLE.COM*	The http Kerberos principal used by Hadoop
dfs.namenode.kerberos.internal.spnego.principal	HTTP/_HOST @*EXAMPLE.COM*	This is the http principal for the HTTP service
dfs.secondary.namenode.kerberos.internal.spnego.principal	HTTP/_HOST @*EXAMPLE.COM*	This is the http principal for the http service
*dfs.secondary.http.address	192.168.142.135:50090	IP address of your secondary NameNode host and port 50090
dfs.web.authentication.kerberos.keytab	/etc/hadoop/conf/spnego.service.keytab	Kerberos keytab file with credentials for http principal
dfs.datanode.kerberos.principal	hdfs/_HOST @*EXAMPLE.COM*	The Kerberos principal that runs the DataNode
dfs.namenode.keytab.file	/etc/hadoop/conf/hdfs.keytab	keytab file containing NameNode service and host principals
dfs.secondary.namenode.keytab.file	/etc/hadoop/conf/hdfs.keytab	keytab file containing NameNode service and host principals
dfs.datanode.keytab.file	/etc/hadoop/conf/hdfs.keytab	keytab file for DataNode
*dfs.https.port	50470	The https port to which the NameNode binds
*dfs.https.address	192.168.142.135:50470	The https address for NameNode (IP address of host + port 50470)
dfs.datanode.address	0.0.0.0:1019	The DataNode server address and port for data transfer.
dfs.datanode.http.address	0.0.0.0:1022	The DataNode http server address and port

*These values may change for your cluster

The files `core-site.xml` and `hdfs-site.xml` are included as downloads for your reference. They also contain Kerberos-related properties set up for other components such as Hive, Oozie, and HBase.

MapReduce-Related Configurations

For MapReduce (version 1), the `mapred-site.xml` file needs to be configured to work with Kerberos. It needs to specify the keytab file locations as well as principal names for the JobTracker and TaskTracker daemons. Use Table 4-3 as a guide, and remember that `mapred` principals are specific to a particular node.

Table 4-3. mapred Principals

Property Name	Property Value	Description
`mapreduce.jobtracker.` `kerberos.principal`	`mapred/_HOST@EXAMPLE.COM`	mapred principal used to start JobTracker daemon
`mapreduce.jobtracker.` `keytab.file`	`/etc/hadoop/conf/mapred.keytab`	Location of the keytab file for the mapred user
`mapreduce.tasktracker.` `kerberos.principal`	`mapred/_HOST@EXAMPLE.COM`	mapred principal used to start TaskTracker daemon
`mapreduce.tasktracker.` `keytab.file`	`/etc/hadoop/conf/mapred.keytab`	Location of the keytab file for the mapred user

`mapred.task.tracker.`
`task-controller`
	`org.apache.`
	`hadoop.mapred.`
	`LinuxTaskController`
		TaskController class used to launch the child JVM

`mapreduce.tasktracker.group`	`mapred`	Group for running TaskTracker
`mapreduce.jobhistory.keytab`	`/etc/hadoop/conf/` `mapred.keytab`	Location of the keytab file for the mapred user
`mapreduce.jobhistory.principal`	`mapred/_HOST@EXAMPLE.COM`	mapred principal used to start JobHistory daemon

For YARN, the `yarn-site.xml` file needs to be configured for specifying the keytab and principal details; Table 4-4 holds the details.

Table 4-4. *YARN Principals*

Property Name	Property Value	Description
yarn.resourcemanager.principal	yarn/_HOST@*EXAMPLE.COM*	yarn principal used to start ResourceManager daemon
yarn.resourcemanager.keytab	/etc/hadoop/conf/yarn.keytab	Location of the keytab file for the yarn user
yarn.nodemanager.principal	yarn/_HOST@*EXAMPLE.COM*	yarn principal used to start NodeManager daemon
yarn.nodemanager.keytab	/etc/hadoop/conf/yarn.keytab	Location of the keytab file for the yarn user
yarn.nodemanager.container-executor.class	org.apache.hadoop.yarn.server. nodemanager. LinuxContainerExecutor	Executor class for launching applications in yarn
yarn.nodemanager.linux-containerexecutor.group	yarn	Group for executing Linux containers

For MapReduce (version 1), the TaskController class defines which Map or Reduce tasks are launched (and controlled) and uses a configuration file called task-controller.cfg. This configuration file is present in the Hadoop configuration folder (/etc/hadoop/conf/) and should have the configurations listed in Table 4-5.

Table 4-5. *TaskController Configurations*

Property Name	Property Value	Description
hadoop.log.dir	/var/log/hadoop-0.20-mapreduce	Hadoop log directory (will vary as per your Hadoop distribution). This location is used to make sure that proper permissions exist for writing to logfiles.
mapreduce. tasktracker.group	mapred	Group that the Task Tracker belongs to
banned.users	mapred, hdfs, and bin	Users who should be prevented from running MapReduce
min.user.id	1000	User ID above which MapReduce tasks will be allowed to run

Here's a sample task-controller.cfg:

```
hadoop.log.dir=/var/log/hadoop-0.20-mapreduce/
mapred.local.dir=/opt/hadoop/hdfs/mapred/local
mapreduce.tasktracker.group=mapred
banned.users=mapred,hdfs,bin
min.user.id=500
```

Please note that the value for min.user.id may change depending on the operating system. Some of the operating systems use a value of 0 instead of 500.

For YARN, you need to define containerexecutor.cfg with the configurations in Table 4-6.

Table 4-6. *YARN* `containerexecutor.cfg` *Configurations*

Property Name	Property Value	Description
yarn.nodemanager.log-dirs	/var/log/yarn	Hadoop log directory (will vary as per your Hadoop distribution). This location is used to make sure that proper permissions exist for writing to logfiles.
yarn.nodemanager.linux-containerexecutor.group	yarn	Group that the container belongs to
banned.users	hdfs, yarn, mapred, *and* bin	Users who should be prevented from running MapReduce
min.user.id	1000	User ID above which MapReduce tasks will be allowed to run

As a last step, you have to set the following variables on all DataNodes in file /etc/default/hadoop-hdfs-datanode. These variables provide necessary information to Jsvc, a set of libraries and applications for making Java applications run on Unix more easily, so it can run the DataNode in secure mode.

```
export HADOOP_SECURE_DN_USER=hdfs
export HADOOP_SECURE_DN_PID_DIR=/var/lib/hadoop-hdfs
export HADOOP_SECURE_DN_LOG_DIR=/var/log/hadoop-hdfs
export JSVC_HOME=/usr/lib/bigtop-utils/
```

If the directory /usr/lib/bigtop-utils doesn't exist, set the JSVC_HOME variable to the /usr/libexec/bigtop-utils as following:

```
export JSVC_HOME=/usr/libexec/bigtop-utils
```

So, finally, having installed, configured, and implemented Kerberos and modified various Hadoop configuration files (with Kerberos implementation information), you are ready to start NameNode and DataNode services with authentication!

Starting Hadoop Services with Authentication

Start the NameNode first. Execute the following command as root and substitute the correct path (to where your Hadoop startup scripts are located):

```
su -l hdfs -c "export HADOOP_LIBEXEC_DIR=/usr/lib/hadoop/libexec && /usr/lib/hadoop/sbin/
hadoop-daemon.sh --config /etc/hadoop/conf start namenode";
```

After the NameNode starts, you can see Kerberos-related messages in NameNode log file indicating successful authentication (for principals hdfs and http) using keytab files:

2013-12-10 14:47:22,605 INFO security.UserGroupInformation (UserGroupInformation. java:loginUserFromKeytab(844)) - Login successful for user hdfs/pract_hdp_sec@EXAMPLE.COM using keytab file /etc/hadoop/conf/hdfs.keytab

2013-12-10 14:47:24,288 INFO server.KerberosAuthenticationHandler (KerberosAuthenticationHandler. java:init(185)) - Login using keytab /etc/hadoop/conf/hdfs.keytab, for principal HTTP/pract_hdp_sec@EXAMPLE.COM

Now start the DataNode: Execute the following command as root and substitute the correct path (to where your Hadoop startup scripts are located):

```
su -l hdfs -c "export HADOOP_LIBEXEC_DIR=/usr/lib/hadoop/libexec &&
/usr/lib/hadoop/sbin/hadoop-daemon.sh --config /etc/hadoop/conf start datanode"
```

After the DataNode starts, you can see the following Kerberos-related messages in the DataNode log file indicating successful authentication (for principal hdfs) using keytab file:

2013-12-08 10:34:33,791 INFO security.UserGroupInformation (UserGroupInformation. java:loginUserFromKeytab(844)) - Login successful for user hdfs/pract_hdp_sec@EXAMPLE.COM using keytab file /etc/ hadoop/conf/hdfs.keytab

2013-12-08 10:34:34,587 INFO http.HttpServer (HttpServer.java:addGlobalFilter(525)) - Added global filter 'safety' (class=org.apache.hadoop.http.HttpServer$QuotingInputFilter)

2013-12-08 10:34:35,502 INFO datanode.DataNode (BlockPoolManager.java:doRefreshNamenodes(193)) - Starting BPOfferServices for nameservices: <default>

2013-12-08 10:34:35,554 INFO datanode.DataNode (BPServiceActor.java:run(658)) - Block pool <registering> (storage id unknown) service to pract_hdp_sec/192.168.142.135:8020 starting to offer service

Last, start the SecondaryNameNode. Execute the following command as root and substitute the correct path (to where your Hadoop startup scripts are located):

```
su -l hdfs -c "export HADOOP_LIBEXEC_DIR=/usr/lib/hadoop/libexec &&
/usr/lib/hadoop/sbin/hadoop-daemon.sh --config /etc/hadoop/conf start secondarynamenode";
```

Congratulations, you have successfully "kerberized" HDFS services! You can now start MapReduce services as well (you have already set up the necessary principals and configuration in MapReduce configuration files).

Please understand that the commands I have used in this section may vary with the version of the operating system (and the Hadoop distribution). It is always best to consult your operating system and Hadoop distributor's manual in case of any errors or unexpected behavior.

Securing Client-Server Communications

With earlier Hadoop versions, when daemons (or services) communicated with each other, they didn't verify that the other service is really what it claimed to be. So, it was easily possible to start a rogue TaskTracker to get access to data blocks. Impersonating services could easily get access to sensitive data, destroy data, or bring the cluster down! Even now, unless you have Kerberos installed and configured and also have the right communication protocols encrypted, the situation is not very different. It is very important to secure inter-process communication for Hadoop. Just using an authentication mechanism (like Kerberos) is not enough. You also have to secure all the means of communication Hadoop uses to transfer data between its daemons as well as communication between clients and the Hadoop cluster.

Inter-node communication in Hadoop uses the RPC, TCP/IP, and HTTP protocols. Specifically, RPC (remote procedure call) is used for communication between NameNode, JobTracker, DataNodes, and Hadoop clients. Also, the actual reading and writing of file data between clients and DataNodes uses TCP/IP protocol, which is not secured by default, leaving the communication open to attacks. Last, HTTP protocol is used for communication by web consoles, for communication between NameNode/Secondary NameNode, and also for MapReduce shuffle data transfers. This HTTP communication is also open to attacks unless secured.

Therefore, you must secure all these Hadoop communications in order to secure the data stored within a Hadoop cluster. Your best option is to use encryption. Encrypted data can't be used by malicious attackers unless they have means of decrypting it. The method of encryption you employ depends on the protocol involved. To encrypt TCP/IP communication, for example, an SASL wrapper is required on top of the Hadoop data transfer protocol to ensure secured data transfer between the Hadoop client and DataNode. The current version of Hadoop allows network encryption (in conjunction with Kerberos) by setting explicit values in configuration files core-site.xml and hdfs-site.xml. To secure inter-process communications between Hadoop daemons, which use RPC protocol, you need to use SASL framework. The next sections will take a closer look at encryption, starting with RPC-based communications.

Safe Inter-process Communication

Inter-process communication in Hadoop is achieved through RPC calls. That includes communication between a Hadoop client and HDFS and also among Hadoop services (e.g., between JobTracker and TaskTrackers or NameNode and DataNodes).

SASL (Simple Authentication and Security Layer) is the authentication framework that can be used to guarantee that data exchanged between the client and servers is encrypted and not vulnerable to "man-in-the-middle" attacks (please refer to Chapter 1 for details of this type of attack). SASL supports multiple authentication mechanisms (e.g., MD5-DIGEST, GSSAPI, SASL PLAIN, CRAM-MD5) that can be used for different contexts.

For example, if you are using Kerberos for authentication, then SASL uses a GSSAPI (Generic Security Service Application Program Interface) mechanism to authenticate any communication between Hadoop clients and Hadoop daemons. For a secure Hadoop client (authenticated using Kerberos) submitting jobs, delegation token authentication is used, which is based on SASL MD5-DIGEST protocol. A client requests a token to NameNode and passes on the received token to TaskTracker, and can use it for any subsequent communication with NameNode.

When you set the hadoop.rpc.protection property in Hadoop configuration file core-site.xml to privacy, the data over RPC will be encrypted with symmetric keys. Here's the XML:

```
<property>
<name>hadoop.rpc.protection</name>
<value>privacy</value>
<description>authentication, integrity & confidentiality guarantees that data exchanged between
client and server is encrypted
</description>
</property>
```

Encryption comes at a price, however. As mentioned in Table 4-1, setting hadoop.rpc.protection to privacy means Hadoop performs integrity checks, encryption, and authentication, and all of this additional processing will degrade performance.

Encrypting HTTP Communication

Hadoop uses HTTP communication for web consoles, communication between NameNode/Secondary NameNode, and for MapReduce (shuffle data). For a MapReduce job, the data moves between the Mappers and the Reducers via the HTTP protocol in a process called a *shuffle*. The Reducer initiates a connection to the Mapper, requesting data, and acts as a SSL client. The steps for enabling HTTPS to encrypt shuffle traffic are detailed next.

Certificates are used to secure the communication that uses HTTP protocol. You can use the Java utility keytool to create and store certificates. Certificates are stored within *KeyStores* (files) and contain *keys* (private key and identity) or *certificates* (public keys and identity). For additional details about KeyStores, please refer to Chapter 8 and Appendix C. A *TrustStore* file contains certificates from trusted sources and is used by the secure HTTP (https) clients. Hadoop HttpServer uses the KeyStore files.

After you create the HTTPS certificates and distribute them to all the nodes, you can configure Hadoop for HTTP encryption. Specifically, you need to configure SSL on the NameNode and all DataNodes by setting property dfs.https.enable to true in the Hadoop configuration file hdfs-site.xml.

Most of the time, SSL is configured to authenticate the server only, a mode called *one-way SSL*. For one-way SSL, you only need to configure the KeyStore on the NameNode (and each DataNode), using the properties shown in Table 4-7. These parameters are set in the ssl-server.xml file on the NameNode and each of the DataNodes.

Table 4-7. *SSL Properties to Encrypt HTTP Communication*

Property	Default Value	Description
`ssl.server.keystore.type`	jks	KeyStore file type
`ssl.server.keystore.location`	NONE	KeyStore file location. The mapred user should own this file and have exclusive read access to it.
`ssl.server.keystore.password`	NONE	KeyStore file password
`ssl.server.truststore.type`	jks	TrustStore file type
`ssl.server.truststore.location`	NONE	TrustStore file location. The mapred user must be file owner with exclusive read access.
`ssl.server.truststore.password`	NONE	TrustStore file password
`ssl.server.truststore.reload.interval`	10000	TrustStore reload interval, in milliseconds

You can also configure SSL to authenticate the client; this mode is called *mutual authentication* or *two-way SSL*. To configure two-way SSL, set the property `dfs.client.https.need-auth` to `true` in the Hadoop configuration file `hdfs-site.xml` (on the NameNode and each DataNode), in addition to setting the property `dfs.https.enable` to `true`.

Appendix C has details of setting up KeyStore and TrustStore to use for HTTP encryption.

To configure an encrypted shuffle, you need to set the properties listed in Table 4-8 in the `core-site.xml` files of all nodes in the cluster.

Table 4-8. `core-site.xml` *Properties for Enabling Encrypted Shuffle (for MapReduce)*

Property	Value	Explanation
`hadoop.ssl.enabled`	true	For MRv1, setting this value to `true` enables both the Encrypted Shuffle and the Encrypted Web UI features. For MRv2, this property only enables the Encrypted WebUI; Encrypted Shuffle is enabled with a property in the `mapred-site.xml` file as described in "Encrypting HTTP Communication."
`hadoop.ssl.require.client.cert`	true	When set to `true`, client certificates are required for all shuffle operations and all browsers used to access Web UIs.
`hadoop.ssl.hostname.verifier`	DEFAULT	The hostname verifier to provide for `HttpsURLConnections`. Valid values are `DEFAULT`, `STRICT`, `STRICT_I6`, `DEFAULT_AND_LOCALHOST`, and `ALLOW_ALL`.
`hadoop.ssl.keystores.factory.class`	`org.apache.hadoop.security.ssl.FileBasedKeyStoresFactory`	The `KeyStoresFactory` implementation to use.
`hadoop.ssl.server.conf`	`ssl-server.xml`	Resource file from which SSL server KeyStore information is extracted. This file is looked up in the classpath; typically it should be in the `/etc/hadoop/conf/` directory.
`hadoop.ssl.client.conf`	`ssl-client.xml`	Resource file from which SSL server KeyStore information is extracted. This file is looked up in the classpath; typically it should be in the `/etc/hadoop/conf/` directory.

To enable Encrypted Shuffle for MRv2, set the property mapreduce.shuffle.ssl.enabled in the mapred-site.xml file to true on every node in the cluster.

To summarize, for configuring Encrypted Shuffle (for MapReduce jobs) and Encrypted Web UIs, the following configuration files need to be used/modified:

- core-site.xml/hdfs-site.xml: for enabling HTTP encryption and defining implementation
- mapred-site.xml: enabling Encrypted Shuffle for MRv2
- ssl-server.xml: storing KeyStore and TrustStore settings for server
- ssl-client.xml: storing KeyStore and TrustStore settings for the client

Securing Data Communication

Data transfer (read/write) between clients and DataNodes uses the Hadoop Data Transfer Protocol. Because the SASL framework is not used here for authentication, a SASL *handshake* or *wrapper* is required if this data transfer needs to be secured or encrypted. This wrapper can be enabled by setting the property dfs.encrypt.data.transfer to true in configuration file hdfs-site.xml. When the SASL wrapper is enabled, a data encryption key is generated by NameNode and communicated to DataNodes and the client. The client uses the key as a credential for any subsequent communication. NameNode and DataNodes use it for verifying the client communication.

If you have a preference regarding the actual algorithm that you want to use for encryption, you can specify that using the property dfs.encrypt.data.transfer.algorithm. The possible values are 3des or rc4 (default is usually 3DES.) 3DES, or "triple DES," is a variation of the popular symmetric key algorithm DES that uses three keys (instead of the single key DES uses) to add strength to the protocol. You encrypt with one key, decrypt with the second, and encrypt with a third. This process gives a strength equivalent to a 112-bit key (instead of DES's 56-bit key) and makes the encryption stronger, but is slow (due to multiple iterations for encryption). Please refer to Chapter 8 for additional details on DES protocol. RC4 is another symmetric key algorithm that performs encryption much faster as compared to 3DES, but is potentially unsafe (Microsoft and Cisco are both phasing out this algorithm and have clear guidelines to their users to avoid any usage of it).

Please note that since RPC protocol is used to send the Data Encryption Keys to the clients, it is necessary to configure the hadoop.rpc.protection setting to privacy in the configuration file core-site.xml (for client and server both), to ensure that the transfer of keys themselves is encrypted and secure.

Summary

In this chapter you learned how to establish overall security or a "fence" for your Hadoop cluster, starting with the client. Currently, PuTTY offers the best open source options for securing your client. I discussed using a key pair and passphrase instead of the familiar login/password alternative. The reason is simple—to make it harder for malicious attacks to break through your security. Everyone has used PuTTY, but many times they don't think about the underlying technology and reason for using some of the available options. I have tried to shed some light on those aspects of PuTTY.

I am not sure if MIT had Hadoop in mind when they developed Kerberos; but the current usage of Kerberos with Hadoop might make you think otherwise! Again, it is (by far) the most popular alternative for Hadoop authentication.

Dealing with KeyStores and TrustStores is always a little harder for non-Java personnel. If you need another example, Appendix C will help further your understanding those concepts.

The use of SASL protocol for RPC encryption and the underlying technology for encrypting data transfer protocol are complex topics. This chapter's example of implementing a secure cluster was merely intended to introduce the topic.

Where do you go from here? Is the job finished now that the outer perimeter of your cluster is secure? Certainly not! This is where it begins—and it goes on to secure your cluster further by specifying finer details of authorization. That's the subject of the next chapter.

CHAPTER 5

■ ■ ■

Implementing Granular Authorization

Designing fine-grained authorization reminds me of a story of a renowned bank manager who was very disturbed by a robbery attempt made on his safe deposit vault. The bank manager was so perturbed that he immediately implemented multiple layers of security and passwords for the vault. The next day, a customer request required that he open the vault. The manager, in all his excitement, forgot the combination, and the vault had to be forced open (legally, of course).

As you may gather, designing fine-grained security is a tricky proposition. Too much security can be as counterproductive as too little. There is no magic to getting it just right. If you analyze all your processes (both manual and automated) and classify your data well, you can determine who needs access to which specific resources and what level of access is required. That's the definition of fine-grained authorization: every user has the correct level of access to necessary resources. Fine-tuning Hadoop security to allow access driven by functional need will make your Hadoop cluster less vulnerable to hackers and unauthorized access—without sacrificing usability.

In this chapter, you will learn how to determine security needs (based on application) and then examine ways to design high-level security and fine-grained authorization for applications, using directory and file-level permissions. To illustrate, I'll walk you through a modified real-world example involving traffic ticket data and access to that data by police, the courts, and reporting agencies. The chapter wraps up with a discussion of implementing fine-grained authorization using Apache Sentry, revisiting the traffic ticket example to highlight Sentry usage with Hive, a database that works with HDFS. By the end of this chapter, you will have a good understanding of how to design fine-grained authorization.

Designing User Authorization

Defining the details of fine-grained authorization is a multistep process. Those steps are:

1. Analyze your environment,

2. Classify data for access,

3. Determine who needs access to what data,

4. Determine the level of necessary access, and

5. Implement your designed security model.

The following sections work through this complete process to define fine-grained authorization for a real-world scenario.

75

Call the Cops: A Real-World Security Example

I did some work for the Chicago Police Department a few years back involving the department's ticketing system. The system essentially has three parts: mobile consoles in police cars, a local database at the local police station, and a central database at police headquarters in downtown Chicago. Why is fine-tuned authorization important in this scenario? Consider the potential for abuse without it: if the IT department has modification permissions for the data, for example, someone with a vested interest could modify data for a particular ticket. The original system was developed using Microsoft SQL Server, but for my example, I will redesign it for a Hadoop environment. Along the way, you'll also learn how a Hadoop implementation is different from a relational database–based implementation.

Analyze and Classify Data

The first step is inspecting and analyzing the system (or application) involved. In addition, reviewing the high-level objective and use cases for the system helps clarify access needs. Don't forget maintenance, backup, and disaster recovery when considering use cases. A system overview is a good starting point, as is reviewing the manual processes involved (in their logical order). In both cases, your goals are to understand the functional requirements within each process, to understand how processes interact with each other, to determine what data is generated within each process and to track how that data is communicated to the next process. Figure 5-1 illustrates the analysis of a system.

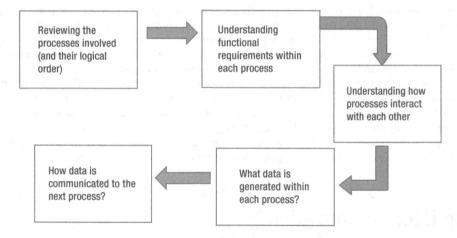

Figure 5-1. *Analyzing a system or an application*

In my example, the first process is the generation of ticket data by a police officer (who issues the ticket). That data gets transferred to the database at a local police station, and obviously needs to have modification rights for the ticketing officer, his or her supervisor at the station, and of course upper management at police headquarters.

Other police officers at the local station need read permissions for this data, as they might want to have a look at all the tickets issued on a particular day or at a person's driving history while deciding whether to issue a ticket or only a warning. Thus, a police officer looks up the ticket data (using the driver's Social Security number, or SSN) at the local police station database (for the current day) as well as at the central database located at police headquarters.

As a second process, the ticket data from local police stations (from all over the Chicago area) gets transmitted to the central database at police headquarters on a nightly basis.

The third and final process is automated generation of daily reports every night for supervisors at all police stations. These reports summarize the day's ticketing activity and are run by a reporting user (created by IT).

Details of Ticket Data

This ticket data is not a single entity, but rather a group of related entities that hold all the data. Understanding the design of the database holding this data will help in designing a detailed level of security.

Two *tables*, or *files* in Hadoop terms, hold all the ticket data. Just as tables are used to store data in a relational database, HDFS uses files. In this case, assume Hadoop stored the data as a comma-delimited text file. (Of course, Hadoop supports a wide range of formats to store the data, but a simple example facilitates better understanding of the concepts.) The table and file details are summarized in Figure 5-2.

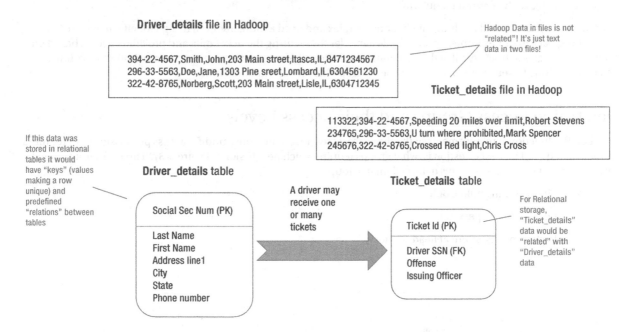

Figure 5-2. Details of ticket data: classification of information and storage in tables versus files

The first table, Driver_details, holds all the personal details of the driver: full legal name, SSN, current address, phone number, and so on. The second table, Ticket_details, has details of the ticket: ticket number, driver's SSN, offense code, issuing officer, and so forth.

Also, these tables are "related" to each other. The relational notation indicates the fact that every driver (featuring in Driver_details) may have one or more tickets to his name, the details of which are in Ticket_details. How can a ticket be related to a driver? By using the SSN. The SSN is a *primary key* (indicated as *PK*) or unique identifier for the Driver_details table because an SSN identifies a driver uniquely. Since a driver may have multiple tickets, however, the SSN is not a unique identifier for the Ticket_details table and is only used to relate the tickets to a driver (indicated as *FK* or *foreign key*).

Please understand that the ticket data example is simplistic and just demonstrates how granular permissions can be used. In addition, it makes these assumptions:

- The example uses Hadoop 2.x, since we will need to append data to all our data files and earlier versions didn't support appends. All the day's tickets from local police stations will be appended every night to appropriate data files located at police headquarters.

- Records won't be updated, but a status flag will be used to indicate the active record (the most recent record being flagged active and earlier ones inactive).

- There is no concurrent modification to records.

- There are no failures while writing data that will compromise the integrity of the system.

- The functional need is that only the police officer (who issues the ticket), that officer's supervisor, and higher management should have rights to modify a ticket—but this desired granularity is not possible with HDFS! Hive or another NoSQL database needs to be used for that purpose. For now, I have just provided modification rights to all police officers. In the next section, however, you will learn how to reimplement this example using Hive and Sentry to achieve the desired granularity.

A production system would likely be much more complex and need a more involved design for effective security.

Getting back to our example, how do we design roles for securing the ticket data and providing access based on need? Our design must satisfy all of the functional needs (for all processes within the system) without providing too much access (due to sensitivity of data). The next part of this section explains how.

Determine Access Groups and their Access Levels

Based on the functional requirements of the three processes, read and write (modify) access permissions are required for the ticket data. The next question is, what groups require which permissions (Figure 5-3)? Three subgroups need partial read and write access to this data; call them Group 1:

- Ticket-issuing police officer

- Local police supervisor

- Higher management at headquarters

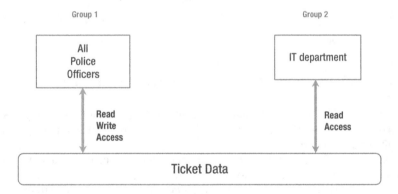

Figure 5-3. *Group access to ticket data with detailed access permissions*

Group 2, the IT department at police headquarters, needs read access. Figure 5-3 illustrates this access. Table 5-1 lists the permissions.

Table 5-1. *Permission Details for Groups and Entities (Tables)*

Table	Group 1	Group 2
Driver_details	Read/write	Read
Ticket_details	Read/write	Read

So, to summarize, analyze and classify your data, then determine the logical groups that need access to appropriate parts of the data. With those insights in hand, you can design roles for defining fine-grained authorization and determine the groups of permissions that are needed for these roles.

Logical design (even a very high-level example like the ticketing system) has to result in a physical implementation. Only then can you have a working system. The next section focuses on details of implementing the example's design.

Implement the Security Model

Implementing a security model is a multistep process. Once you have a good understanding of the roles and their permissions needs, you can begin. These are the steps to follow:

1. Secure data storage.

2. Create users and groups as necessary.

3. Assign ownerships, groups and permissions.

Understanding a few basic facts about Hadoop file permissions will help you in this process.

Ticket Data Storage in Hadoop

For the ticketing system example, I will start with implementation of data storage within HDFS. As you saw earlier, data in Hadoop is stored in the files Driver_details and Ticket_details. These files are located within the root data directory of Hadoop, as shown in Figure 5-4. To better understand the figure, consider some basic facts about HDFS file permissions.

```
Permission groups:   [root@sandbox ~]# hadoop fs -ls /
first character      Found 6 items
indicates            -rw-rw-r--   1 root    hdfs        18 2013-11-12 04:43 /Driver_details
directory or file,   -rw-rw-r--   1 root    hdfs        18 2013-11-12 04:44 /Ticket_details
next 3 for owner,    drwxr-xr-x   - hdfs    hdfs         0 2013-11-12 04:07 /apps
then next 3 for      drwx------   - mapred  hdfs         0 2013-11-19 16:17 /mapred
owner's group and    drwxrwxrwx   - hdfs    hdfs         0 2013-06-28 08:21 /tmp
last 3 for other     drwxr-xr-x   - hdfs    hdfs         0 2013-11-12 04:06 /user
groups               [root@sandbox ~]# _
                                         Owner      Group                          File name
```

Figure 5-4. HDFS directory and file permisssions

- HDFS files have three sets of permissions, those for owner, group, and others. The permissions are specified using a ten-character string, such as -rwxrwxrwx.

- The first character indicates directory or file (- for file or d for directory), the next three characters indicate permissions for the file's owner, the next three for the owner's group, and last three for other groups.

- Possible values for any grouping are r (read permission), w (write permission), x (permission to execute), or - (a placeholder). Note that x is valid only for executable files or directories.

In Figure 5-4, the owner of the files Driver_details and ticket_details (root) has rw- permissions, meaning read and write permissions. The next three characters are permissions for group (meaning all the users who belong to the group this file is owned by, in this case hdfs). The permissions for group are rw-, indicating all group members have read and write permissions for this file. The last three characters indicate permissions for others (users who don't own the file and are not a part of the same group this file is owned by). For this example, others have read permissions only (r--).

Adding Hadoop Users and Groups to Implement File Permissions

As a final step in implementing basic authorization for this system, I need to define appropriate users and groups within Hadoop and adjust file permissions.

First, I create groups for this server corresponding to the example's two groups: Group 1 is called POfficers and Group 2 is ITD.

```
[root@sandbox ~]# groupadd POfficers
[root@sandbox ~]# groupadd ITD
```

Listing and verifying the groups is a good idea:

```
[root@sandbox ~]# cut -d: -f1 /etc/group | grep POfficers
```

I also create user Puser for group POfficers and user Iuser for group ITD:

```
[root]# useradd Puser -gPOfficers
[root]# useradd Iuser -gITD
```

Next, I set up passwords:

```
[root]# passwd Puser
Changing password for user Puser.
New password:
Retype password:
Passwd: all authentication tokens updated successfully.
```

Now, as a final step, I allocate owners and groups to implement the permissions. As you can see in Figure 5-5, owners for the files Driver_details and Ticket_details are changed to the dummy user Puser, and group permissions are set to write; so users from group POfficers (all police officers) will have read/write permissions and users from other groups (viz. IT department) will have read permission only.

```
[root@sandbox home]#
[root@sandbox home]# sudo -u hdfs hadoop fs -chown Puser:POfficers /Ticket_detai
ls
[root@sandbox home]# sudo -u hdfs hadoop fs -chown Puser:POfficers /Driver_detai
ls
[root@sandbox home]# hadoop fs -ls /
Found 6 items
-rw-rw-r--   1 Puser   POfficers           18 2013-11-12 04:43 /Driver_details
-rw-rw-r--   1 Puser   POfficers           18 2013-11-12 04:44 /Ticket_details
drwxr-xr-x   - hdfs    hdfs                 0 2013-11-12 04:07 /apps
drwx------   - mapred  hdfs                 0 2013-11-19 16:17 /mapred
drwxrwxrwx   - hdfs    hdfs                 0 2013-06-28 08:21 /tmp
drwxr-xr-x   - hdfs    hdfs                 0 2013-11-12 04:06 /user
[root@sandbox home]# _
```

Figure 5-5. *Changing owner and group for HDFS files*

Comparing Table 5-1 to the final permissions for all the entities (same-named files in HDFS), you will see that the objective has been achieved: Puser owns the files Driver_details and Ticket_details and belongs to group POfficers (Group 1). The permissions -rw-rw-r-- indicate that any one from Group 1 has read/write permissions, while users belonging to any other group (e.g., Group 2) only have read permissions.

This example gave you a basic idea about fine-tuning authorization for your Hadoop cluster. Unfortunately, the real world is complex, and so are the systems we have to work with! So, to make things a little more real-world, I'll extend the example, and you can see what happens next to the ticket.

Extending Ticket Data

Tickets only originate with the police. Eventually, the courts get involved to further process the ticket. Thus, some of the ticket data needs to be shared with the judicial system. This group needs read as well as modifying rights on certain parts of the data, but only after the ticket is processed through traffic court. In addition, certain parts of the ticket data need to be shared with reporting agencies who provide this data to insurance companies, credit bureaus, and other national entities as required.

These assumptions won't change the basic groups, but will require two new ones: one for the judiciary (Group 3) and another for reporting agencies (Group 4). Now the permissions structure looks like Figure 5-6.

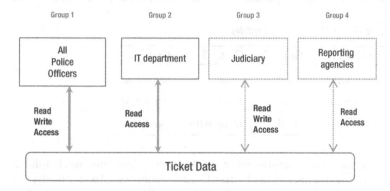

Figure 5-6. *Group access to ticket data with detailed access permissions, showing new groups*

With the added functionality and groups, data will have to be added as well. For example, the table Judgement_details will contain the ticket's judicial history, such as case date, final judgment, ticket payment details, and more. Hadoop will store this table in a file by the same name (Figure 5-7).

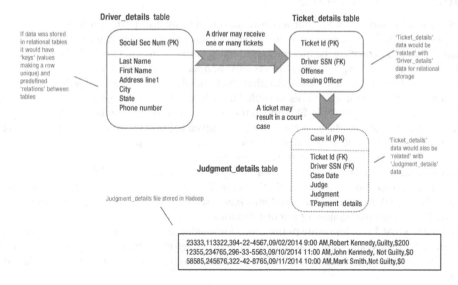

Figure 5-7. *Details of ticket data—classification of information—with added table for legal details*

Like Figure 5-2, Figure 5-7 also illustrates how data would be held in tables if a relational database was used for storage. This is just to compare data storage in Hadoop with data storage in a relational database system. As I discussed earlier, data stored within a relational database system is related: driver data (the Driver_details table) is related to ticket data (the Ticket_details table) using SSN to relate or link the data. With the additional table (Judgement_details), court judgment for a ticket is again related or linked with driver and ticket details using SSN.

Hadoop, as you know, uses files for data storage. So, as far as Hadoop is concerned, there is one additional data file for storing data related to judiciary—Judgement_details. There is no concept of relating or linking data stored within multiple files. You can, of course, link the data programmatically, but Hadoop doesn't do that automatically for you. It is important to understand this difference when you store data in HDFS.

The addition of a table will change the permissions structure as well, as you can see in Table 5-2.

Table 5-2. *Permission Details for Groups and Entities*

Entity (Table)	Group 1	Group 2	Group 3	Group 4
Driver_details	Read/write	Read	Read	No access
Ticket_details	Read/write	Read	Read	No access
Judgement_details	Read	Read	Read/write	Read

Adding new groups increases the permutations of possible permissions , but isn't helpful in addressing complex permission needs (please refer to the section "Role-Based Authorization with Apache Sentry" to learn about implementing granular permissions). For example, what if the police department wanted only the ticket-issuing officer and the station superintendent to have write permission for a ticket? The groups defined in Figure 5-7 and Table 5-2 clearly could not be used to implement this requirement. For such complex needs, Hadoop provides *access control lists* (*ACLs*), which are very similar to ACLs used by Unix and Linux.

Access Control Lists for HDFS

As per the HDFS permission model, for any file access request HDFS enforces permissions for the most specific user class applicable. For example, if the requester is the file owner, then owner class permissions are checked. If the requester is a member of group owning the file, then group class permissions are checked. If the requester is not a file owner or member of the file owner's group, then others class permissions are checked.

This permission model works well for most situations, but not all. For instance, if all police officers, the manager of the IT department, and the system analyst responsible for managing the ticketing system need write permission to the Ticket_details and Driver_details files, the four existing groups would not be sufficient to implement these security requirements. You could create a new owner group called Ticket_modifiers, but keeping the group's membership up to date could be problematic due to personnel turnover (people changing jobs), as well as wrong or inadequate permissions caused by manual errors or oversights.

Used for restricting access to data, ACLs provide a very good alternative in such situations where your permission needs are complex and specific. Because HDFS uses the same (POSIX-based) permission model as Linux, HDFS ACLs are modeled after POSIX ACLs that Unix and Linux have used for a long time. ACLs are available in Apache Hadoop 2.4.0 as well as all the other major vendor distributions.

You can use the HDFS ACLs to define file permissions for specific users or groups in addition to the file's owner and group. ACL usage for a file does result in additional memory usage for NameNode, however, so your best practice is to reserve ACLs for exceptional circumstances and use individual and group ownerships for regular security implementation.

To use ACLs, you must first enable them on the NameNode by adding the following configuration property to hdfs-site.xml and restarting the NameNode:

```
<property>
<name>dfs.namenode.acls.enabled</name>
<value>true</value>
< /property>
```

Once you enable ACLs, two new commands are added to the HDFS CLI (command line interface): setfacl and getfacl. The setfacl command assigns permissions. With it, I can set up write and read permissions for the ticketing example's IT Manager (ITMgr) and Analyst (ITAnalyst):

```
> sudo -u hdfs hdfs dfs -setfacl -m user:ITMgr:rw- /Driver_details
> sudo -u hdfs hdfs dfs -setfacl -m user:ITAnalyst:rw- /Driver_details
```

With getfacl, I can verify the permissions:

```
> hdfs dfs -getfacl /Driver_details
# file: /Driver_details
# owner: Puser
# group: POfficers
user::rw-
user:ITAnalyst:rw-
user:ITMgr:rw-
group::r--
mask::rw-
other::r--
```

When ACL is enabled the file listing shows a + in permissions:

```
> hdfs dfs -ls /Driver_details
-rw-rw-r--+ 1 Puser POfficers          19 2014-09-19 18:42 /Driver_details
```

You might have situations where specific permissions need to be applied to all the files in a directory or to all the subdirectories and files for a directory. In such cases, you can specify a default ACL for a directory, which will be automatically applied to all the newly created child files and subdirectories within that directory:

```
> sudo -u hdfs hdfs dfs -setfacl -m default:group:POfficers:rwx /user
```

Verifying the permissions shows the default settings were applied:

```
> hdfs dfs -getfacl /user

# file: /user
# owner: hdfs
# group: hdfs
user::rwx
group::r-x
other::r-x
```

```
default:user::rwx
default:group::r-x
default:group:POfficers:rwx
default:mask::rwx
default:other::r-x
```

Note that in our simple example I left rw- access for all users from group POfficers, so the ACLs really do not restrict anything. In a real-world application, I would most likely have restricted the group POfficers to have less access (probably just read access) than the approved ACL-defined users.

Be aware that hdfs applies the default ACL only to newly created subdirectories or files; application of a default ACL or subsequent changes to the default ACL of a parent directory are not automatically applied to the ACL of existing subdirectories or files.

You can also use ACLs to block access to a directory or a file for a specific user without accidentally revoking permissions for any other users. Suppose an analyst has been transferred to another department and therefore should no longer have access to ticketing information:

```
> sudo -u hdfs hdfs dfs -setfacl -m user:ITAnalyst:--- /Driver_details
```

Verify the changes:

```
> hdfs dfs -getfacl /Driver_details

# file: /Driver_details
# owner: Puser
# group: POfficers
user::rw-
user:ITAnalyst:---
user:ITMgr:rw-
group::r--
mask::rw-
other::r--
```

The key to effectively using ACLs is to understand the order of evaluation for ACL entries when a user accesses a HDFS file. The permissions are evaluated and enforced in the following order:

1. If the user owns the file, then the owner permissions are enforced.

2. If the user has an ACL entry, then those permissions are enforced.

3. If the user is a member of group (of file ownership), then those permissions are used.

4. If there is an ACL entry for a group and the user is a member of that group, then those permissions are used.

5. If the user is a member of a file group or any other group with ACL entry denying access to the file, then the user is denied access (to the file). If user is a member of multiple groups, then union of permissions for all matching entries is enforced.

6. Last, if no other permissions are applicable, then permissions for the group others are used.

To summarize, HDFS ACLs are useful for implementing complex permission needs or to provide permissions to a specific user or group different from the file ownership. Remember, however, to use ACLs judiciously, because files with ACLs result in higher memory usage for NameNode. If you do plan to use ACLs, make sure to take this into account when sizing your NameNode memory.

Role-Based Authorization with Apache Sentry

Sentry is an application that provides role-based authorization for data stored in HDFS and was developed and committed by Cloudera to the Apache Hadoop community. It provides granular authorization that's very similar to that of a relational database. As of this writing, Sentry is the most mature open source product that offers RBAC (role-based authorization control) for data stored within HDFS, although another project committed by Hortonworks (Argus) is a challenger. Sentry currently works in conjunction with Hive (database/data warehouse made available by the Apache Software Foundation) and Impala (query engine developed by Cloudera and inspired by Google's Dremel).

Hive Architecture and Authorization Issues

Hive is a database that works with HDFS. Its query language is syntactically very similar to SQL and is one of the reasons for its popularity. The main aspects of the database to remember are the following:

- Hive structures data into familiar database concepts such as tables, rows, columns, and partitions.

- Hive supports primitive data types: integers, floats, doubles, and strings.

- Hive tables are HDFS directories (and files within).

- Partitions (for a Hive table) are subdirectories within the "table" HDFS directory.

- Hive privileges exist at the database or table level and can be granted to a user, group, or role.

- Hive privileges are select (read), update (modify data), and alter (modify metadata).

Hive isn't perfect, however. It uses a repository (Metastore) for storing metadata related to tables, so you can potentially have a mismatch between table metadata and HDFS permissions if permissions for underlying HDFS objects are changed directly. Hive doesn't have the capability to prevent or identify such a situation. Therefore, it's possible that a user is granted select permissions on a table, but has update or write permissions on the corresponding directory/files within HDFS, through the user's operating system user or group. Also, Hive has no way of providing permissions for specific parts of table data or partial table data. There is no way to provide column-level permissions, define views (for finer data access control), or define server level roles.

Sentry addresses some of these issues. It provides roles at the server, database, and table level and can work with Hive external tables —which you can use for partial data access control for users.

Figure 5-8 illustrates Hive's architecture and where it fits in respect to HDFS.

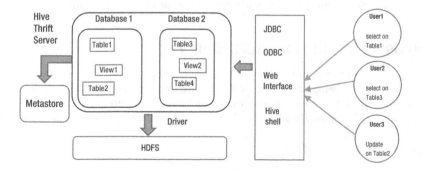

Figure 5-8. *Hive architecture and its authorization*

Sentry Architecture

A security module that integrates with Hive and Impala, Sentry offers advanced authorization controls that enable more secure access to HDFS data. We will focus on Sentry integration with Hive (since it is used more extensively). Sentry uses *rules* to specify precise permissions for a database object and *roles* to combine or consolidate the rules, thereby making it easy to group permissions for different database objects while offering flexibility to create rules for various types of permissions (such as select or insert).

Creating Rules and Roles for Sentry

Sentry grants precise control to specify user access to subsets of data within a database or a schema or a table using a *rule*. For example, if a database db1 has table called Employee, then a rule providing access for Insert can be:

```
server=MyServer->db=db1->table=Employee->action=Insert
```

A *role* is a set of rules to access Hive objects. Individual rules are comma separated and grouped to form a role. For example, the Employee_Maint role can be specified as:

```
Employee_Maint = server=Myserver->db=db1->table=Employee->action=Insert, \
server=server1->db=db1->table=Employee_Dept->action=Insert, \
server=server1->db=db1->table=Employee_salary->action=Insert
```

Here, the Employee_Maint role enables any user (who has the role) to insert rows within tables Employee, Employee_Dept, and Employee_salary.

Role-based authorization simplifies managing permissions since administrators can create templates for groupings of privileges based on functional roles within their organizations.

Multidepartment administration empowers central administrators to deputize individual administrators to manage security settings for each separate database or schema using database-level roles. For example, in the following code, the DB2_Admin role authorizes all permissions for database db2 and Svr_Admin authorizes all permissions for server MyServer:

```
DB2_Admin = server=MyServer->db=db2
Svr_Admin = server=MyServer
```

Creating rules and roles within Sentry is only the first step. Roles need to be assigned to users and groups if you want to use them. How does Sentry identify users and groups? The next section explains this.

Understanding Users and Groups within Sentry

A *user* is someone authenticated by the authentication subsystem and permitted to access the Hive service. Because the example assumes Kerberos is being used, a user will be a Kerberos principal. A *group* is a set of one or more users that have been granted one or more authorization roles. Sentry currently supports HDFS-backed groups and locally configured groups (in the configuration file policy.xml). For example, consider the following entry in policy.xml:

```
Supervisor = Employee_Maint, DB2_Admin
```

If Supervisor is a HDFS-backed group, then all the users belonging to this group can execute any HiveQL statements permitted by the roles Employee_Maint and DB2_Admin. However, if Supervisor is a local group, then users belonging to this group (call them ARoberts and MHolding) have to be defined in the file policy.xml:

```
[users]
ARoberts = Supervisor
MHolding = Supervisor
```

Figure 5-9 demonstrates where Sentry fits in the Hadoop architecture with Kerberos authentication.

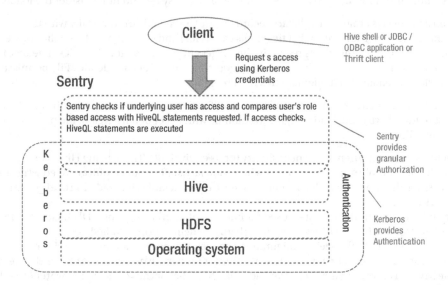

Figure 5-9. *Hadoop authorization with Sentry*

To summarize, after reviewing Hive and Sentry architectures, you gained an understanding of the scope of security that each offers. You had a brief look at setting up rules, roles, users, and groups. So, you are now ready to reimplement the ticketing system (using Sentry) defined in the earlier sections of this chapter.

Implementing Roles

Before reimplementing the ticketing system with the appropriate rules, roles, users, and groups, take a moment to review its functional requirements. A ticket is created by the police officer who issues the ticket. Ticket data is stored in a database at a local police station and needs to have modification rights for all police officers. The IT department located at police headquarters needs read permission on this data for reporting purposes. Some of the ticket data is shared by the judicial system, and they need read as well as modifying rights to parts of data, because data is modified after a ticket is processed through traffic court. Last, certain parts of this data need to be shared with reporting agencies that provide this data to insurance companies, credit bureaus, and other national agencies as required. Table 5-3 summarizes the requirements; for additional detail, consult Figure 5-7.

Table 5-3. *Permission Details for Groups and Entities*

Entity (Table)	Police Officers	IT Department	Judiciary	Reporting Agencies
Driver_details	Read/write	Read	Read	No access
Ticket_details	Read/write	Read	Read	No access
Judgement_details	Read	Read	Read/write	Read

The original implementation using HDFS file permissions was easy but did not consider the following issues:

- When a ticket gets created, a judiciary record (a case) is created automatically with the parent ticket_id (indicating what ticket this case is for) and case details. The police officer should have rights to insert this record in the Judgement_details table with ticket details, but shouldn't be allowed to modify columns for judgment and other case details. File permissions aren't flexible enough to implement this requirement.

- The judge (assigned for a case) should have modification rights for columns with case details, but shouldn't have modification rights to columns with ticket details. Again, file permissions can't handle this.

To implement these requirements, you need Sentry (or its equivalent). Then, using Hive, you need to create external tables with relevant columns (the columns where judiciary staff or police officers need write access) and provide write access for the appropriate departments to those external tables instead of Ticket_details and Judgement_details tables.

For this example, assume that the cluster (used for implementation) is running CDH4.3.0 (Cloudera Hadoop distribution 4.3.0) or later and has HiveServer2 with Kerberos authentication installed.

As a first step, you need to make a few configuration changes. Change ownership of the Hive warehouse directory (/user/hive/warehouse or any other path specified as value for property hive.metastore.warehouse.dir in Hive configuration file hive-site.xml) to the user hive and group hive. Set permissions on the warehouse directory as 770 (rwxrwx---), meaning read, write, and execute permissions for owner and group; but no permissions for others or users not belonging to the group hive. You can set the property hive.warehouse.subdir.inherit.perms to true in hive-site.xml, to make sure that permissions on the subdirectories will be set to 770 as well. Next, change the property hive.server2.enable.doAs to false. This will execute all queries as the user running service Hiveserver2. Last, set the property min.user.id to 0 in configuration file taskcontroller.cfg. This is to ensure that the hive user can submit MapReduce jobs.

Having made these configuration changes, you're ready to design the necessary tables, rules, roles, users, and groups.

Designing Tables

You will need to create the tables Driver_details, Ticket_details, and Judgement_details, as well as an external table, Judgement_details_PO, as follows:

```
CREATE TABLE  Driver_details (SocialSecNum STRING,
Last Name STRING,
First Name STRING,
Address STRUCT<street:STRING, city:STRING, state:STRING, zip:INT>,
Phone BIGINT)
ROW FORMAT DELIMITED FIELDS TERMINATED BY '\;'
LOCATION "/Driver_details";
```

```
CREATE TABLE  Ticket_details (TicketId BIGINT,
DriverSSN STRING,
Offense STRING,
Issuing Officer STRING)
ROW FORMAT DELIMITED FIELDS TERMINATED BY '\;'
LOCATION "/Ticket_details";

CREATE TABLE  Judgement_details (CaseID BIGINT,
TicketId BIGINT,
DriverSSN STRING,
CaseDate STRING,
Judge STRING,
Judgement STRING,
TPaymentDetails STRING)
ROW FORMAT DELIMITED FIELDS TERMINATED BY '\;'
LOCATION "/Judgement_details";

CREATE EXTERNAL TABLE  Judgement_details_PO (CaseID BIGINT,
TicketId BIGINT,
DriverSSN STRING)
ROW FORMAT DELIMITED FIELDS TERMINATED BY '\;'
LOCATION "/user/hive/warehouse/Judgement_details";
```

If you refer to Figure 5-5, you will observe that I am using the same columns (as we have in Hadoop files or tables) to create these tables and just substituting the data type as necessary (e.g., the Last Name is a character string, or data type STRING; but TicketId is a big integer or BIGINT). The last table, Judgement_details_PO, is created as a Hive *external table*, meaning Hive only manages metadata for this table and not the actual datafile. I created this table as an external table with the first two columns of the table Judgement_details because I need certain resources to have permissions to modify these two columns only—not the other columns in that table.

Designing Rules

I need to design rules to provide the security required to implement the ticketing system. The example has four tables, and various roles are going to need Read (Select) or Modify (Insert) rights, because there are no "updates" for Hive or HDFS data. I will simply append (or Insert) the new version of a record. So, here are the rules:

```
server=MyServer->db=db1->table=Driver_details->action=Insert
server=MyServer->db=db1->table=Ticket_details->action=Insert
server=MyServer->db=db1->table=Judgement_details->action=Insert
server=MyServer->db=db1->table=Judgement_details_PO->action=Insert
server=MyServer->db=db1->table=Driver_details->action=Select
server=MyServer->db=db1->table=Ticket_details->action=Select
server=MyServer->db=db1->table=Judgement_details->action=Select
```

These rules simply perform Select or Modify actions for all the tables.

Designing Roles

Let's design roles using the rules we created. The first role is for all police officers:

```
PO_role = server=Myserver->db=db1->table= Driver_details ->action=Insert, \
server=MyServer->db=db1->table= Driver_details ->action=Select, \
server=MyServer->db=db1->table= Ticket_details ->action=Insert, \
server=MyServer->db=db1->table= Ticket_details ->action=Select, \
server=MyServer->db=db1->table= Judgement_details ->action=Select, \
server=MyServer->db=db1->table= Judgement_details_PO ->action=Insert
```

Notice that this role allows all the police officers to have read/write permissions to tables Driver_details and Ticket_details but only read permission to Judgement_details. The reason is that police officers shouldn't have permission to change the details of judgment. You will also observe that police officers have write permission to Judgement_details_PO and that is to correct the first two columns (that don't have any judicial information)—in case there is any error!

The next role is for employees working at the IT department:

```
IT_role = server=MyServer->db=db1->table= Driver_details ->action=Select, \
server=MyServer->db=db1->table= Ticket_details ->action=Select, \
server=MyServer->db=db1->table= Judgement_details ->action=Select
```

The IT employees have only read permissions on all the tables because they are not allowed to modify any data. The role for Judiciary is as follows:

```
JU_role = server=MyServer->db=db1->table= Judgement_details ->action=Insert, \
server=MyServer->db=db1->table= Driver_details ->action=Select, \
server=MyServer->db=db1->table= Ticket_details ->action=Select
```

The judiciary has read permissions for driver and ticket data (because they are not supposed to modify it) but write permission to enter the judicial data because only they are allowed to modify it.

Last, for the Reporting agencies the role is simple:

```
RP_role = server=MyServer->db=db1->table=Judgement_details->action=Select
```

The Reporting agencies have read permissions on the Judgement_details table only because they are allowed to report the judgement. All other data is confidential and they don't have any permissions on it.

Setting Up Configuration Files

I have to set up the various configuration files for Sentry to incorporate the roles that we have set up earlier. The first file is sentry-provider.ini and that defines per-database policy files (with their locations), any server level or database level roles, and Hadoop groups with their assigned (server level or database level) roles. Here's how sentry-provider.ini will look for our example:

```
[databases]
# Defines the location of the per DB policy file for the db1 DB/schema
db1 = hdfs://Master:8020/etc/sentry/customers.ini
```

```
[groups]
# Assigns each Hadoop group to its set of roles
db1_admin = db1_admin_role
admin = admin_role

[roles]
# Implies everything on MyServer -> db1. Privileges for
# db1 can be defined in the global policy file even though
# db1 has its only policy file. Note that the Privileges from
# both the global policy file and the per-DB policy file
# are merged. There is no overriding.
db1_admin_role = server=MyServer->db=db1

# Implies everything on server1
admin_role = server=MyServer
```

In the example's case, there is a specific policy file for database db1 (`customers.ini`) and is defined with its location. Administrator roles for the server and database db1 are defined (`admin_role`, `db1_admin_role`). Appropriate Hadoop groups (`db1_admin`, `admin`) are assigned to those administrator roles.

The next file is `db1.ini`. It is the per-database policy file for database db1:

```
[groups]
POfficers = PO_role
ITD = IT_role
Judiciary = JU_role
Reporting = RP_role

[roles]
PO_role = server=MyServer->db=db1->table= Driver_details ->action=Insert, \
server=MyServer->db=db1->table= Driver_details ->action=Select, \
server=MyServer->db=db1->table= Ticket_details ->action=Insert, \
server=MyServer->db=db1->table= Ticket_details ->action=Select, \
server=MyServer->db=db1->table= Judgement_details ->action=Select, \
server=MyServer->db=db1->table= Judgement_details_PO ->action=Insert

IT_role = server=MyServer->db=db1->table= Driver_details ->action=Select, \
server=MyServer->db=db1->table= Ticket_details ->action=Select, \
server=MyServer->db=db1->table= Judgement_details ->action=Select

JU_role = server=MyServer->db=db1->table= Judgement_details ->action=Insert, \
server=MyServer->db=db1->table= Driver_details ->action=Select, \
server=MyServer->db=db1->table= Ticket_details ->action=Select

RP_role = server=MyServer->db=db1->table=Judgement_details->action=Select
```

Notice above that I have defined all the roles (designed earlier) in the `roles` section. The groups section maps Hadoop groups to the defined roles. Now, I previously set up Hadoop groups `POfficers` and `ITD`. I will need to set up two additional groups (`Judiciary` and `Reporting`) because I mapped roles to them in `db1.ini` file.

The last step is setting up Sentry configuration file `sentry-site.xml`:

```
<configuration>
  <property>
    <name>hive.sentry.provider</name>
    <value>org.apache.sentry.provider.file.HadoopGroupResourceAuthorizationProvider</value>
  </property>

  <property>
    <name>hive.sentry.provider.resource</name>
    <value>hdfs://Master:8020/etc/sentry/authz-provider.ini</value>
  </property>

  <property>
    <name>hive.sentry.server</name>
    <value>Myserver</value>
  </property>
</configuration>
```

Last, to enable Sentry, we need to add the following properties to `hive-site.xml`:

```
<property>
<name>hive.server2.session.hook</name>
<value>org.apache.sentry.binding.hive.HiveAuthzBindingSessionHook</value>
</property>

<property>
<name>hive.sentry.conf.url</name>
<value>hdfs://Master:8020/etc/sentry-site.xml</value>
</property>
```

This concludes reimplementation of the ticketing system example using Apache Sentry. It was possible to specify the correct level of authorization for our ticketing system because Sentry allows us to define rules and roles that limit access to data as necessary. Without this flexibility, either too much access would be assigned or no access would be possible.

Summary

One of the few applications that offers role-based authorization for Hadoop data, Sentry is a relatively new release and still in its nascent state. Even so, it offers a good start in implementing role-based security, albeit nowhere close to the type of security an established relational database technology offers. True, Sentry has a long way to go in offering anything comparable to Oracle or Microsoft SQL Server, but currently it's one of the few options available. That's also the reason why the best practice is to supplement Sentry capabilities with some of Hive's features!

You can use Hive to supplement and extend Sentry's functionality. For example, in the ticketing example, I used the external table feature of Hive to create a role that provided write permission on only some columns of the table. Sentry by itself is not capable of offering partial write permission on a table, but you can use it in combination with Hive to offer such a permission. I encourage you to study other useful Hive features and create your own roles that can extend Sentry's functionality. The Apache documentation at `https://cwiki.apache.org/confluence/display/Hive/LanguageManual+DDL` provides many useful suggestions

Last, the chapter's ticketing example proved that you can provide partial data access (number of columns starting from first column) to a role by defining an external table in Hive. Interestingly, you can't provide access to only some columns (e.g., columns four to eight) for a table using Sentry. Of course, there are other ways of implementing such a request using features that Hive provides!

■ ■ ■

## PART III

Audit Logging and Security Monitoring

■ ■ ■

## CHAPTER 6

Hadoop Logs: Relating and Interpretation

The other day, a very annoyed director of business intelligence (at a client site) stormed into my office and complained about one of the contractors deleting some ledger records from a production server. She had received a daily summary audit log report that showed 300 ledger records (financial transaction entries) had been deleted! To start with, the contractor in question shouldn't have had access to them. So I investigated, and it turned out that the ERP (Enterprise resource planning) software that client was using had a bug that provided access through the "Public" role. I wouldn't have discovered the bug if I didn't have audit logging enabled, which proves how important audit logging can be from a security perspective.

The purpose of HDFS audit logging is to record all HDFS access activity within Hadoop. A MapReduce audit log has entries for all jobs submitted. In addition, the Hadoop daemon log files contain startup messages, internal diagnostic information, errors, informational or warning messages, configuration logs, and so forth. You can filter the information that's not required later, but it's helpful to log all access, including authorized access. Even authorized users can perform tasks for which they are not authorized. For example, a police officer might perform an unauthorized update to his girlfriend's ticket record without appropriate approvals. Besides, for audited applications or any SOX-compliant applications, it is mandatory to audit all access to data objects (e.g., tables) within an application, as well as to audit all job activity that changes any data within an audited application.

In this chapter, I will discuss how to enable auditing for Hadoop and how to capture auditing data. Log4j is at the heart of Hadoop logging, be it audit logs or Hadoop daemon logs. I will begin with a high-level discussion of the Log4j API and how to use it for audit logging, and then discuss the Log4j logging levels and their purpose. After an overview of daemon logs and the information they capture, you will learn how to correlate auditing with Hadoop daemon logs to implement security effectively.

Using Log4j API

A Java-based utility or framework, Apache Log4j was created by by Ceki Gülcü and has since become a project of the Apache Software Foundation. Logging is an essential part of any development cycle and in the absence of a debugger (which is usually the case), it is the only tool for troubleshooting application code. It's very important to use the correct type of logging—one that's reliable, fast, and flexible. Log4j fulfills these requirements:

- **Reliability** is the expectation that relevant error or status messages are displayed without any exceptions. Custom logging routines can be prone to bugs in that some of the messages are not displayed due to faulty logic. Log4j doesn't have that problem. This logging system is well tested and has been popular for a long time. Reliability of the logging output logic can certainly be guaranteed with Log4j.

- **Speed** refers to the response time of logging routine used. With Log4j, the Logger class is instantiated (an instance created) as opposed to interacting with an interface, resulting in a superfast response. Deciding what to log (based on logging level) only involves a decision based on Logger hierarchy, which is fast. Outputting of a log message is fast due to use of preformatting using Layouts and Appenders; typically, actual logging is about 100 to 300 microseconds. With SimpleLayout (the simplest Layout option for Log4j, explained in the "Layout" section), Log4j can log as quickly as a print statement (which simply prints input text to a console or a file)!

- **Flexibility** refers to the ease of change to a logging system (without modifying the application binaries that use it) and the ease of use for the application using the modified logging. For example, with Log4j, you can direct output to two destinations, like the console and a log file, using multiple logging destinations, which are also called Appenders. Simply modify the log4j. properties configuration file to make this change; no code changes are needed.

The easiest way to include status or error messages is, of course, to insert them directly in your code. So, what's the advantage of using Log4j for logging as opposed to inserting comments in your application code or using a custom logging module? Well, inserting comments and removing them is a tedious and time-consuming process that relies on the expertise of the programmer—who might just forget to remove them after testing. Getting the percentage of comments correct (sometimes too many, other times too few) is difficult, and selectively displaying those comments is impossible. Also, any changes to comments involve recompilation of code. Last, a custom logging module may have bugs or may not have as extensive functionality as Log4j API.

Via a configuration file, Log4j allows you to set logging behavior at runtime without modifying application binaries. A major concern with logging is its impact on performance. Any logging by nature slows down an application, but with Log4j the impact on performance is minuscule. For example, an independent test of the latest release of Log4j 2 (Version 2) showed that it can output up to 18 million messages per second (for full results, see Christian Grobmeier, "Log4j": Performance Close to Insane," www.javacodegeeks.com/2013/07/Log4j-2-performance-close-to-insane.html). With Log4j the impact is limited to a range from nanoseconds to microseconds, depending on your Log4j configuration, logging level, and Appenders.

The main components of Log4j logging framework are the Logger, Appender, Layout, and Filters. So you can better understand how they work together, Figure 6-1 illustrates where they fit within the framework.

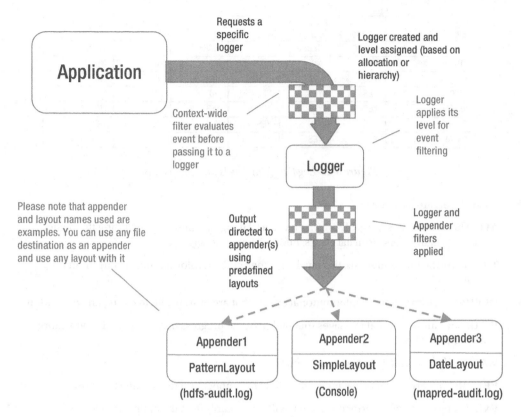

Figure 6-1. *Log4j framework and its main components*

The sections that follow will discuss each of these components in detail and provide information about what they do and what their exact role is within the framework.

Loggers

A *Logger* is a named entity that is associated with a configuration (LoggerConfig) and subsequently with a logging level. For Log4j logging to function, you need to have a root Logger with a related configuration defined. The root Logger defines the default configuration (Appender, Layout, etc.). So what are these logging levels and how do they correlate?

Logging Levels for Log4j

There are seven logging levels for Log4j API. They log information in order of severity and each of the levels is inclusive of all higher levels. For example, log level INFO includes informational messages, warnings (higher-level WARN included), nonfatal errors (higher-level ERROR included) and fatal errors (higher-level FATAL included). Similarly, log level WARN includes warnings, nonfatal errors, and fatal errors. Figure 6-2 summarizes these inclusions.

Row data shows possible logging levels that can be used with Hadoop daemons or services (such as NameNode, JobTracker etc.)

Column data shows level of messages you will actually get in your log files for a Hadoop daemon's configured level

Event Level	Logger Configuration level					
	TRACE	DEBUG	INFO	WARN	ERROR	FATAL
TRACE	YES	NO	NO	NO	NO	NO
DEBUG	YES	YES	NO	NO	NO	NO
INFO	YES	YES	YES	NO	NO	NO
WARN	YES	YES	YES	YES	NO	NO
ERROR	YES	YES	YES	YES	YES	NO
FATAL	YES	YES	YES	YES	YES	YES

Figure 6-2. *Log4j logging levels and inclusions*

The seven log levels are as follows:

- **ALL**: This is the lowest possible logging level, and it logs all messages including the higher levels (e.g., fatal errors, nonfatal errors, informational messages, etc.)

- **TRACE**: As the name suggests, this level logs finer-grained informational events than the DEBUG level.

- **DEBUG**: Logs fine-grained informational events that are most useful to debug an application.

- **INFO**: Logs informational messages that highlight the progress of the application at a more coarse-grained level.

- **WARN**: Logs potentially harmful situations.

- **ERROR**: Logs error events that might still allow the application to continue running.

- **FATAL**: Logs very severe error events that will presumably lead the application to abort.

Please note that enabled TRACE and DEBUG levels can be considered a serious security flaw in production systems and may be reported by vulnerability scanners as such. So, please use these log levels only when troubleshooting issues and make sure that they are disabled immediately afterward.

Logger Inheritance

Logger names are case-sensitive and named hierarchically. A Logger is said to be an *ancestor* of another Logger if its name followed by a dot is a prefix of the descendant Logger name. A Logger is said to be a *parent* of a child Logger if there are no ancestors between it and the descendant Logger. So, for example, the Logger named L1.L2 is parent of the Logger named L1.L2.L3. Also, L1 is parent of L1.L2 and ancestor (think grandparent) of L1.L2.L3. The *root* Logger is at the top of the Logger hierarchy.

A Logger can be assigned a default log level. If a level is not assigned to a Logger, then it inherits one from its closest ancestor with an assigned level. The inherited level for a given Logger L1 is equal to the first non-null level in the Logger hierarchy, starting at L1 and proceeding upward in the hierarchy toward the root Logger. To make sure that all Loggers inherit a level, the root Logger always has an assigned level. Figure 6-3 contains an example of level inheritance.

Logger Name	Assigned level	Inherited level
Root	Lroot	Lroot
L1	L1	L1
L1.L2	None	L1
L1.L2.L3	L3	L3

Figure 6-3. *Logger level inheritance*

As you can see, the root Logger, L1, and L1.L2.L3 have assigned logging levels. The Logger L1.L2 has no logging level assigned to it and inherits the logging level L1 from its parent L1. A logging request is said to be enabled if its level is higher than or equal to the level of its Logger. Otherwise, the request is disabled.

Most Hadoop distributions have five standard Loggers defined in log4j.properties in the /etc/Hadoop/conf or $HADOOP_INSTALL/hadoop/conf directories (Figure 6-4). For Log4j logging to function, a *root* Logger (with related configuration) must be defined. The *security* Logger logs the security audit information. *Audit* Loggers log HDFS and MapReduce auditing information, while a *job summary* Logger logs summarized information about MapReduce jobs. Some distributions also have Loggers defined for Hadoop metrics, JobTracker, or TaskTracker.

Logger Name	Log4j property	Default log level
Root logger	hadoop.root.logger	INFO
Security logger	hadoop.security.logger	INFO
HDFS Audit logger	hdfs.audit.logger	WARN
MapReduce audit logger	mapred.audit.logger	WARN
Job summary logger	hadoop.mapreduce.jobsummary.logger	INFO

Figure 6-4. *Loggers and default log levels*

Figure 6-5 is a sample entry for HDFS audit Logger from log4j.properties.

```
#
# hdfs audit logging                    Logger level        Property specifying
#                                                            logger for hdfs
hdfs.audit.logger=INFO,NullAppender                         audit logging
hdfs.audit.log.maxfilesize=256MB
hdfs.audit.log.maxbackupindex=20
log4j.logger.org.apache.hadoop.hdfs.server.namenode.FSNamesystem.audit=${hdfs.audit.logger}
log4j.additivity.org.apache.hadoop.hdfs.server.namenode.FSNamesystem.audit=false
log4j.appender.RFAAUDIT=org.apache.log4j.RollingFileAppender
log4j.appender.RFAAUDIT.File=${hadoop.log.dir}/hdfs-audit.log        Output written to
log4j.appender.RFAAUDIT.layout=org.apache.log4j.PatternLayout        file hdfs-audit.log
log4j.appender.RFAAUDIT.layout.ConversionPattern=%d{ISO8601} %p %c{2}: %m%n
log4j.appender.RFAAUDIT.MaxFileSize=${hdfs.audit.log.maxfilesize}
log4j.appender.RFAAUDIT.MaxBackupIndex=${hdfs.audit.log.maxbackupindex}
```

Figure 6-5. *HDFS Audit Logger*

The maxfilesize setting is the critical size (here 256MB) after which the log file will "roll" and create a new log file; maxbackupindex (20 in this case) is the number of backup copies of the log file to be created. In this example, when the log file rolls over 21 times, the oldest file will be erased. Properties of other Loggers are specified in a similar manner in the log4j.properties file.

Appenders

For the Log4j framework, an output destination is called an *Appender*. Currently, Appenders exist for the console, files, GUI components, remote socket servers, JMS, NT Event Loggers, and remote UNIX Syslog daemons. In other words, you can define any of these as your output destinations for logging. As of Log4j Version 2, you also can log asynchronously, to pass the control back from the Logger to the application while I/O operations are performed in the background by a separate thread or process. Asynchronous logging can improve your application's performance.

Appender Additivity

Multiple Appenders can be attached to a Logger. Each enabled logging request for a given Logger will be forwarded to all the Appenders in that Logger as well as the Appenders higher in the hierarchy. This is a default behavior known as *Appender additivity* and can easily be disabled by setting the Additivity flag to false in the log4j.properties configuration file.

Consider the example in Figure 6-6. If a console Appender is added to the root Logger, then all enabled logging requests will display on the console. In addition, if a file Appender is added to the Loggers L1, L1.L2, and L1.L2.L3, then logging requests for L1, L1.L2, and L1.L2.L3 will be written to the appropriate files and displayed on the console. Now suppose you set Logger L4's Additivity flag to false. This effectively disconnects L4 and its children from the upward propagation of log output. Because the parent of Logger L4.L5 (which is L4 in the example) has its Additivity flag set to false, L4.L5's output will be directed only to the Appenders in L4.L5 (in this case none) and its ancestors up to and including L4 (File4), but will not propagate to L1, L2, or L3. Figure 6-6 tabulates the results.

Logger	Appender	Additivity	Output	Comment
Root	Console	not applicable	Console	No default appender for root
L1	File1	True	Console, File1	Appenders of "L1" and root
L1.L2	None	True	Console, File1	Appenders of "L1" and root.
L1.L2.L3	File2	True	Console, File1, File2	Appenders in "L1.L2.L3", "L1" and root
L4	File4	**False**	File4	No appender accumulation since additivity is set to false
L4.L5	None	True	File4	Only appenders of L4 since additivity in "L4" is set to false

Figure 6-6. *Appender additivity for Log4j framework*

The Appenders frequently used by the major Hadoop distributions are:

- **Console Appender**: Displays log messages on the console
- **File Appender**: Writes log messages to a specific file, which you define in log4j.properties
- **Rolling file Appender**: Writes log messages to files and rolls them based on size
- **Daily rolling file Appender**: Writes log messages to files and rolls them on a daily basis

Using the same entry as for the HDFS Audit Logger (Figure 6-5), consider the Appender section presented in Figure 6-7.

```
#
# hdfs audit logging                            hdfs-audit.log will roll off if
#                                               size bigger than 256MB and 20
hdfs.audit.logger=INFO,NullAppender             log files will be maintained
hdfs.audit.log.maxfilesize=256MB
hdfs.audit.log.maxbackupindex=20
log4j.logger.org.apache.hadoop.hdfs.server.namenode.FSNamesystem.audit=${hdfs.audit.logger}
log4j.additivity.org.apache.hadoop.hdfs.server.namenode.FSNamesystem.audit=false
log4j.appender.RFAAUDIT=org.apache.log4j.RollingFileAppender
log4j.appender.RFAAUDIT.File=${hadoop.log.dir}/hdfs-audit.log                    Additivity 'false';
log4j.appender.RFAAUDIT.layout=org.apache.log4j.PatternLayout                    output to 'hdfs-
log4j.appender.RFAAUDIT.layout.ConversionPattern=%d{ISO8601} %p %   Rolling file  audit.log' only
log4j.appender.RFAAUDIT.MaxFileSize=${hdfs.audit.log.maxfilesize}  appender used
log4j.appender.RFAAUDIT.MaxBackupIndex=${hdfs.audit.log.maxbackup  with file name
                                                                  'hdfs-audit.log'
```

Figure 6-7. *Rolling file Appender for HDFS Audit Logger*

In Figure 6-7, I used the RollingFileAppender with HDFS audit Logger. The output is formatted as per the Layout (PatternLayout) and the defined conversion pattern (I will discuss Layout and conversion patterns shortly), and looks like this:

```
2014-02-09 16:00:00,683 INFO FSNamesystem.audit: allowed=true   ugi=hdfs (auth:SIMPLE)
ip=/127.0.0.1   cmd=getfileinfo src=/user/sqoop2/.Trash/Current dst=null       perm=null
```

■ **Note**   HDFS audit output may result in a large file. Therefore, it is a good idea to have it roll off to a new file on a daily basis or by size.

Layout

A *Layout* is an output format for a log entry. It can be associated with an Appender and can format the logging request as per your specifications before that request is delivered via an Appender.

It's important to structure and present information in a way that makes reading and interpretation easy. Often it is necessary to pass logging information to another error-processing program running on a remote machine. So, it is important to decide on a structure for logging information. This is what the Layout objects provide.

Layouts use conversion patterns to format and output the log message. A *conversion pattern* consists of a format modifier and conversion characters. For example, the modifier t outputs the name of the thread that generated the logging event, and the conversion characters %5p display (or write) the log level using five characters with space padding on left. So, log level INFO is displayed (or written) as "INFO".

A Layout can be specified for an Appender in the log4j.properties file. For example, I specified PatternLayout as a layout (for our HDFS audit log Appender) in Figure 6-8.

```
#
# hdfs audit logging
#
hdfs.audit.logger=INFO,NullAppender
hdfs.audit.log.maxfilesize=256MB
hdfs.audit.log.maxbackupindex=20
log4j.logger.org.apache.hadoop.hdfs.server.namenode.FSNamesystem.audit=${ho
log4j.additivity.org.apache.hadoop.hdfs.server.namenode.FSNamesystem.audit=      'PatternLayout' specified
log4j.appender.RFAAUDIT=org.apache.log4j.RollingFileAppender                      for HDFS Audit Logger's
log4j.appender.RFAAUDIT.File=${hadoop.log.dir}/hdfs-audit.log                     Appender
log4j.appender.RFAAUDIT.layout=org.apache.log4j.PatternLayout
log4j.appender.RFAAUDIT.layout.ConversionPattern=%d{ISO8601} %p %c{2}: %m%n
log4j.appender.RFAAUDIT.MaxFileSize=${hdfs.audit.log.maxfilesize}
log4j.appender.RFAAUDIT.MaxBackupIndex=${hdfs.audit.log.maxbackupindex}           Conversion pattern
                                                                                  for PatternLayout
```

Figure 6-8. *PatternLayout for HDFS Audit Logger*

The conversion pattern %d{ISO8601} %p %c{2}: %m%n from Figure 6-8 outputs as:

```
2014-01-27 20:34:55,508 INFO FSNamesystem.audit: allowed=true   ugi=mapred (auth:SIMPLE)
ip=/127.0.0.1   cmd=setPermission        src=/tmp/mapred/system/jobtracker.info  dst=null
perm=mapred:supergroup:rw-------
```

The first field is the date/time in ISO8601 (YYYY-MM-DD HH:mm:ss,SSS) format. The second field is the level or priority of the log statement. The third is the category, the fourth field is the message itself, and the fifth field is the line separator (newline or /n).

Apache Log4j offers several Layout objects:

- **Simple Layout**: org.apache.log4j.SimpleLayout provides a very basic structure for the logging message. It includes only the level of the logging information and the logging message itself. This is how the log message for HDFS Audit Logger (from Figure 6-8) will be output if Simple Layout is used instead of PatternLayout:

  ```
  INFO allowed=true ugi=hdfs (auth:SIMPLE) ip=/127.0.0.1
  cmd=getfileinfo src=/user/sqoop2/.Trash/Current dst=null perm=null
  ```

- **Thread-Time-Category-Context Layout (TTCCLayout)**: This Layout outputs the invoking thread, time (in milliseconds since application started), the category or Logger used to create this logging event, and nested diagnostic context. All these properties are optional and if they are all disabled, the Layout will still write out the logging level and the message itself, just like Simple Layout. If you specify the following options in log4j.properties:

  ```
  #configuring the Appender CONSOLE
  log4j.appender.CONSOLE=org.apache.log4j.ConsoleAppender
  log4j.appender.CONSOLE.layout=org.apache.log4j.TTCCLayout
  #configuring the Layout TTCCLayout
  log4j.appender.CONSOLE.layout.ThreadPrinting=false
  log4j.appender.CONSOLE.layout.ContextPrinting=false
  log4j.appender.CONSOLE.layout.CategoryPrefixing=false
  log4j.appender.CONSOLE.layout.DateFormat= ISO8601
  ```

You get the following output:

```
INFO allowed=true ugi=hdfs (auth:SIMPLE) ip=/127.0.0.1
cmd=getfileinfo src=/user/sqoop2/.Trash/Current dst=null perm=null
```

- **DateLayout**: As the name suggests, this Layout provides date formats such as NULL (no date/time displayed), RELATIVE (displays time elapsed after application start), DATE (dd MMM YYYY HH:mm:ss,SSS pattern; final SSS is time elapsed after application start), ABSOLUTE (HH:mm:ss,SSS pattern), and ISO8601 (yyyy-MM-dd HH:mm:ss,SSS pattern).

- **HTMLLayout**: Your application might need to present log information in a nice, visually appealing HTML-formatted file. `org.apache.log4j.HTMLLayout` is the relevant object. A big advantage of having the log file in HTML format is that it can be published as a web page for remote viewing.

- **XMLLayout**: To render logging information in a portable (across multiple application modules) format, Log4j provides the `org.apache.log4j.xml.XMLLayout` object. It is important to note that the final output is *not* a well-formed XML file. This Layout object produces logging information as a number of `<log4j:event>` elements.

- **PatternLayout**: You can use this Layout to "format" or output log messages using a consistent pattern to facilitate their use by an external entity. The relevant Layout object is `org.apache.log4j.PatternLayout`. The formatting is specified by *format modifiers* (e.g. m writes the log message, p writes the log level information) in a conversion pattern such as `%d{ISO8601} %p %c{2}: %m%n`. The display (or write) information is specified by *conversion characters*. For example, `%10c` instructs that the Logger name must be 10 characters, and if it's shorter, to add space padding on left. Specifying `%-10c` indicates space padding should be added to the right. For more details on the PatternLayout class and conversion characters, see: `http://logging.apache.org/log4j/1.2/apidocs/org/apache/log4j/PatternLayout.html`.

Filters

Filters evaluate log events and either allow them to be published or not. There are several types of Filters, and they screen out events based on such criteria as number of events (BurstFilter); a log-event message matching a regular expression (RegexFilter); or the event ID, type, and message (StructuredDataFilter). The type of filter determines where you need to specify it:

- Context-wide Filters are configured as a part of the configuration (LoggerConfig) and evaluate events before passing them to Loggers for further processing.

- Logger Filters are configured for a Logger and are evaluated after the Context-wide Filters and the log level for the Logger.

- Appender Filters are configured for an Appender and determine if a specific Appender should publish the event.

- Appender Reference Filters are configured for a Logger and determine if a Logger should route the event to an Appender.

Please note that all of these Filters need to be specified in the appropriate section (for a Logger or an Appender) in your log4j.properties file. For example, Figure 6-9 shows a section from log4j.properties that defines a RegexFilter to capture HDFS auditing events for login root only:

```
#
# hdfs audit logging
#
hdfs.audit.logger=INFO,console
log4j.logger.org.apache.hadoop.hdfs.server.namenode.FSNamesystem.audit=${hdfs.au
dit.logger}
log4j.additivity.org.apache.hadoop.hdfs.server.namenode.FSNamesystem.audit=false
log4j.appender.DRFAAUDIT=org.apache.log4j.DailyRollingFileAppender
log4j.appender.DRFAAUDIT.File=${hadoop.log.dir}/hdfs-audit.log
log4j.appender.DRFAAUDIT.filter.1=org.apache.log4j.varia.StringMatchFilter      Capture events
log4j.appender.DRFAAUDIT.filter.1.StringToMatch=root                            matching 'root'
log4j.appender.DRFAAUDIT.filter.1.AcceptOnMatch=true
log4j.appender.DRFAAUDIT.filter.2=org.apache.log4j.varia.DenyAllFilter          Filter out all
log4j.appender.DRFAAUDIT.layout=org.apache.log4j.PatternLayout                  other events
log4j.appender.DRFAAUDIT.layout.ConversionPattern=%r %d{ISO8601} %p %c{2}: %m%n
log4j.appender.DRFAAUDIT.DatePattern=.yyyy-MM-dd
```

Figure 6-9. RegexFilter for HDFS Audit Logger

You can similarly use other types of Filters to prevent capture of unwanted events, which will help keep the size of audit log small and make focusing on specific issues easier.

Reviewing Hadoop Audit Logs and Daemon Logs

As you've learned, you can use the Log4j component to generate log output for many purposes (e.g., debugging, operational stats, auditing). The logging data Log4j outputs is, in turn, generated by system daemon processes, and a particular type of data may exist in multiple places. How do you connect and analyze data from disjoint sources to get the total view of system operations, history, and state? The key is Hadoop's audit logs. This section will discuss which daemon processes generate which data, what kind of data is captured by auditing, and how you can use Hadoop audit logs for security proposes.

To get a complete system picture, you need to understand what kind of data is logged by Hadoop daemons or processes (that generate logs) and where these log files reside. You also need to understand how the captured data differs with configured logging level. The auditing data from HDFS, for example, doesn't have details of jobs executed. That data exists elsewhere, so connecting a job with HDFS access audits requires some work. You have to know where logs for JobTracker, TaskTracker (MapReduce V1), and ResourceManager (MapReduce V2) are or where log data for Task attempts is stored. You will need it for a complete audit of data access (who/what/where), and you certainly may need it in case of a security breach.

It is a major issue with Hadoop auditing that there is no direct or easy way to relate audit data with Job data. For example, JobTracker and TaskTracker logs (along with task attempt log data) can provide details of jobs executed and all the statistics related to jobs. But how can you relate this data with audit data that only has details of all HDFS access? You will learn a couple of possible ways later in this chapter.

Audit Logs

Auditing in Hadoop is implemented using the Log4j API, but is not enabled by default. Hadoop provides an HDFS audit log that captures all access to HDFS and the MapReduce audit log, which captures information about all submitted jobs for a Hadoop cluster. The location of audit logs is specified using the environment variable HADOOP_LOG_DIR defined in the hadoop-env.sh configuration file located in $HADOOP_INSTALL/hadoop/conf directory ($HADOOP_INSTALL is the directory where Hadoop is installed). The audit log file names are defined in the `log4j.properties` file, and the defaults are `hdfs-audit.log` (for the HDFS audit log) and `mapred-audit.log` (for the MapReduce audit log). You can't define audit logging for YARN using `log4j.properties` yet; this is still being worked on (see "Add YARN Audit Logging to log4j.properties," `https://issues.apache.org/jira/browse/HADOOP-8392`).

To enable auditing, you need to modify the `log4j.properties` configuration file by changing the logging level of the appropriate Logger from WARN to INFO. You'll find the file in the `/etc/Hadoop/conf` directory or the `$HADOOP_INSTALL/hadoop/conf` directory, where `$HADOOP_INSTALL` is the Hadoop installation directory. `log4j.properties` defines the logging configuration for NameNode and the other Hadoop daemons (JobTracker, TaskTracker, NodeManager, and ResourceManager). For example, to enable HDFS auditing, look for this line in the `log4j.properties` file:

```
log4j.logger.org.apache.hadoop.hdfs.server.namenode.FSNamesystem.audit=WARN
```

Replace WARN with INFO to enable HDFS auditing and ensure a log line written to the HDFS audit log for every HDFS event.

Likewise, to enable MapReduce auditing, set its Logger to the INFO level:

```
log4j.logger.org.apache.hadoop.mapred.AuditLogger=INFO
```

Figure 6-10 shows a section from `log4j.properties` defining the HDFS auditing configuration.

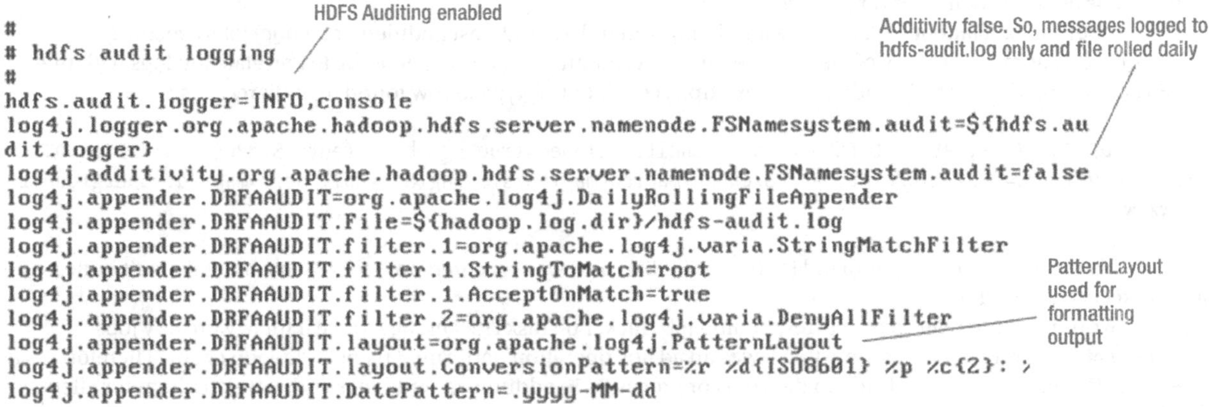

Figure 6-10. *HDFS audit logging configuration*

Hadoop Daemon Logs

Hadoop daemon logs are logs generated by Hadoop daemons (NameNode, DataNode, JobTracker, etc.) and located under `/var/log/hadoop`; the actual directories may vary as per the Hadoop distribution used. The available logs are as follows:

- NameNode logs (`hadoop-hdfs-namenode-xxx.log`) containing information about file opens and creates, metadata operations such as renames, mkdir, and so forth.

- DataNode logs (`hadoop-hdfs-datanode-xxx.log`) containing information about DataNode access and modifications to data blocks.

- Secondary NameNode logs (`hadoop-hdfs-secondarynamenode-xxx.log`) containing information about application of edits to FSimage, new FSimage generation, and transfer to NameNode.

- JobTracker logs (`hadoop-xxx-mapreduce1-jobtracker-xxx.log`), containing information about jobs executed. JobTracker creates an xml file (`job_xxx_conf.xml`) for every job that runs on the cluster. The XML file contains the job configuration. In addition, JobTracker creates runtime statistics for jobs. The statistics include task attempts, start times of tasks attempts, and other information.

- TaskTracker logs (`hadoop-xxx-mapreduce1-tasktracker-xxx.log`), containing information about tasks executed. TaskTracker creates logs for task attempts that include standard error logs, standard out logs, and Log4j logs.

- ResourceManager (`yarn-xxx-resourcemanager-xxx.log`) and Job History server logs (`mapred-xxx-historyserver-xxx.log`), containing information about job submissions, views, or modifications. These are available only if you use MapReduce V2 or YARN.

As with audit logs, you can specify the logging level of the Hadoop daemons in the configuration file `log4j.properties`, and each daemon can have a different level of logging if required. For example, you could set the Audit Logger for HDFS to the INFO level and instruct TaskTracker to log at level TRACE:

```
log4j.logger.org.apache.hadoop.hdfs.server.namenode.FSNamesystem.audit=INFO
log4j.logger.org.apache.hadoop.mapred.TaskTracker=TRACE
```

Please note that other components (e.g., Hive, HBase, Pig, Oozie, etc.) have corresponding `log4j.properties` files in their own configuration directories.

Any operational Hadoop cluster has a number of scheduled (and unscheduled or ad hoc) jobs executing at various times, submitted by any of the approved users. As mentioned, it is challenging to correlate job logs with the HDFS access logs captured via auditing. For example, consider this typical row found in audit records:

```
2013-10-07 08:17:53,438 INFO FSNamesystem.audit: allowed=true ugi=hdfs (auth:SIMPLE) ip=/127.0.0.1
cmd=setOwner src=/var/lib/hadoop-hdfs/cache/mapred/mapred/staging dst=null perm=mapred:supergroup:r
wxrwxrwt
```

All this row says is that a command (`setOwner` in this case) was executed on a source file, but it doesn't indicate if it was executed as part of a job.

You would need to refer to the corresponding JobTracker or TaskTracker logs to see if there were any jobs executing at that time, or else assume that it was an ad hoc operation performed using a Hadoop client. Therefore, you need to maintain logs of other Hadoop daemons or processes in addition to audit logs and correlate them for effective troubleshooting.

Correlating and Interpreting Log Files

Hadoop generates a lot of logs. There are audit logs and daemon logs that separately provide a lot of information about the processing done at the sources from which they are gathered. However, they don't form a cohesive, complete picture of all the processing performed at your Hadoop cluster. That's the reason you need to correlate these logs while troubleshooting an issue or investigating a security breach.

Correlating Hadoop audit data with logs generated by Hadoop daemons is not straightforward and does require a little effort, but the results are well worth it. Using a username or job number as well as Linux filters (e.g. sed or stream editor utility), you can relate the data and identify security breaches.

What to Correlate?

Hadoop daemons log a lot of useful information, and you can also enable and gather audit logs. Assuming you have all these logs available, what should you correlate? Well, that depends on the event you are trying to investigate.

Consider a possible security breach in Chapter 3's ticketing system example. As you remember, all the police stations send their ticketing data nightly to the central repository at police headquarters. The central repository holds the ticketing data in a Hive table that has partitions for each day. Every day, an IT professional runs automated process to add a new partition using the data received.

One day, one of the IT professionals decided to help out his girlfriend by removing her speeding ticket entry. He was caught due to analysis conducted using correlated logs. He removed the ticket entry from the ticketing table, but forgot to remove the corresponding entries from judiciary-related tables, and the system flagged errors when the case was due for a hearing. Subsequently, a thorough investigation was conducted. Let's follow the trail as it unfolded; the unprofessional IT professional goes by the username RogueITGuy.

When the error was detected, the system administrator checked access to HDFS using the following:

- **HDFS audit log:** This provided details of all commands users executed on a cluster. Because Ticket_details was the table that was missing a record, investigators focused on it and filtered out access by user root and HDFS superuser hdfs (since both are system users with controlled passwords) to get a list of users who accessed Ticket_details. To filter, investigators (the team including the system administrator) used the following shell command:

  ```
  grep Ticket_details hdfs-audit.log | grep -v 'ugi=root' | grep -v 'ugi=hdfs'
  ```

  (The -v option for command grep filters records with the keyword specified after the option.) The results included normal user activity plus the following suspicious activity by a user RogueITGuy:

  ```
  2014-03-06 22:26:08,280 INFO FSNamesystem.audit: allowed=true ugi=RogueITGuy
  (auth:SIMPLE) ip=/127.0.0.1    cmd=getfileinfo
  src=/Ticketing/Ticket_details_20140220
        dst=null        perm=null

  2014-03-06 22:26:08,296 INFO FSNamesystem.audit: allowed=true ugi=RogueITGuy
  (auth:SIMPLE) ip=/127.0.0.1    cmd=rename
      src=/Ticketing/Ticket_details_20140220
      dst=/Ticketing/Ticket_stg/Ticket_details_20140220
      perm=RogueITGuy:supergroup:rw-r--r–

  2014-03-06 22:27:02,666 INFO FSNamesystem.audit: allowed=true ugi=RogueITGuy
  (auth:SIMPLE) ip=/127.0.0.1    cmd=open
      src=/Ticketing/Ticket_stg/Ticket_details_20140220        dst=null
      perm=null
  ```

Investigators concluded the following:

- User RogueITGuy (ugi=RogueITGuy) loaded a new version of daily staging file Ticket_details_20140220 (cmd=rename src=/Ticketing/Ticket_details_20140220 dst=/Ticketing/Ticket_stg/Ticket_details_20140220).

- File was loaded to HDFS location that points to external staging table Ticket_details_stg, which is used to load data to the Ticket_details table by creating and overwriting the partition for a particular day.

- The first entry (cmd=getfileinfo src=/Ticketing/Ticket_details_20140220) was to make sure he had the correct (modified with his girlfriend's ticket entry removed) file uploaded from his PC.

- The third entry was to make sure that the modified file was uploaded to the staging location correctly.

- **Hive log:** If this user overwrote a partition with the modified file, he would have done that using Hive. So, investigators looked at the Hive logs next (in /var/log/hive for Cloudera CDH4; may vary as per your distribution and configuration):

```
grep 'ugi=RogueITGuy' hadoop-cmf-hive1-HIVEMETASTORE-localhost.localdomain.log.out
| grep 'ticket_details' | grep -v 'get_partition'
```

They searched for activity by RogueITGuy in the table Ticket_details and, after reviewing the output, filtered out 'get_partition' entries, since that command does not modify a partition. Here's what they saw:

2014-03-06 22:42:36,948 INFO
org.apache.hadoop.hive.metastore.HiveMetaStore.audit: ugi=**RogueITGuy**
ip=/127.0.0.1   cmd=source:/127.0.0.1 **get_table** : db=default tbl=**ticket_details**

2014-03-06 22:42:37,184 INFO
org.apache.hadoop.hive.metastore.HiveMetaStore.audit: ugi=**RogueITGuy**
ip=/127.0.0.1   cmd=source:/127.0.0.1 **append_partition**: db=default
tbl=**ticket_details[2014,2,20]**

Investigators drew the following conclusions:

- The partition for 2/20/14 was overwritten (ugi=RogueITGuy ip=/127.0.0.1 cmd=source:/127.0.0.1 append_partition: db=default tbl=ticket_details[2014,2,20]) for table Ticket_details by RogueITGuy.

- The file Ticket_details_20140220 was uploaded on 3/6/14 22:26 and the Hive partition was overwritten on 3/6/14 22:42 by the same user—RogueITGuy. Case closed!

Last, investigators checked the jobs submitted by RogueITGuy. Several *job-related logs* provided details of jobs users executed. Investigators started by reviewing the *MapReduce audit logs,* which contain all the user, date/time, and result details of submitted jobs. For Cloudera their location is /var/log/hadoop-0.20-mapreduce/mapred-audit.log. Investigators next issued the following command:

```
grep 'RogueITGuy' mapred-audit.log
```

It yielded a couple of jobs:

```
2014-03-06 22:28:01,590 INFO mapred.AuditLogger: USER=RogueITGuy        IP=127.0.0.1
        OPERATION=SUBMIT_JOB    TARGET=job_201403042158_0008    RESULT=SUCCESS
2014-03-06 22:42:07,415 INFO mapred.AuditLogger: USER=RogueITGuy        IP=127.0.0.1
        OPERATION=SUBMIT_JOB    TARGET=job_201403042158_0009    RESULT=SUCCESS
2014-03-06 22:45:55,399 INFO mapred.AuditLogger: USER=RogueITGuy        IP=127.0.0.1
        OPERATION=SUBMIT_JOB    TARGET=job_201403042158_0010    RESULT=SUCCESS
2014-03-06 22:47:39,380 INFO mapred.AuditLogger: USER=RogueITGuy        IP=127.0.0.1
        OPERATION=SUBMIT_JOB    TARGET=job_201403042158_0011    RESULT=SUCCESS
2014-03-06 22:48:46,991 INFO mapred.AuditLogger: USER=RogueITGuy        IP=127.0.0.1
        OPERATION=SUBMIT_JOB    TARGET=job_201403042158_0012    RESULT=SUCCESS
```

Investigators checked the JobTracker and TaskTracker logs using the web interface for JobTracker at `http://JobTrackerHost:50030/JobTracker.jsp`. Jobs job_201403042158_00010, job_201403042158_0011, and job_201403042158_0012 were Select statements that didn't modify any data, but jobs job_201403042158_0008 and job_201403042158_0009 led to conclusive proof! Investigators reviewed the `hive.query.string` property in the job.xml file for these jobs and retrieved the query that was executed, which was:

```
FROM Ticket_details_stg INSERT OVERWRITE TABLE Ticket_details PARTITION (Yr=2014,Mo=2,Dy=20) SELECT
TicketId,DriverSSN,Offense,IssuingOfficer
```

The query used the data from the `Ticket_details_stg` table (a daily staging table) to overwrite a partition for date 2/20/14 for table `Ticket_details`. The HDFS audit logs already established that RogueITGuy had loaded a temporary data file to staging table.

Together, the logs made clear that RogueITGuy edited the daily temporary data file and removed the record that contained ticket entry for his girlfriend. Then he uploaded the new file to the staging table and used the staging table to overwrite a partition for the `Ticket_details` table to make sure that the ticket entry was removed. Using the HDFS audit log, Hive log, MapReduce audit log and `job.xml` files, investigators obtained conclusive evidence of unauthorized activities performed by RogueITGuy and were able to successfully conclude the investigation.

As a result, RogueITGuy lost his job, and his girlfriend had to pay the ticket. She was so touched by his devotion, however, that she agreed to marry him. So, in the end, even RogueITGuy thanked correlated logs!

How to Correlate Using Job Name?

There are several ways you can correlate the logs. The easiest is using login name or job name, because log messages contain this information. You saw how the RogueITGuy username led to correlating the various log files to investigate unauthorized activities. Relating the logs using job names was an important step, as well. To track down the security breach, investigators had to extract relevant information from the logs and use job name to relate multiple logs to get details of what activities were performed for a particular job.

I will walk you through that process now, starting with the MapReduce audit log (`mapred-audit.log`), which has entries as shown in Figure 6-11.

```
[cloudera@localhost hadoop-0.20-mapreduce]$ tail -8 mapred-audit.log
2014-03-05 23:28:54,899 INFO mapred.AuditLogger: USER=hdfs       IP=127.0.0.1      OPERATION=SUBMIT_JOB        TARGET=job_201403042158_0005       RE
SULT=SUCCESS
2014-03-06 21:26:57,491 INFO mapred.AuditLogger: USER=hdfs       IP=127.0.0.1      OPERATION=SUBMIT_JOB        TARGET=job_201403042158_0006       RE
SULT=SUCCESS
2014-03-06 21:28:59,579 INFO mapred.AuditLogger: USER=hdfs       IP=127.0.0.1      OPERATION=SUBMIT_JOB        TARGET=job_201403042158_0007       RE
SULT=SUCCESS
2014-03-06 22:28:01,590 INFO mapred.AuditLogger: USER=RogueITGuy       IP=127.0.0.1       OPERATION=SUBMIT_JOB        TARGET=job_201403042158_00
08     RESULT=SUCCESS
2014-03-06 22:42:07,415 INFO mapred.AuditLogger: USER=RogueITGuy       IP=127.0.0.1       OPERATION=SUBMIT_JOB        TARGET=job_201403042158_00
09     RESULT=SUCCESS
2014-03-06 22:45:55,399 INFO mapred.AuditLogger: USER=RogueITGuy       IP=127.0.0.1       OPERATION=SUBMIT_JOB        TARGET=job_201403042158_00
10     RESULT=SUCCESS
2014-03-06 22:47:39,380 INFO mapred.AuditLogger: USER=RogueITGuy       IP=127.0.0.1       OPERATION=SUBMIT_JOB        TARGET=job_201403042158_00
11     RESULT=SUCCESS
2014-03-06 22:48:46,991 INFO mapred.AuditLogger: USER=RogueITGuy       IP=127.0.0.1       OPERATION=SUBMIT_JOB        TARGET=job_201403042158_00
12     RESULT=SUCCESS
[cloudera@localhost hadoop-0.20-mapreduce]$ █
```

Figure 6-11. *MapReduce audit log*

Notice the highlighted entry with the job name job_201403042158_0008. The HDFS audit log has multiple entries for this job. How do you filter them out?

If you look at the first occurrence of an entry for this job (in `hdfs-audit.log`), you will observe that it has the pattern `cmd=getfileinfo` along with job name job_201403042158_0008. This holds true for Cloudera's Hadoop distribution (CDH4) and if you have use a different distribution, you will need to identify a unique pattern for the first and last occurrences of a particular job. The good news is that you only have to perform this exercise *once for a Hadoop distribution*. You simply have to establish a unique pattern for the first and last occurrence of the job name that separates it from subsequent occurrences; then you can use it for all your searches.

Subsequently, you can use the Linux utility awk to get the line number for first occurrence of this pattern:

```
awk '/cmd\=getfileinfo/ && /job_201403042158_0008\t/ { print NR }' hdfs-audit.log
```

The awk utility looks for the first line that matches the patterns cmd=getfileinfo and job_201403042158_0008 and uses the built-in variable NR to output line number.

Also, you can get the line number for last occurrence of a job name by using the patterns cmd=delete and /src=/tmp/mapred/system/ job_201403042158_0008 like:

```
awk '/cmd\=delete/ && /src=\/tmp\/mapred\/system\/job_201403042158_0008/ { print NR }'
hdfs-audit.log
```

After that, you can just use a stream editor, such as sed, to print lines starting with the first pattern and ending with the second pattern. For example, sed -n 1,20p hdfs-audit.log will display lines 1 to 20 from file hdfs-audit.log on the screen.

```
sed -n `awk '/cmd\=getfileinfo/ && /job_201403042158_0008\t/ { print NR }' hdfs-audit.log`,`awk
'/cmd\=delete/ && /src=\/tmp\/mapred\/system\/ job_201403042158_0008/ { print NR }' hdfs-audit.log`p
hdfs-audit.log
```

The sed command uses line numbers obtained in earlier steps (marked with ***bold and italic***) as start and end to print all the lines in between. You can redirect the output of command sed to a file and review the HDFS audit records, instead of watching them on the screen (as implied by the last sed command). You can use this sed command to extract job details from hdfs-audit.log for any jobs (for CDH4)—just substitute the job name!

Now, in this case, you didn't get much information from hdfs-audit.log entries, except that this job did Hive-related processing and also showed the location of job.xml:

```
2014-03-06 22:27:59,817 INFO FSNamesystem.audit: allowed=true   ugi=RogueITGuy (auth:SIMPLE)
ip=/127.0.0.1   cmd=create      src=/user/RogueITGuy/.staging/job_201403042158_0008/libjars/hive-
builtins-0.10.0-cdh4.4.0.jar    dst=null         perm=RogueITGuy:supergroup:rw-r--r–

2014-03-06 22:28:02,184 INFO FSNamesystem.audit: allowed=true   ugi=RogueITGuy (auth:SIMPLE)
ip=/127.0.0.1   cmd=getfileinfo src=/user/RogueITGuy/.staging/job_201403042158_0008/job.xml
dst=null        perm=null

2014-03-06 22:28:02,324 INFO FSNamesystem.audit: allowed=true   ugi=RogueITGuy
(auth:SIMPLE)     ip=/127.0.0.1    cmd=getfileinfo src=/tmp/hive-RogueITGuy/hive_2014-03-06_22-
27-55_562_981696949097457901-1/-mr-10004/164c8515-a032-4b6f-a551-9bc285ce37c4       dst=null
perm=null
```

Why not just use grep command to retrieve the job details for job job_201403042158_0008 in hdfs-audit.log? The reason is that all the lines pertaining to job job_201403042158_0008 may not contain the job name pattern and you want to make sure you don't miss any relevant lines from log file hdfs-audit.log.

Using Job Name to Retrieve Job Details

You can use the same technique of finding a unique pattern for the first occurrence to retrieve records relevant to a job from the JobTracker or TaskTracker logs. For example, to look for a pattern in the JobTracker log file and get the line number of the first occurrence of a job, such as job_201403042158_0008, use:

```
awk '/job_201403042158_0008/ && /nMaps/ && /nReduces/ { print NR }'
hadoop-cmf-mapreduce1-JOBTRACKER-localhost.localdomain.log.out
```

To retrieve the line number for last occurrence for 'job_201403042158_0008', use:

```
awk '/job_201403042158_0008/ && /completed successfully/ { print NR }'
hadoop-cmf-mapreduce1-JOBTRACKER-localhost.localdomain.log.out
```

You can use command sed to get details from the JobTracker log file for CDH4 by specifying the job name. For example, the sed command to print out all records for job_201403042158_0008 is:

```
sed -n `awk '/job_201403042158_0008/ && /nMaps/ && /nReduces/ { print NR }' hadoop-cmf-mapreduce1-
JOBTRACKER-localhost.localdomain.log.out`,`awk '/job_201403042158_0008/ && /completed successfully/
{ print NR }' hadoop-cmf-mapreduce1-JOBTRACKER-localhost.localdomain.log.out`p hadoop-cmf-
mapreduce1-JOBTRACKER-localhost.localdomain.log.out
```

The command's output provides valuable details such as the nodes tasks were executed on or where the task output is located:

```
2014-03-06 22:28:01,394 INFO org.apache.hadoop.mapred.JobInProgress: job_201403042158_0008: nMaps=1
nReduces=0 max=-1

2014-03-06 22:28:01,764 INFO org.apache.hadoop.mapred.JobInProgress: Input size for job
job_201403042158_0008 = 74. Number of splits = 1

2014-03-06 22:28:01,765 INFO org.apache.hadoop.mapred.JobInProgress: tip:task_201403042158_0008_m_00
0000 has split on node:/default/localhost.localdomain

2014-03-06 22:28:01,765 INFO org.apache.hadoop.mapred.JobInProgress: Job job_201403042158_0008
initialized successfully with 1 map tasks and 0 reduce tasks.

2014-03-06 22:28:02,089 INFO org.apache.hadoop.mapred.JobTracker: Adding task (JOB_SETUP)
'attempt_201403042158_0008_m_000002_0' to tip task_201403042158_0008_m_000002, for tracker
'tracker_localhost.localdomain:localhost.localdomain/127.0.0.1:47799'
```

Using Web Browser to Retrieve Job Details

You can also review the JobTracker and TaskTracker log records easily using the browser interface. The runtime statistics for a job or XML file for a job are best reviewed using the browser interface. The URL for the records is composed of the tracker's name and web access port. If your JobTracker host is called 'MyJobHost' and uses port 50030 for web access, for example, then the JobTracker logs can be reviewed at http://MyJobHost:50030/logs/. Likewise, logs for a TaskTracker running on host 'MyTaskHost' and using port 50060 can be reviewed at http://MyTaskHost:50060/logs/. Check your configuration file (mapred-site.xml) for particulars of hosts running specific daemons and ports. Filenames may vary by distributions, but log files will have TaskTracker or JobTracker in their names, making them easy to identify.

Figure 6-12 shows a logs directory and various MapReduce log files for a cluster using MapReduce 1.0.

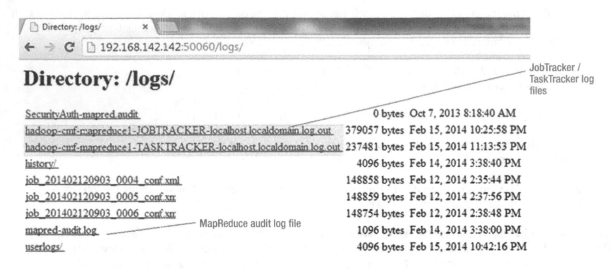

Figure 6-12. *MapReduce log files for MapReduce Version 1*

If you are using YARN, then the corresponding daemons are ResourceManager (instead of JobTracker) and NodeManager (instead of TaskTracker). Please check the YARN configuration file (yarn-site.xml) for web access ports (values of mapreduce.johistory.webapp.address and yarn.resourcemanager.webapp.address). For example, in Figure 6-13, the ResourceManager uses port 8088.

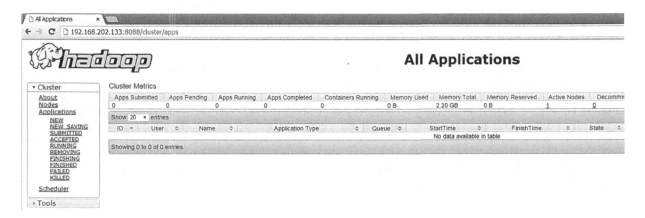

Figure 6-13. *ResourceManager web interface for YARN*

The NodeManager uses port 8042, as shown in Figure 6-14.

Figure 6-14. *NodeManager web interface for YARN*

Last, the Historyserver uses port 19888 (Figure 6-15).

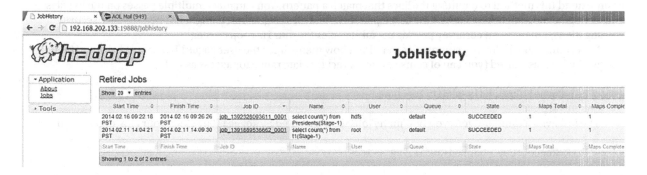

Figure 6-15. *HistoryServer web interface for YARN*

The YARN logs for NodeManager and ResourceManager should be used to get job details when YARN is used. Historyserver holds logs for archived or "retired" jobs. So, if you need to access older job details, that's what you need to check. The patterns to locate first and last lines may change slightly and might need to be adjusted; but you can easily browse through the log files to make those adjustments. An easy way to find out location of the YARN log files is to refer to the log4j.properties file located in /etc/hadoop/conf and see where the appropriate Appenders are pointing.

A thought before I conclude the chapter. You have seen how to relate logs for a job, but what if you want to trace all the activity for a user or you want to trace activity for a whole day? Defining and using awk patterns would be cumbersome, difficult, and error-prone. Instead, try defining Log4j Filters for Appenders, as well as defining additional Appenders to direct relevant output to separate files for an issue, and consolidate all the files for an issue. You can either use Flume for that purpose or simply have your shellscripts do the consolidation for you.

Important Considerations for Logging

Some additional factors will help you make effective use of logging. Although they are not directly relevant to security, I will mention them briefly in this section and you can decide how relevant they are for your individual environments.

Time Synchronization

Hadoop is a distributed system with multiple nodes—often a large number of them. Therefore, Hadoop logs are also distributed across the various nodes within your cluster. Individual log messages are timestamped, and while you are troubleshooting, you need to be sure that 12:00 PM on one node is the same moment of time as specified by 12:00 PM on another node.

For a network, *clock skew* is the time difference in the clocks for different nodes on the network. Usually, a time difference in milliseconds is acceptable; but a larger clock skew needs to be avoided. A number of protocols (e.g., Network Time Protocol, http://en.wikipedia.org/wiki/Network_Time_Protocol) can be used to make sure that there is negligible time skew. It is certainly important to make sure that the generated logs for your cluster are time synchronized.

Hadoop Analytics

In the section "Correlating and Interpreting Log Files," I have discussed how a combination of the Linux stream editor sed and the powerful text processor awk can be used to search for a pattern and print the appropriate lines. You can easily extend this method to counting the lines that match a pattern. You can make multiple passes on the log files and aggregate the matches to analyze the usage patterns. Analytics so generated might not be useful for security investigations, but they can certainly provide useful statistics for your Hadoop cluster.

For example, the following command can tell you how many times the user RogueITGuy accessed your Hadoop cluster since it was started (you can of course easily extract the date range for access as well):

```
grep 'ugi=RogueITGuy' hdfs-audit.log | wc -l
```

The following command tells you how many jobs were executed by RogueITGuy since your cluster restarted:

```
grep 'USER=RogueITGuy' mapred-audit.log | wc -l
```

The following script extracts the start and end date/time for job job_201403042158_0008 (you can then compute the job duration):

```
awk -F ',' '/cmd\=getfileinfo/ && /job_201403042158_0008\t/ { print $1 }' hdfs-audit.log
awk -F ',' '/cmd\=delete/ && /src=\/tmp\/mapred\/system\/job_201403042158_0008/ { print $1 }' hdfs-audit.log
```

You can develop automated scripts that write all the daily job analysis or HDFS access analysis to files and add them as partitions for appropriate Hive tables. You can then perform aggregations or use other statistical functions on this data for your own analytical system.

Of course, the analytics that are more relevant to you may vary, but I am sure you understand the method behind them.

This historical data (stored as Hive tables) can also be used for generating security alerts by defining *variation thresholds*. For example, you can write a Hive query to generate an alert (through Nagios) if a user executes twice (or more) the number of jobs as compared to his monthly average. The use of historical data for security alerts will always rely on sudden change in usage, and you can use the concept as applicable to your environment.

Splunk

Splunk is a very powerful tool for analyzing Hadoop data. Using the Hadoop Connect module of Splunk, you can import any HDFS data and use the indexing capability of Splunk for further searching, reporting, analysis, and visualization for your data. You can also import Hadoop logs, index them, and analyze them.

Splunk provides a powerful search processing language (SPL) for searching and analyzing real-time and historical data. It can also provide capability of real-time monitoring of your log data (for patterns/thresholds) and generate alerts when specific patterns occur (within your data). For example, if you are using Hive, you want to know when a partition (for one of your Production tables) is overwritten or added. You might also want to alert your system administrator when one of the users connects to your cluster.

Splunk's most important capability (from security logging perspective) is its ability to correlate data. Splunk supports the following ways to correlate data:

- **Time and geolocation based**: You can correlate data for events that took place over a specific date or time duration and at specific locations. So, if I had used Splunk to conduct investigation for RogueITGuy, I could have asked Splunk to give me all the log data for 3/16/14 (the specific date when the issue occurred).

- **Transaction based**: You can correlate all the data for a business process (or series of business processes) and identify it as a single event. Even though it can't be used for security, it can provide analytics for a job or a business process (such as duration, CPU and RAM resources consumed, etc.).

- **Sub-searches**: Allow you to use the results of one search and use them in another. So, if I had used Splunk to conduct investigation for RogueITGuy, then I could define my sub-searches to HDFS, MapReduce, or Hive access for easier analysis.

- **Lookups**: Allow you to correlate data from external sources. For instance, I could have checked all Hive alerts from Nagios to see if RogueITGuy was involved in any other issues.

- **Joins**: Allows you to link two completely different data sets together based on a username or event ID field. Using Splunk, I could link monitoring data from Ganglia and Hadoop log data using username RogueITGuy and investigate what else he accessed while performing his known illegal activities.

Last, Splunk offers Hunk, which is an analytics tool specifically designed for Hadoop and NoSQL Data. It lets you explore, analyze, and visualize raw, unstructured data. Hunk also offers role-based access to limit access to sensitive data (more information at www.splunk.com/hunk). Take a look and see if it is more useful for your needs!

Summary

In this chapter, I discussed how Hadoop logging can be effectively used for security purposes. The high-level approach is to use Linux utilities and stream editors to process the text in log files and derive the necessary information, but this is, of course, very old-fashioned and hard work. There are easier ways of achieving similar results by using third-party solutions such as Splunk.

A large number of third-party products are available for reducing the work involved in troubleshooting or investigating security breaches. The disadvantage is that you won't have as much control or flexibility while correlating or analyzing the logs. The preference is yours—and most of the times it's dictated by your environment and your requirements. With either approach, be sure to synchronize time on all the nodes you need to consider before you can rely on the logs generated.

Last, it is worthwhile to explore the use of Hadoop logs for analytics—be it security related or otherwise. You can either buy expensive software to perform the analytics or develop your own scripts if you are sure of your requirements—and if they are small in number!

CHAPTER 7

■ ■ ■

Monitoring in Hadoop

Monitoring, as any system administrator will tell you, is ideal for getting to the root of performance issues. Monitoring can help you understand why a system is out of CPU or RAM resources, for example, and notify you when CPU or RAM usage nears a specified percent. What your system administrator may not know (but you can explain after reading this chapter) is that monitoring is equally well suited for ferreting out security issues.

Consider a scenario: You manage a Hadoop cluster (as system administrator) and are concerned about two specific users: Bob, a confirmed hacker, and Steve, who loves to run queries that access volumes of data he is not supposed to access! To stop password loss and avoid server crashes, you would like to be notified when Bob is trying to read the /etc/password file and when Steve is running a huge query that retrieves the whole database. Hadoop monitoring can provide the information you need. Specifically, Hadoop provides a number of Metrics to gain useful security details, which the leading monitoring systems can use to alert you to trouble. In addition, these monitoring systems let you define thresholds (for generating alerts) based on specific Metric values and also let you define appropriate actions (in case thresholds are met) Thus, Hadoop monitoring offers many features you can use for performance monitoring and troubleshooting.

In this chapter's detailed overview of monitoring, I will discuss features that a monitoring system needs, with an emphasis on monitoring distributed clusters. Thereafter, I will discuss the Hadoop Metrics you can use for security purposes, and introduce Ganglia and Nagios, the two most popular monitoring applications for Hadoop. Last, I will discuss some helpful plug-ins for Ganglia and Nagios that provide integration between the two programs, as well as plug-ins that provide security-related functionality.

Overview of a Monitoring System

Monitoring a distributed system is always challenging. Not only are multiple processes interacting with users and each other, but you must monitor the system without affecting the performance of those processes in any way. A system like Hadoop presents an even greater challenge, because the monitoring software has to monitor individual hosts and then consolidate that data in the context of the whole system. It also needs to consider the roles of various components in context of the whole system. For example, the CPU usage on a DataNode is not as important as the CPU usage on NameNode. So, how will the system process CPU consumption alerts or identify separate threshold levels for hosts with different roles within the distributed system? Also, when considering CPU or storage usage for DataNodes, the monitoring system must consider combined usage for all the DataNodes within a cluster. Subsequently, the monitoring system needs to have capability of summarizing monitoring thresholds by role as well.

In addition to the complex resource monitoring capabilities, a monitoring system for distributed systems needs to have access to details of processes executing at any time. This is necessary for generating alerts (e.g., a user process resulting in 90% CPU usage) or performing any preventive action (e.g., a user is accessing critical system files).

Before you can effectively meet the challenges of monitoring a Hadoop system, you need to understand the architecture of a simple monitoring system. In the next section, I'll discuss the components, processing, and features that you need for monitoring a distributed system effectively, as well as how this simple architecture can be adapted to be better suited for monitoring a Hadoop cluster.

Simple Monitoring System

A simple monitoring system needs four key components: a server or coordinator process, connections to poll distributed system hosts and gather the necessary information, a repository to store gathered information, and a graphical user interface as a front-end (Figure 7-1).

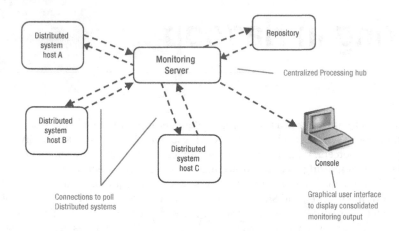

Figure 7-1. *Simple monitoring system*

As you can see, the monitoring server consolidates input received by polling the distributed system hosts and writes detailed (as well as summarized) output to a repository. A console provides display options for the gathered data, which can be summarized using various parameters, such as monitoring event, server, type of alert, and so on.

Unfortunately, simple monitoring system architecture like this doesn't scale well. Consider what would happen if Figure 7-1's system had to monitor thousands of hosts instead of three. The monitoring server would have to manage polling a thousand connections, process and consolidate output, and present it on the console within a few seconds! With every host added to the monitoring system, the load on the monitoring server will increase. After a certain number of hosts, you won't be able to add any more, because the server simply won't be able to support them. Also, the large volume of polling will add to network traffic and impact overall system performance.

Add to that the complexities of a Hadoop cluster where you need to consider a node's role while consolidating data for it, as well as summarizing data for multiple nodes with the same role. The simplistic design just won't suffice, but it can be adapted for monitoring a Hadoop cluster.

Monitoring System for Hadoop

A simple monitoring system follows the same processing arrangement as the traditional client-server design: a single, centralized monitoring server does all the processing, and as the number of hosts increase, so does the processing load. Network traffic also weighs down the load, as polled data from hosts consolidates on the monitoring server.

Just as Hadoop's distributed architecture is a marked improvement in efficiency over traditional client-server processing, a distributed processing model can improve a simple monitoring system as well. If a localized monitoring process captures and stores monitoring data for each node in a Hadoop cluster, for example, there is no longer a centralized server to become a processing bottleneck or a single point of failure. Every node is an active participant performing part of the processing in parallel. Each of these localized processes can then transmit data to other nodes in the cluster and also receive copies of data from other nodes in the cluster. A polling process can poll monitoring data for the whole cluster from any of the nodes within the cluster at any predetermined frequency. The data can be written to a repository and stored for further processing or displayed by a graphical or web based frontend. Figure 7-2 shows a possible design.

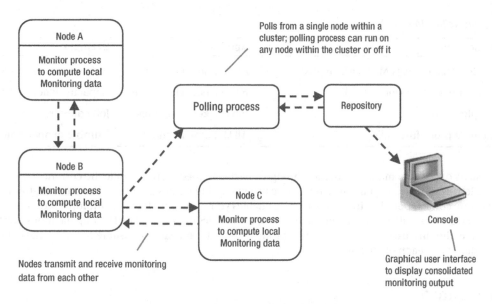

Figure 7-2. *Monitoring system for Hadoop*

With this architecture, even adding 1000 hosts for monitoring would not adversely affect performance. No additional load burdens any of the existing nodes or the polling process, because the polling process can still poll from any of the nodes and doesn't have to make multiple passes. The cluster nodes transmit data to a common channel that is received by all other nodes. So, increasing the number of nodes does not impact polling process or system performance in any way, making the architecture highly scalable. Compared to traditional monitoring systems, the only extra bit of work that you need to do is to apply the monitoring process configuration to all the nodes.

Taking a closer look at Figure 7-2, notice that the monitoring processes on individual nodes compute "local monitoring data." The monitoring data needs to be computed locally; because Hadoop is a multi-node distributed system where data is spread onto its numerous DataNodes and as per the Hadoop philosophy of "taking processing to data," the data is processed locally (where it resides—on the DataNodes). This "local monitoring data" is actually Metric output for individual nodes; it can tell you a lot about your system's security and performance, as you'll learn next.

Hadoop Metrics

Hadoop *Metrics* are simply information about what's happening within your system, such as memory usage, number of open connections, or remaining capacity on a node. You can configure every Hadoop daemon to collect Metrics at a regular interval and then output the data using a plug-in. The collected data can contain information about Hadoop daemons (e.g., the resources used by them), events (e.g., MapReduce job executions), and measurements (e.g., number of files created for NameNode). The output plug-in you use determines the Metric's destination. For example, FileContext writes the Metric to a file, GangliaContext passes the Metric passed on to the Ganglia monitoring system for display and consolidation, and NullContext discards the Metric.

Depending on the information they contain Metrics are classified into four *contexts*: jvm, dfs, rpc, and mapred. Metrics for jvm contain basic statistics for JVM (Java Virtual Machine) such as memory usage or thread counts etc. This context is applicable for all Hadoop daemons. The dfs (distributed file system) context is applicable to NameNode and DataNode. Some of the Metrics for this context output information such as capacity or number of files (for NameNode), number of failed disk volumes, remaining capacity on that particular worker node (for DataNode), et cetera. JobTracker and TaskTracker use the mapred context for their counters. These Metrics contain pre-job counter data, job counters, and post-job counters. The rpc context is used for remote procedure call (RPC) Metrics such as average time taken to process an RPC, number of open connections, and the like, and is applicable to all Hadoop daemons. Table 7-1 summarizes the contexts.

Table 7-1. *Contexts for Hadoop Metrics*

Context	Description	Applicable to	Example
jvm	Basic statistics for JVM (Java Virtual Machine)	All Hadoop daemons	Memory usage, thread count
dfs	Distributed file system	NameNode, DataNode	Capacity, failed disk volumes
mapred	MapReduce	JobTracker, TaskTracker	Job counters
rpc	Remote procedure calls	All Hadoop daemons	Number of open connections

Early versions of Hadoop managed Metrics through a system named Metrics, while the current version of Hadoop uses Metrics2. The management systems have two major differences. Metrics relies on a one-to-one relationship of one context per plug-in, while Metrics2 enables you to output Metrics to multiple plug-ins. The Metrics2 system also uses a slightly different terminology; the Metrics data output by Hadoop daemons is referred to as *sources* and the plug-ins are called *sinks*. Sources produce the data, and sinks consume or output the data. Let me discuss a few Metrics for each of the contexts.

The jvm Context

The jvm Metrics focus on basic JVM statistics. Table 7-2 lists some of these Metrics.

Table 7-2. *Metrics for jvm Context*

Metric	Description
GcCount	Number of garbage collections (automated deallocation of heap memory from unused objects) performed for the JVM
GcTimeMillis	Total time for all garbage collections for a JVM (in milliseconds)
LogFatal	Number of log lines with error level FATAL (using Log4j)
MemHeapCommittedM	Heap memory committed, or the amount of memory guaranteed to be available for use by the JVM (in MB)
MemHeapUsedM	Heap memory currently used by the JVM (includes memory occupied by all objects) (in MB)
ThreadsWaiting	Number of threads in WAITING state (i.e., waiting for another thread to complete an action)

You can infer how dynamic your JVM process is by looking at **GcCount** and **GcTimeMillis** Metrics; larger numbers indicate a lot of memory-based activity. A large number of fatal errors indicate a problem with your system or application, and you need to consult your logs immediately. The memory counter **MemHeapUsedM** tells you about total memory usage, and if you see a large number for **ThreadsWaiting**, you know you need more memory.

The dfs Context

The dfs (distributed file system) Metrics focus on basic file operations (create, delete) or capacity, transactions, and the like. Table 7-3 lists some of these Metrics.

Table 7-3. Metrics for dfs Context

Metric	Desription
CapacityRemaining	Total disk space free in HDFS (in GB)
FilesCreated	Number of files created in a cluster
FilesDeleted	Number of files deleted in a cluster
FilesRenamed	Number of files renamed in a cluster
PercentRemaining	Percentage of remaining HDFS capacity (in GB)
TotalBlocks	Total number of blocks in a cluster
Transactions_avg_time	Average time for a transcation
Transactions_num_ops	Number of transactions

The dfs Metrics can be used for security purposes. You can use them to spot unusual activity or sudden change in activity for your cluster. You can store the daily Metric values (in a Hive table), and calculate an average for last 30 days. Then, if the daily value for a Metric varies by, say, 50% from the average, you can generate an alert. You can also direct the Metrics output to Ganglia, use Ganglia for aggregation and averaging, and then use Nagios to generate alerts based on the 50% variation threshold.

The rpc Context

The rpc (remote procedure call) Metrics focus on process details of remote processes. Table 7-4 lists some important rpcMetrics.

Table 7-4. Metrics for rpc Context

Metric	Desription
RpcProcessingTimeNumOps	Number of processed RPC requests
RpcAuthenticationFailures	Number of failed RPC authentication calls
RpcAuthorizationFailures	Number of failed RPC authorization calls

The rpc Metrics can also be used for security purposes. You can use them to spot unusual RPC activity or sudden changes in RPC activity for your cluster. Again, you can store the daily Metric values in a Hive table (or use Ganglia) and maintain averages for last 30 days. Then, if the daily value for a Metric varies by a certain percentage from the average, such as 50%, you can generate an alert. Metrics such as **RpcAuthenticationFailures** or **RpcAuthorizationFailures** are especially important from the security perspective.

The mapred Context

Metrics for mapred (MapReduce) context provide job-related details (for JobTracker/TaskTracker). Table 7-5 lists some important mapred Metrics.

Table 7-5. *Metrics for mapred Context*

Metric	Desription
jobs_completed	Number of jobs that completed successfully
jobs_failed	Number of jobs that failed
maps_completed	Number of maps that completed successfully
maps_failed	Number of maps that failed
memNonHeapCommittedM	Non-heap memory that is committed (in MB)
memNonHeapUsedM	Non-heap memory that is used (in MB)
occupied_map_slots	Number of used map slots
map_slots	Number of map slots
occupied_reduce_slots	Number of used reduce slots
reduce_slots	Number of reduce slots
reduces_completed	Number of reducers that completed successfully
reduces_failed	Number of reducers that failed
running_1440	Number of long-running jobs (more than 24 hours)
Trackers	Number of TaskTrackers available for the cluster

Metrics for mapred context provide valuable information about the jobs that were executed on your cluster. They can help you determine if your cluster has any performance issues (from a job execution perspective). You can use a monitoring system (like Ganglia) to make sure that you have enough map and reduce slots available at any time. Also, you can make sure that you don't have any long-running jobs—unless you know about them in advance! You can use Nagios with Ganglia to generate appropriate alerts. Just like the other contexts, mapred Metrics can also be monitored for unusual job activity (against average job activity).

You can find Hadoop Metrics listed in Appendix D, "Hadoop Metrics and Their Relevance to Security." Appendix D also includes an example that explains use of specific Metrics and pattern searches for security (I included the security-specific configuration for that example, too).

Metrics and Security

Several Metrics can provide useful security information, including the following:

- **Activity statistics for NameNode:** It's important to monitor the activity on NameNode, as it can provide a lot of information that can alert you to security issues. Being the "brain" of a Hadoop cluster, NameNode is hub of all the file creation activity. If the number of newly created files changes drastically or the number of files whose permissions are changed increases drastically, the Metrics can trigger alerts so you can investigate.

- **Activity statistics for a DataNode:** For a DataNode, if the number of reads or writes by a local client increases suddenly, you definitely need to investigate. Also, if the number of blocks added or removed changes by a large percentage, then Metrics can trigger alerts to warn you.

- **Activity statistics for RPC-related processing:** For the NameNode (or a DataNode), you need to monitor closely the RPCMetrics, such as the number of processed RPC requests, number of failed RPC authentication calls, or number of failed RPC authorization calls. You can compare the daily numbers with weekly averages and generate alerts if the numbers differ by a threshold percentage. For example, if the number of failed RPC authorization calls for a day is 50 and the weekly average is 30, then if the alert threshold is 50% or more of the weekly average, an alert will be generated (50% of 30 is 15, and the daily number (50) is greater than 45).

- **Activity statistics for sudden change in system resources:** It is beneficial to monitor for sudden changes in any of the major system resources, such as available memory, CPU, or storage. Hadoop provides Metrics for monitoring these resources, and you can either define a specific percentage (for generating alerts) or monitor for a percent deviation from weekly or monthly averages. The later method is more precise, as some of the clusters may never hit the target alert percentage even with a malicious attack (e.g., if average memory usage for a cluster is 20% and a malicious attack causes the usage to jump to 60%). If you have defined an alert threshold of 80% or 90%, then you will never get an alert. Alternatively, if you have defined your alert threshold for 50% or more (of average usage), then you will definitely get an alert.

You can use a combination of Ganglia and Nagios to monitor sudden changes to any of your system resources or Metrics values for any of the Hadoop daemons. Again, Appendix D has an example that describes this approach.

If you don't want to use a monitoring system and want to adopt the "old-fashioned" approach of writing the Metrics data to files and using Hive or HBase to load that data in tables, that will work, too. You will of course need to develop shellscripts for scheduling your dataloads, perform aggregations, generate summary reports and generate appropriate alerts.

Metrics Filtering

When you are troubleshooting a security breach or a possible performance issue, reviewing a large amount of Metrics data can take time and be distracting and error-prone. Filtering the Metrics data helps you focus on possible issues and save valuable time. Hadoop allows you to configure Metrics filters by source, context, record, and Metrics. The highest level for filtering is by source (e.g., DataNode5) and the lowest level of filtering is by the Metric name (e.g., FilesCreated). Filters can be combined to optimize the filtering efficiency.

For example, the following file sink accepts Metrics from context dfs only:

```
bcl.sink.file0.class=org.apache.hadoop.metrics2.sink.FileSink
bcl.sink.file0.context=dfs
```

To set up your filters, you first need to add a snippet like the following in your $HADOOP_INSTALL/hadoop/conf/**hadoop-metrics2.properties** file:

```
# Syntax: <prefix>.(source|sink).<instance>.<option>

*.sink.file.class=org.apache.hadoop.metrics2.sink.FileSink
*.source.filter.class=org.apache.hadoop.metrics2.filter.GlobFilter
*.record.filter.class=${*.source.filter.class}
*.metric.filter.class=${*.source.filter.class}
```

After this, you can include any of the following configuration options that will set up filters at various levels:

```
# This will filter out sources with names starting with Cluster2

jobtracker.*.source.filter.exclude=Cluster2*

# This will filter out records with names that match localhost in the source dfs

jobtracker.source.dfs.record.filter.exclude=localhost*

# This will filter out Metrics with names that match cpu* for sink instance file only

jobtracker.sink.file.metric.filter.exclude=cpu*
jobtracker.sink.file.filename=MyJT-metrics.out
```

So, to summarize, you can thus filter out Metric data by source, by a pattern within a source, or by Metric names or patterns within an output file for a sink.

Please remember, when you specify an "include" pattern only, the filter only includes data that matches the filter condition. Also, when you specify an "exclude" pattern only, the matched data is excluded. Most important, when you specify both of these patterns, sources that don't match either pattern are included as well! Last, include patterns have precedence over exclude patterns.

Capturing Metrics Output to File

How do you direct output of NameNode or DataNode Metrics to files? With Metrics2, you can define a sink (output file) into which to direct output from your Metric source by adding a few lines to the hadoop-metrics2.properties configuration file in the directory /etc/Hadoop/conf or $HADOOP_INSTALL/hadoop/conf. In the following example, I am redirecting the NameNode and DataNode Metrics to separate output files as well as the Ganglia monitoring system (remember, Metrics2 can support output to two sinks at once):

```
# Following are entries from configuration file hadoop-metrics2.properties
# collectively they output Metrics from sources NameNode and DataNode to
# a sink named 'tfile' (output to file) and also to a sink named 'ganglia'
# (output to Ganglia)

# Defining sink for file output
*.sink.tfile.class=org.apache.hadoop.metrics2.sink.FileSink

# Filename for NameNode output

namenode.sink.tfile.filename = namenode-metrics.log

# Output the DataNode Metrics to a separate file
datanode.sink.tfile.filename = datanode-metrics.log

# Defining sink for Ganglia 3.1
*.sink.ganglia.class=org.apache.hadoop.metrics2.sink.ganglia.GangliaSink31
```

```
# Default polling period for GangliaSink
*.sink.ganglia.period=10

# Directing output to ganglia servers
namenode.sink.ganglia.servers=gangliahost_1:8649,gangliahost_2:8649
datanode.sink.ganglia.servers=gangliahost_1:8649,gangliahost_2:8649
```

Now that you have all the Metric data in files, you need to make effective use of it. If you don't plan to use a monitoring system, you will have to define file sinks (as output) for all the Hadoop daemons and manually analyze the huge output files or aggregate them as required! At the most, you can define Hive external tables and ease the processing. Alternatively, you can direct the Metrics output to a JMX console for reviewing it.

Please note that with either of these approaches, you won't be able to display the Metric data or aggregations graphically for a quick review. Also, you will need to set up interface with alerting mechanism via shellscripts (accessing the Hive data) and set up interfaces for paging the system administrators (in case of critical events) as well.

However, if you plan to use Ganglia, sending your Metrics to the Ganglia monitoring system is as simple as sending them to a file and provides many more advantages, as you'll learn in the next section.

Security Monitoring with Ganglia and Nagios

The best security monitoring system for your Hadoop cluster is a system that matches your environment and needs. In some cases, making sure that only authorized users have access may be most important, while in other cases, you may need to monitor the system resources and raise an immediate alert if a sudden change in their usage occurs. Some cluster administrators solely want to monitor failed authentication requests. The leaders in Hadoop security monitoring, Ganglia (http://ganglia.sourceforge.net) and Nagios (www.nagios.org), meet this challenge by providing flexibility and varied means of monitoring the system resources, connections, and any other part of your Hadoop cluster that's technically possible to monitor.

Both are open source tools with different strengths that complement each other nicely. Ganglia is very good at gathering Metrics, tracking them over time, and aggregating the results; while Nagios focuses more on providing an alerting mechanism. Since gathering Metrics and alerting are both equally essential aspects of monitoring, Ganglia and Nagios work best together. Both these tools have agents running on all hosts for a cluster and gather information via a polling process that can poll any of the hosts to get the necessary information.

Ganglia

Ganglia was designed at the University of California, Berkeley and started as an open source monitoring project meant to be used with large distributed systems. Ganglia's open architecture makes it easy to integrate with other applications and gather statistics about their operations. That's the reason Ganglia can receive and process output data from Hadoop Metrics with ease and use it effectively.

For a monitored cluster, each host runs a daemon process called *gmond* that collects and broadcasts the local Metrics data (like CPU usage, memory usage, etc.) to all the hosts within the cluster. A polling process (*gmetad*) can then query any of the hosts, read all the Metrics data and route it to a central monitoring server. The central host can display the Metrics, aggregate them, or summarize them for further use. *Gmond* has little overhead and hence can easily be run on every machine in the cluster without affecting user performance. Ganglia's web interface can easily display the summary usage for last hour, day, week, or month as you need. Also, you can get details of any of these resource usages as necessary.

Ganglia Architecture

Broadly, Ganglia has four major components: gmond, gmetad, rrdtool and gweb. gmond runs on all the nodes in a cluster and gathers Metrics data, *gmetad* polls the data from *gmond*, *rrdtool* stores the polled data, and *gweb* is the interface that provides visualization and analysis for the stored data. Figure 7-3 illustrates how Ganglia's components fit into the basic Hadoop distributed monitoring system shown in Figure 7-2.

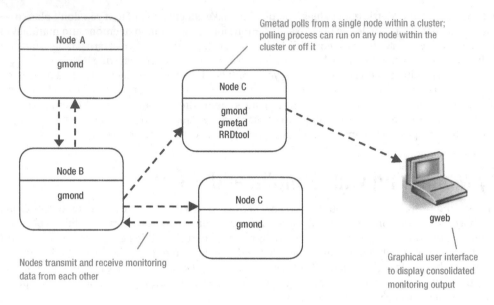

Figure 7-3. *Ganglia monitoring system for Hadoop*

Take a closer look at what each of the Ganglia components does:

- **gmond:** gmond needs to be installed on every host you want monitored. It interacts with the host operating system to acquire Metrics such as load Metrics (e.g., average cluster load), process Metrics (e.g., total running processes) or rpc Metrics (e.g., RpcAuthenticationFailures). It is modular and uses operating system–specific plugins to take measurements. Since only the necessary plugins are installed at compile time, gmond has a very small footprint and negligible overhead.

  gmond is not invoked as per request from an external polling engine (for measurement), but rather polls according to a schedule defined by a local configuration file. Measurements are shared with other hosts (from the cluster) via a simple listen/announce protocol broadcasted at the same multicast address. Every gmond host also records the Metrics it receives from other hosts within the cluster.

  Therefore, every host in a Ganglia cluster knows the current value of every Metric recorded by every other host in the same cluster. That's the reason only one host per cluster needs to be polled to get Metrics of the entire cluster, and any individual host failures won't affect the system at all! Also, this design reduces the number of hosts that need to be polled exponentially, and hence is easily scalable for large clusters.

- **gmetad:** gmetad is the polling process within the Ganglia monitoring system. It needs a list of hostnames that specifies at least one host per cluster. An XML-format dump of the Metrics for a cluster can be requested by gmetad from any host in the cluster on port 8649, which is how gmetad gets Metrics data for a cluster.

- **RRDtool:** RRDtool is the Ganglia component used for storing the Metrics data polled by gmetad from any of the cluster hosts. Metrics are stored in "round-robin" fashion; when no space remains to store new values, old values are overwritten. As per the specified data retention requirements, *RRDtool* aggregates the data values or "rolls them up." This way of data storage allows us to quickly analyze recent data as well as maintain years of historical data using a small amount of disk space. Also, since all the required disk space is allocated in advance, capacity planning is very easy.

- **gweb:** gweb is the visualization interface for Ganglia. It provides instant access to any Metric from any host in the cluster without specifying any configuration details. It visually summarizes the entire grid using graphs that combine Metrics by cluster and provides drop-downs for additional details. If you need details of a specific host or Metric, you can specify the details and create a custom graph of exactly what you want to see.

  gweb allows you to change the time period in graphs, supports extracting data in various textual formats (CSV, JSON, and more), and provides a fully functional URL interface so that you can embed necessary graphs into other programs via specific URLs. Also, gweb is a PHP program, which is run under the Apache web server and is usually installed on the same physical hardware as gmetad, since it needs access to the RRD databases created by gmetad.

Configuring and Using Ganglia

With a clearer understanding of Ganglia's major components, you're ready to set it up and put it to work for security-related monitoring and outputting specific Hadoop Metrics.

To install Ganglia on a Hadoop cluster you wish to monitor, perform the following steps:

1. Install Ganglia components gmetad, gmond, and gweb on one of the cluster nodes or hosts. (For my example, I called the host GMaster).

2. Install Ganglia component gmond on all the other cluster nodes.

The exact command syntax or means of install will vary according to the operating system you use. Please refer to the Ganglia installation instructions for specifics. In all cases, however, you will need to modify configuration files for Ganglia to work correctly and also for Hadoop to output Metrics through Ganglia as expected (the configuration files gmond.conf, gmetad.conf, and hadoop-metrics2.properties need to be modified).

To begin, copy gmond.conf (with the following configuration) to all the cluster nodes:

```
/* the values closely match ./gmond/metric.h definitions in 2.5.x */
globals {
  daemonize = yes
  setuid = yes
  user = nobody
  debug_level = 0
  max_udp_msg_len = 1472
  mute = no
  deaf = no
  allow_extra_data = yes
```

```
  host_dmax = 86400 /*secs. Expires hosts in 1 day */
  host_tmax = 20 /*secs */
  cleanup_threshold = 300 /*secs */
  gexec = no
  send_metadata_interval = 0 /*secs */
}

/*
 * The cluster attributes specified will be used as part of the <CLUSTER>
 * tag that will wrap all hosts collected by this instance.
 */
cluster {
  name = "pract_hdp_sec"
  owner = "Apress"
  latlong = "N43.47 E112.34"
  url = "http://www.apress.com/9781430265443"
}

/* The host section describes attributes of the host, like the location */
host {
  location = "Chicago"
}

/* Feel free to specify as many udp_send_channels as you like */
udp_send_channel {
  bind_hostname = yes #soon to be default
  mcast_join = 239.2.11.71
  port = 8649
  ttl = 1
}

/* You can specify as many udp_recv_channels as you like as well. */
udp_recv_channel {
  mcast_join = 239.2.11.71
  port = 8649
  bind = 239.2.11.71
  retry_bind = true
}

/* You can specify as many tcp_accept_channels as you like to share
   an xml description of the state of the cluster */
tcp_accept_channel {
  port = 8649
}

/* Each Metrics module that is referenced by gmond must be specified and
   loaded. If the module has been statically linked with gmond, it does
   not require a load path. However all dynamically loadable modules must
   include a load path. */
```

```
modules {
  module {name = "core_metrics"}
  module {name = "cpu_module"  path = "modcpu.so"}
  module {name = "disk_module" path = "moddisk.so"}
  module {name = "load_module" path = "modload.so"}
  module {name = "mem_module"  path = "modmem.so"}
  module {name = "net_module"  path = "modnet.so"}
  module {name = "proc_module" path = "modproc.so"}
  module {name = "sys_module"  path = "modsys.so"}
}
```

In the Globals section, the daemonize attribute, when true, will make gmond run as a background process. A debug_level greater than 0 will result in gmond running in the foreground and outputting debugging information. The mute attribute, when true, will prevent gmond from sending any data, and the deaf attribute, when true, will prevent gmond from receiving any data. If host_dmax is set to a positive number, then gmond will flush a host after it has not heard from it for host_dmax seconds. The cleanup_threshold is the minimum amount of time before gmond will cleanup any hosts or Metrics with expired data. The send_metadata_interval set to 0 means that gmond will only send the metadata packets at startup and upon request from other gmond nodes running remotely.

Several Ganglia Metrics detect sudden changes in system resources and are well suited for security monitoring:

- cpu_aidle (percentage of CPU cycles idle since last boot; valid for Linux)

- cpu_user (percentage of CPU cycles spent executing user processes)

- load_five (reported system load, averaged over five minutes)

- mem_shared (amount of memory occupied by system and user processes)

- proc_run (total number of running processes)

- mem_free (amount of memory free)

- disk_free (total free disk space)

- bytes_in (number of bytes read from all non-loopback interfaces)

- bytes_out (number of bytes written to all non-loopback interfaces)

You can add them to your gmond.conf file in the following format:

```
collection_group {
  collect_every = 40
  time_threshold = 300
  metric {
    name = "bytes_out"
    value_threshold = 4096
    title = "Bytes Sent"
  }
}
```

As you can see in the example, Metrics that need to be collected and sent out at the same interval can be grouped under the same collection_group. In this example, collect_every specifies the sampling interval, time_threshold specifies the maximum data send interval (i.e., data is sent out at that interval), and value_threshold is Metric variance threshold (i.e., value is sent if it exceeds the value_threshold value).

The second configuration file is gmetad.conf, which needs to reside on the host (GMaster) only. Keep in mind that the code that follows is only an example, and you can set up your own data sources or change settings as you need for round-robin archives:

```
# Format:
# data_source "my cluster" [polling interval] address1:port addreses2:port ...
#
data_source "HDPTaskTracker" 50 localhost:8658
data_source "HDPDataNode" 50 localhost:8659
data_source "HDPNameNode" 50 localhost:8661
data_source "HDPJobTracker" 50 localhost:8662
data_source "HDPResourceManager" 50 localhost:8664
data_source "HDPHistoryServer" 50 localhost:8666
#
# Round-Robin Archives
# You can specify custom Round-Robin archives here
#
RRAs "RRA:AVERAGE:0.5:1:244" "RRA:AVERAGE:0.5:24:244" RRA:AVERAGE:0.5:168:244"
"RRA:AVERAGE:0.5:672:244" "RRA:AVERAGE:0.5:5760:374"
#
# The name of this Grid. All the data sources above will be wrapped in a GRID
# tag with this name.
# default: unspecified
gridname "HDP_GRID"
#
# In earlier versions of gmetad, hostnames were handled in a case
# sensitive manner. If your hostname directories have been renamed to lower
# case, set this option to 0 to disable backward compatibility.
# From version 3.2, backwards compatibility will be disabled by default.
# default: 1   (for gmetad < 3.2)
# default: 0   (for gmetad >= 3.2)
case_sensitive_hostnames 1
```

Last, you need to customize the hadoop-metrics2.properties configuration file in the directory /etc/Hadoop/conf or $HADOOP_INSTALL/hadoop/conf. You can define appropriate sources (in this case, either the dfs, jvm, rpc, or mapred Metrics), sinks (just Ganglia or a combination of Ganglia and output files), and filters (to filter out Metrics data that you don't need).

To set up your sources and sinks, use code similar to the following:

```
# syntax: [prefix].[source|sink|jmx].[instance].[options]
# See package.html for org.apache.hadoop.metrics2 for details

*.period=60

*.sink.ganglia.class=org.apache.hadoop.metrics2.sink.ganglia.GangliaSink31
*.sink.ganglia.period=10

# default for supportsparse is false
*.sink.ganglia.supportsparse=true
```

```
.sink.ganglia.slope=jvm.metrics.gcCount=zero,jvm.metrics.memHeapUsedM=both
.sink.ganglia.dmax=jvm.metrics.threadsBlocked=70,jvm.metrics.memHeapUsedM=40

# Associate sinks with server and ports
namenode.sink.ganglia.servers=localhost:8661
datanode.sink.ganglia.servers=localhost:8659
jobtracker.sink.ganglia.servers=localhost:8662
tasktracker.sink.ganglia.servers=localhost:8658
maptask.sink.ganglia.servers=localhost:8660
reducetask.sink.ganglia.servers=localhost:8660
resourcemanager.sink.ganglia.servers=localhost:8664
nodemanager.sink.ganglia.servers=localhost:8657
historyserver.sink.ganglia.servers=localhost:8666
resourcemanager.sink.ganglia.tagsForPrefix.yarn=Queue
```

Setting supportsparse to true helps in reducing bandwidth usage. Otherwise the Metrics cache is updated every time the Metric is published and that can be CPU/network intensive. Ganglia slope can have values of zero (the Metric value always remains the same), positive (the Metric value can only be increased), negative (the Metric value can only be decreased), or both (the Metric value can either be increased or decreased). The dmax value indicates how a long a particular value will be retained. For example, the value for JVM Metric threadsBlocked (from the preceding configuration) will be retained for 70 seconds only.

As I discussed earlier in the "Metrics Filtering," section, filters are useful in situations where you are troubleshooting or need to focus on a known issue and need specific Metric data only. Of course, you can limit the Metrics data you are capturing through settings in gmond.conf (as you learned earlier in this section), but filters can be useful when you need Metric data limited (or captured) temporarily—and quickly!

Monitoring HBase Using Ganglia

Ganglia can be used to monitor HBase just as you have seen it used for monitoring Hadoop. There is a configuration file called hadoop-metrics.properties located in directory $HBASE_HOME/conf (where $HBASE_HOME is the HBase install directory). You need to configure all the "contexts" for HBase to use Ganglia as an output:

```
# Configuration of the "hbase" context for Ganglia
hbase.class=org.apache.hadoop.metrics.ganglia.GangliaContext
hbase.period=60
hbase.servers=localhost:8649

# Configuration of the "jvm" context for Ganglia
jvm.class=org.apache.hadoop.metrics.ganglia.GangliaContext
jvm.period=60
hbase.servers=localhost:8649

# Configuration of the "rpc" context for Ganglia
rpc.class=org.apache.hadoop.metrics.ganglia.GangliaContext
rpc.period=60
hbase.servers=localhost:8649
```

For the hbase context, you can see values for metrics like averageLoad (average number of regions served by each region server) or numRegionServers (number of online region servers) on the HBase master server.

Also, for the jvm context, you can see Metrics like MemHeapUsedM (heap memory used, in MB) and MemHeapCommittedM (heap memory committed, in MB). If more than one jvm is running (i.e., more than one HBase process) Ganglia aggregates the Metrics values instead of reporting them per instance.

This concludes the HBase monitoring section. I have listed all the HBase Metrics in Appendix D for your reference.

Before I conclude the discussion about Ganglia, I want you to have a quick look at the Ganglia web interface. Please review Figure 7-4. It shows the Ganglia dashboard displaying summary graphs for the previous month. You can see the average and maximum load, CPU usage, memory usage, and network usage. From the dashboard you can select detailed graphs for any of these resources or create custom graphs for the specific Metrics you need.

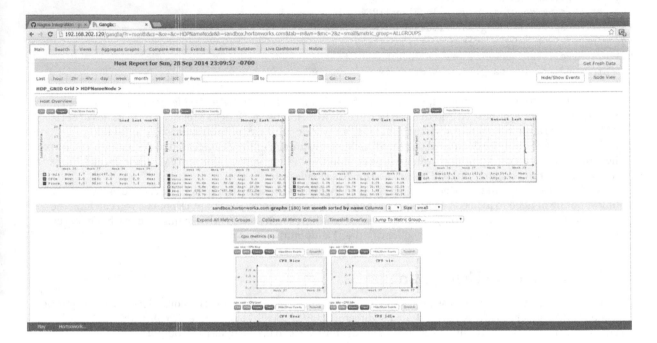

Figure 7-4. *Ganglia dashboard*

■ **Note**   Ganglia is available at `http://ganglia.sourceforge.net/`. Plug-ins for Ganglia are available at `https://github.com/ganglia/`. The user community URL for Ganglia is: `http://ganglia.info/?page_id=67`.

Nagios

Nagios is a specialized scheduling and notification engine. It doesn't monitor any processes or resources, but instead schedules execution of plug-ins (executable programs—Nagios plug-ins are not the same as Hadoop Metrics plug-ins) and takes action based on execution status. For example, status 0 is Success, 1 is Warning, 2 is Critical, and 3 is Unknown. You can configure the Nagios service to map specific actions for each of these outputs for all the plug-ins defined within the configuration files. In addition, you can define your own plug-ins and define the frequency for monitoring them as well as actions mapped to each of the possible outputs.

In addition to codes, the plug-ins can also return a text message, which can be written to a log and also be displayed on the web interface. If the text message contains a pipe character, the text after it is treated as performance data. The performance data contains Metrics from the monitored hosts and can be passed to external systems (like Ganglia) for use.

Most of the time, Nagios is used for monitoring along with Ganglia. The reason is that both these open source tools complement each other nicely, since they have different strengths. For example, Ganglia is more focused on gathering Metrics and tracking them over a time period, while Nagios focuses more on being an alerting mechanism. Since gathering Metrics and alerting are both essential aspects of monitoring, they work best in conjunction. Both Ganglia and Nagios have agents running on all hosts for a cluster and gather information.

Getting back to Nagios, let me start with Nagios architecture.

Architecture

The Nagios daemon or service runs on a host and has plug-ins running on all the remote hosts that need to be monitored. (To integrate Nagios with Ganglia, be sure the Ganglia process *gmond* is running on every host that has a Nagios plug-in running). The remote Nagios plug-ins send information and updates to the Nagios service, and the Nagios web interface displays it. When issues are detected, the Nagios daemon notifies predefined administrative contacts using email or page (text message sent to a phone). Historical log data is available in a log file defined in the configuration file. As you can see in Figure 7-5, the Nagios monitoring system has three major components:

- **Server:** The server is responsible for managing and scheduling plug-ins. At regular intervals, the server checks the plug-in status and performs action as per the status. In case of alerts, configured administrative resources are notified.

- **Plug-ins:** Nagios provides a standard set of user-configurable plug-ins, plus you can add more as required. Plug-ins are executable programs (mostly written in C, Java, Python, etc). that perform a specific task and return a result to the Nagios server.

- **Browser interface of Nagios:** These are web pages generated by CGI that display summary information about monitored resources.

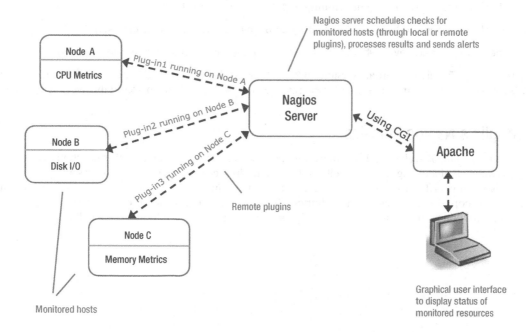

Figure 7-5. Nagios architecture

■ **Note** Nagios is freely available at `http://www.nagios.org`. You can download official Nagios plug-ins from the Nagios Plug-In Development Team at `http://nagiosplug.sourceforge.net`. In addition, the Nagios community is continuously developing new plug-ins, which you can find at `http://exchange.nagios.org`.

Although using Ganglia and Nagios in conjunction is an effective approach to security monitoring, the applications are not integrated by default. You need to integrate them through plug-ins, as the next section explains.

Nagios Integration with Ganglia

Nagios has no built-in Metrics. Remote or local plug-ins are executed and their status compared by Nagios with user-specified status/notification mapping to perform any necessary notification tasks. Services like NRPE (Nagios Remote Plugin Executor) or NSCA (Nagios Service Check Acceptor) are used for remote executions. If you're using Ganglia for monitoring, however, all the Metrics Nagios needs (for CPU, memory, disk I/O, etc.) are already available. You simply have to point Nagios at Ganglia to collect these Metrics! To help you, as of version 2.2.0 the Ganglia project started including a number of official Nagios plug-ins in its gweb versions (for details, see `https://github.com/ganglia/ganglia-web/wiki/Nagios-Integration`). In Nagios, you can then use these plug-ins to create commands and services to compare Metrics captured (or generated) by Ganglia against alert thresholds defined in Nagios.

Originally, five Ganglia plug-ins were available:

- `check_heartbeat` (check heartbeat to verify if the host is available)
- `check_metric` (check a single Metric on a specific host)
- `check_multiple_metrics` (check multiple Metrics on a specific host)
- `check_host_regex` (check multiple Metrics across a regex-defined range of hosts)
- `check_value_same_everywhere` (check value or values are the same across a set of hosts)

Now, the current Ganglia web tarball (version 3.6.2) contains 10 plug-ins for Nagios integration! You can download it at `http://sourceforge.net/projects/ganglia/files/ganglia-web/3.6.2/` to check out the five new plugins.

Using Ganglia's Nagios Plug-ins

When extracted, the Ganglia web tarball contains a subdirectory called `nagios` that contains the shellscripts as well as PHP scripts for each of the plug-ins. The shellscript for a plug-in accepts values for parameters and passes them on to the corresponding PHP script. The PHP script processes the values and uses an XML dump of the grid state (state of the cluster containing details of all the Metrics; obtained by gmetad) to acquire current Metric values as per the request. A return code (indicating the status of request) is passed back to Nagios. Figure 7-6 illustrates the process.

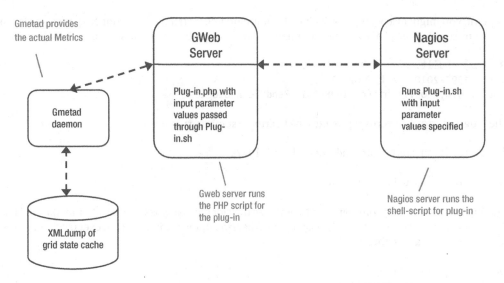

Figure 7-6. *Ganglia-Nagios integration processing*

Remember to enable the server-side PHP script functionality before using it and to verify the following parameter values in configuration file conf.php (used by gweb):

```
$conf['nagios_cache_enabled'] = 1;
$conf['nagios_cache_file']= $conf['conf_dir']."/nagios_ganglia.cache";
$conf['nagios_cache_time'] = 45;
```

The location of conf.php varies as per the operating system, Hadoop distribution, and other factors. Your best option is to use the find command:

```
find / -name conf.php -print
```

The steps to follow for using Nagios as a scheduling and alerting mechanism for any of the five Ganglia plug-ins are very similar. Therefore, I will demonstrate the process with two of the plug-ins: check_heartbeat and check_multiple_metrics. I also will assume you have installed Ganglia, PHP, and Nagios and you are using the Hortonworks Hadoop distribution.

The check_heartbeat plug-in is a heartbeat counter used by Ganglia to make sure a host is functioning normally. This counter is reset every time a new Metric packet is received for the host. To use this plug-in with Nagios, first copy the check_heartbeat.sh script from the Nagios subdirectory in the Ganglia web tarball (in my case, /var/www/html/ganglia/nagios) to your Nagios plug-ins directory (in my case, /usr/lib64/nagios/plugins). Make sure that the GANGLIA_URL inside the script is correct. Substitute your localhost name and check if http://localhost/ganglia takes you to the Ganglia homepage for your installation. Then check if this is the setting in check_heartbeat.sh:

```
GANGLIA_URL=http://<localhost>/ganglia/nagios/check_heartbeat.php
```

At this point, you might also want to verify if PHP command line installation on your Nagios server is functional; you can do that by running the php -version command. You should see a response similar to the following:

```
PHP 5.3.3 (cli) (built: Aug  6 2014 05:54:27)
Copyright (c) 1997-2010 The PHP Group
Zend Engine v2.3.0, Copyright (c) 1998-2010 Zend Technologies
```

Run the plug-in script and verify it provides the heartbeat status correctly:

```
> ./check_heartbeat.sh host=pract_hdp_sec threshold=75

OK Last beacon received 0 days, 0:00:07
```

Next, define this plug-in as a command for Nagios (see the sidebar "Nagios Commands and Macros" for details). The threshold is the amount of time since the last reported heartbeat; that is, if the last packet received was 50 seconds ago, you would specify 50 as the threshold:

```
define command {
command_name check_ganglia_heartbeat
command_line $USER1$/check_heartbeat.sh host=$HOSTADDRESS$ threshold=$ARG1$
}
```

Note the use of the macros $HOSTADDRESS$ (substituted to IPaddress of the host), $USER1$ (user-defined macro defined in a resource file), and $ARG1$ (first argument to the command). Using macros provides the information contained in them automatically to a command (since the referenced value is available). So, the command check_ganglia_heartbeat can be used for checking the heartbeat on any host within your cluster. Similarly, the argument value passed to this command lets you change that parameter at runtime. Please refer to the sidebar "Nagios Commands and Macros" for further details about macros.

NAGIOS COMMANDS AND MACROS

For Nagios, a command can be defined to include service checks, service notifications, service event handlers, host checks, host notifications, and host event handlers. Command definitions can contain macros that are substituted at runtime; this is one of the main features that makes Nagios flexible (please refer to http://nagios.sourceforge.net/docs/3_0/macros.html for more information on macros).

Macros can provide information from hosts, services, and other sources. For example, $HOSTNAME$ or $HOSTADDRESS$ are frequently used macros. Macros can also pass arguments using $ARGn$ (nth argument passed to a command). Nagios supports up to 32 argument macros ($ARG1$ through $ARG32$). The syntax for defining a command is as follows:

```
define command{
command_name<command_name>
command_line<command_line>
}
```

where <command_name> is the name of the command and <command_line> is what Nagios actually executes when the command is used.

You can define the commands in the Nagios main configuration file called `nagios.cfg`. Most of the time the file resides in `/etc/nagios`, but location may vary for your install. The main configuration file defines individual object configuration files for commands, services, contacts, templates, and so forth. In addition, there may be a specific section for Hadoop servers. For example, the Hortonworks `nagios.cfg` has the following section:

```
# Definitions for hadoop servers
cfg_file=/etc/nagios/objects/hadoop-hosts.cfg
cfg_file=/etc/nagios/objects/hadoop-hostgroups.cfg
cfg_file=/etc/nagios/objects/hadoop-servicegroups.cfg
cfg_file=/etc/nagios/objects/hadoop-services.cfg
cfg_file=/etc/nagios/objects/hadoop-commands.cfg
```

I will define the command `check_ganglia_heartbeat` in configuration file `/etc/nagios/objects/hadoop-commands.cfg`. The last step is defining a service for Nagios. Within Nagios, use of the term *service* is very generic or nonspecific. It may indicate an actual service running on the host (e.g., POP, SMTP, HTTP, etc.) or some other type of Metric associated with the host (free disk space, CPUusage, etc.). A service is defined in configuration file `/etc/nagios/objects/hadoop-services.cfg` and has the following syntax:

```
define service {
        host_name               localhost
        use                     hadoop-service
        service_description     GANGLIA::Ganglia Check Heartbeat
        servicegroups           GANGLIA
        check_command           check_ganglia_heartbeat!50
        normal_check_interval   0.25
        retry_check_interval    0.25
        max_check_attempts      4
}
```

Please note that `check_command` indicates the actual command that would be executed on the specified host. The parameter `normal_check_interval` indicates the number of time units to wait before scheduling the next check of the service. One time unit is 60 seconds (that's the default), and therefore 0.25 indicates 15 seconds. `retry_check_interval` defines the number of time units to wait before scheduling a recheck of the service if it has changed to a non-okaystate, and `max_check_attempts` indicates the number of retries in such a situation.

The command `check_multiple_metrics` checks multiple Ganglia Metrics and generates a single alert. To use it, copy the `check_multiple_metrics.sh` script from the Nagios subdirectory in the Ganglia web tarball to your Nagios plug-ins directory. Make sure that `GANGLIA_URL` inside the script is set to `http://localhost/ganglia/nagios/check_heartbeat.php`, and also remember to substitute `localhost` with the appropriate host name.

Define the corresponding command `check_ganglia_multiple_metrics` in the configuration file `/etc/nagios/objects/hadoop-commands.cfg`:

```
define command {
command_name check_ganglia_multiple_metrics
command_line $USER1$/check_multiple_metrics.sh host=$HOSTADDRESS$ checks='$ARG1$'
}
```

You can add a list of checks delimited with a colon. Each check consists of `Metric_name,operator,critical_value`. Next, define a corresponding service in the configuration file /etc/nagios/objects/hadoop-services.cfg:

```
define service {
        host_name               localhost
        use                     hadoop-service
        service_description     GANGLIA::Ganglia check Multiple Metric service
        servicegroups           GANGLIA
        check_command           check_ganglia_multiple_metrics!disk_free,less,10:load_one,more,5
        normal_check_interval   0.25
        retry_check_interval    0.25
        max_check_attempts      4
}
```

Note the `check_command` section that defines the command to be executed:

`check_ganglia_multiple_metrics!disk_free,less,10:load_one,more,5`.

This indicates that an alert will be generated if free disk space (for the host) falls below 10GB or if 1-minute load average goes over 5.

After successfully defining your Ganglia plug-ins, you can use the Nagios web interface to check and manage these plug-ins. As you can see in Figure 7-7, the new `check_heartbeat` and `check_multiple_metrics` plug-ins are already in place and being managed by Nagios.

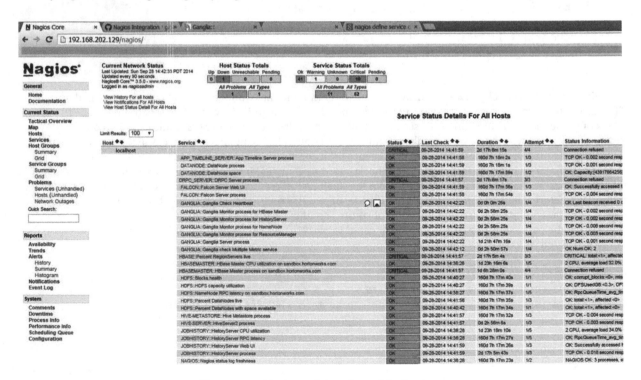

Figure 7-7. *Nagios web interface with plug-ins*

If you'd like more practice, you can follow the same steps and add the other three plug-ins.

The Nagios Community

The real strength of Nagios is in its active user community that's constantly working towards making a more effective use of Nagios and adding plug-ins to enhance its functionality. To see the latest plug-ins your fellow users have developed, visit the community page at http://exchange.nagios.org/directory/Plugins. For security purposes, you'll find many plug-ins that you can use effectively, such as:

- **check_ssh_faillogin**: Monitors the ssh failed login attempts; available at http://exchange.nagios.org/directory/Plugins/Security/check_ssh_faillogin/details.

- **show_users:** Shows logged users. Can alert on certain users being logged in using a whitelist, blacklist, or both. Details at: http://exchange.nagios.org/directory/Plugins/System-Metrics/Users/Show-Users/details

- **check_long_running_procs.sh:** Checks long-running processes; available at http://exchange.nagios.org/directory/Plugins/System-Metrics/Processes/Check-long-running-processes/details.

You can use the same process as you followed for using the Ganglia plug-ins to use any new plug-in. You will need to copy it to the Nagios plug-ins directory, then define a command and service. Of course, follow any specific install instructions for individual plug-ins or install any additional packages that are required for their functioning.

Summary

In this chapter, I have discussed monitoring for Hadoop as well as popular open-source monitoring tools. Remember, monitoring involves a good understanding of both the resources that need to be monitored and the environment that you plan to monitor. Though I can tell you what needs to be monitored for a Hadoop cluster, you know your environment's individual requirements best. I have tried to provide some general hints, but from my experience, monitoring is always as good as your own system administrator's knowledge and understanding of your environment.

The "relevance" (how "up to date" or "state of the art" a system is) is also a very valid consideration. You have to be conscious on a daily basis of all the innovations in your area of interest (including the malicious attacks) and tune your monitoring based on them. Remember, the best system administrators are the ones who are most alert and responsive.

Last, please try to look beyond the specific tools and version numbers to understand the principles and intentions behind the monitoring techniques described in this chapter. You may not have access to the same tools to monitor, but if you follow the principles, you will be able to set up effective systems for monitoring—and in the end, that's both our goal.

## PART IV

Encryption for Hadoop

■ ■ ■

## CHAPTER 8

Encryption in Hadoop

Recently, I was talking with a friend about possibly using Hadoop to speed up reporting on his company's "massive" data warehouse of 4TB. (He heads the IT department of one of the biggest real estate companies in the Chicago area.) Although he grudgingly agreed to a possible performance benefit, he asked very confidently, "But what about encrypting our HR [human resources] data? For our MS SQL Server–based HR data, we use symmetric key encryption and certificates supplemented by C# code. How can you implement that with Hadoop?"

As Hadoop is increasingly used within corporate environments, a lot more people are going to ask the same question. The answer isn't straightforward. Most of the Hadoop distributions now have Kerberos installed and/or implemented and include easy options to implement authorization as well as encryption in transit, but your options are limited for at-rest encryption for Hadoop, especially with file-level granularity.

Why do you need to encrypt data while it's at rest and stored on a disk? Encryption is the last line of defense when a hacker gets complete access to your data. It is a comforting feeling to know that your data is still going to be safe, since it can't be decrypted and used without the key that scrambled it. Remember, however, that encryption is used for countering unauthorized access and hence can't be replaced by authentication or authorization (both of which control authorized access).

In this chapter, I will discuss encryption at rest, and how you can implement it within Hadoop. First, I will provide a brief overview of symmetric (secret key) encryption as used by the DES and AES algorithms, asymmetric (public key) encryption used by the RSA algorithm, key exchange protocols and certificates, digital signatures, and cryptographic hash functions. Then, I will explain what needs to be encrypted within Hadoop and how, and discuss the Intel Hadoop distribution, which is now planned to be offered partially with Cloudera's distribution and is also available open source via Project Rhino. Last, I will discuss how to use Amazon Web Services's Elastic MapReduce (or VMs preinstalled with Hadoop) for implementing encryption at rest.

Introduction to Data Encryption

Cryptography can be used very effectively to counter many kinds of security threats. Whether you call the data scrambled, disguised, or encrypted, it cannot be read, modified, or manipulated easily. Luckily, even though cryptography has its origin in higher mathematics, you do not need to understand its mathematical basis in order to use it. Simply understand that a common approach is to base the encryption on a *key* (a unique character pattern used as the basis for encryption and decryption) and an *algorithm* (logic used to scramble or descramble data, using the key as needed). See the "Basic Principles of Encryption" sidebar for more on the building blocks of encryption.

BASIC PRINCIPLES OF ENCRYPTION

As children, my friends and I developed our own special code language to communicate in school. Any messages that needed to be passed around during class contained number sequences like "4 21 8 0 27 18 24 0 6 18 16 12 17 10" to perplex our teachers if we were caught.

Our code is an example of a simple *substitution cipher* in which numbers (signifying position within the alphabet) were substituted for letters and then a 3 was added to each digit; 0 was used as a word separator. So, the above sequence simply asked the other guy "are you coming"? While our code was very simple, data encryption in real-world applications uses complex ciphers that rely on complex logic for substituting the characters. In some cases, a key, such as a word or mathematical expression, is used to transpose the letters. So, for example, using "myword" as a key, ABCDEFGHIJKLMNOPQRSTUVWXYZ could map to **myword**abcefghijklnpqstuvwxyz, meaning the cipher text for the phrase "Hello world" would be "Brggj ujngo". To add complexity, you can substitute the position of a letter in the alphabet for x in the expression $2x + 5 \leq 26$ to map ABCDEFGHIJKLMNOPQRSTUVWXYZ to gikmoqsuwyabcdefhjlnprtvxz. Complex substitution ciphers can be used for robust security, but a big issue is the time required to encrypt and decrypt them.

The other method of encryption is *transposition* (also called reordering, rearranging, or permutation). A transposition is an encryption where letters of the original text are rearranged to generate the encrypted text. By spreading the information across the message, transposition makes the message difficult to comprehend. A very simple example of this type of encryption is *columnar transposition*, which involves transposing rows of text to columns. For example, to transpose the phrase "CAN YOU READ THIS NOW" as a six-column transposition, I could write the characters in rows of six and arrange one row after another:

```
C A N Y O U
R E A D T H
I S N O W
```

The resulting cipher text would then be read down the columns as: "cri aes nan ydo otw uh". Because of the storage space needed and the delay involved in decrypting the cipher text, this algorithm is not especially appropriate for long messages when time is of the essence.

Although substitution and transposition ciphers are not used alone for real-world data encryption, their combination forms a basis for some widely used commercial-grade encryption algorithms.

Popular Encryption Algorithms

There are two fundamental key-based encryptions: symmetric and asymmetric. Commonly called *secret keys*, symmetric algorithms use the same key for encryption as well as decryption. Two users share a secret key that they both use to encrypt and send information to the other as well as decrypt information from the other—much as my childhood friends and I used the same number-substitution key to encode the notes we passed in class. Because a separate key is needed for each pair of users who plan to use it, key distribution is a major problem in using symmetric encryption. Mathematically, n users who need to communicate in pairs require $n \times (n - 1)/2$ keys. So, the number of keys increases almost exponentially with number of users. Two popular algorithms that use symmetric key are DES and AES (more on these shortly).

Asymmetric or *public key* systems don't have the issues of key distribution and exponential number of keys. A public key can be distributed via an e-mail message or be copied to a shared directory. A message encrypted using it can be decrypted using the corresponding private key, which only the authorized user possesses. Since a user (within a system) can use any other user's public key to encrypt a message meant for him (that user has a corresponding private key to decrypt it), the number of keys remains small—two times the number of users. The popular encryption algorithm RSA uses public key. Public key encryption, however, is typically 10,000 times slower than symmetric key encryption because the modular exponentiation that public key encryption uses involves multiplication and division, which is slower than the bit operations (addition, exclusive OR, substitution, shifting) that symmetric algorithms use. For this reason, symmetric encryption is used more commonly, while public key encryption is reserved for specialized applications where speed is not a constraint. One place public key encryption becomes very useful is symmetric key exchange: it allows for a protected exchange of a symmetric key, which can then be used to secure further communications.

Symmetric and asymmetric encryptions, and DES, AES, and RSA in particular, are used as building blocks to perform such computing tasks as signing documents, detecting a change, and exchanging sensitive data, as you'll learn in the "Applications of Encryption" section. For now, take a closer look at each of these popular algorithms.

Data Encryption Standard (DES)

Developed by IBM from its Lucifer algorithm, the *data encryption standard* (*DES*) was officially adopted as a US federal standard in November 1976 for use on all public- and private-sector unclassified communication. The DES algorithm is a complex combination of two fundamental principles of encryption: substitution and transposition. The robustness of this algorithm is due to repeated application of these two techniques for a total of 16 cycles. The DES algorithm is a block algorithm, meaning it works with a 64-bit data block instead of a stream of characters. It splits an input data block in half, performs substitution on each half separately, fuses the key with one of the halves, and finally swaps the two halves. This process is performed 16 times and is detailed in the "DES Algorithm" sidebar.

DES ALGORITHM

For the DES algorithm, the first cycle of encryption begins when the first 64 data bits are transposed by initial permutation. First, the 64 transposed data bits are divided into left and right halves of 32 bits each. A 64-bit key (56 bits are used as the key; the rest are parity bits) is used to transform the data bits. Next, the key gets a left shift by a predetermined number of bits and is transposed. The resultant key is combined with the right half (substitution) and the result is combined with the left half after a round of permutation. This becomes the new right half. The old right half (one before combining with key and left half) becomes the new left half. This cycle (Figure 8-1) is performed 16 times. After the last cycle is completed, a final transposition (which is the inverse of the initial permutation) is performed to complete the algorithm.

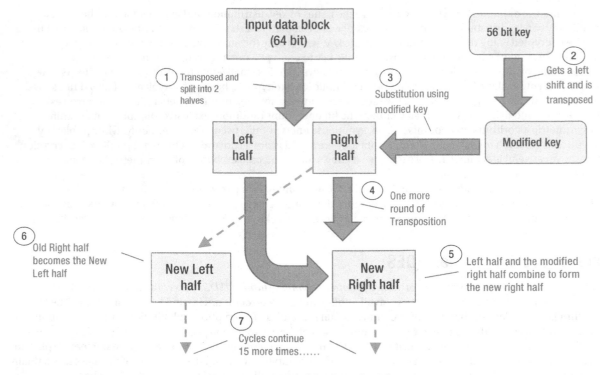

Figure 8-1. *Cycle of the DES algorithm*

Because DES limits its arithmetic and logical operations to 64-bit numbers, it can be used with software for encryption on most of the current 64-bit operating systems.

The real weakness of this algorithm is against an attack called differential cryptanalysis in which a key can be determined from chosen cipher texts in 258 searches. The cryptanalytic attack has not exposed any significant, exploitable vulnerability in DES, but the risks of using the 56-bit key are increasing with easy availability of computing power. Although the computing power or time needed to break DES is still significant, a determined hacker can certainly decrypt text encrypted with DES. If a triple-DES approach (invoking DES three times for encryption using the sequence: encryption via Key1, decryption using Key2, encryption using Key3) is used, the effective key length becomes 112 (if only two of the three keys are unique) or 168 bits (if Key1, Key2, and Key3 are all unique), increasing the difficulty of attack exponentially. DES can be used in the short term, but is certainly at end-of-life and needs to be replaced by a more robust algorithm.

Advanced Encryption Standard (AES)

In 1997, the US National Institute of Standards and Technology called for a new encryption algorithm; subsequently, *Advanced Encryption Standard* (*AES*) became the new standard in 2001. Originally called *Rijndael*, AES is also a block cipher and uses multiple cycles, or rounds, to encrypt data using an input data block size of 128. Encryption keys of 128, 192, and 256 bits require 10, 12, or 14 cycles of encryption, respectively. The cycle of AES is simple, involving a substitution, two permuting functions, and a keying function (see the sidebar "AES Algorithm" for more detail). There are no known weaknesses of AES and it is in wide commercial use.

AES ALGORITHM

To help you visualize the operations of AES, let me first assume input data to be 9 bytes long and represent the AES matrix as a 3×3 array with the data bytes b0 through b8.

Depicted in Figure 8-2, each round of the AES algorithm consists of the following four steps:

1. **Substitute**: To diffuse the data, each byte of a 128-bit data block is substituted using a substitution table.

2. **Shift row:** The rows of data are permuted by a left circular shift; the first (leftmost, high order) n elements of row n are shifted around to the end (rightmost, low order). Therefore, a row n is shifted left circular $(n - 1)$ bytes.

3. **Mix columns**: To transform the columns, the three elements of each column are multiplied by a polynomial. For each element the bits are shifted left and exclusive-ORed with themselves to diffuse each element of the column over all three elements of that column.

4. **Add round key**: Last, a portion of the key unique to this cycle (subkey) is exclusive-ORed or added to each data column. A subkey is derived from the key using a series of permutation, substitution, and ex-OR operations on the key.

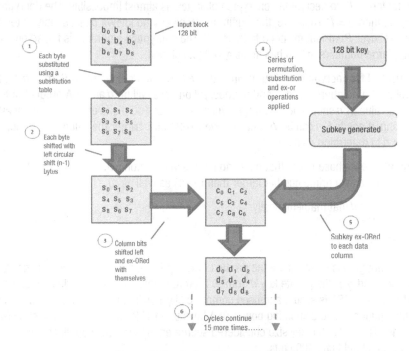

Figure 8-2. *Cycle of the AES algorithm*

Rivest-Shamir-Adelman Encryption

With DES, AES, and other symmetric key algorithms, each pair of users needs a separate key. Each time a user $(n + 1)$ is added, n more keys are required, making it hard to track keys for each additional user with whom you need to communicate. Determining as well as distributing these keys can be a problem—as can maintaining security for the distributed keys because they can't all be memorized. Asymmetric or public key encryption, however, helps you avoid this and many other issues encountered with symmetric key encryption. The most famous algorithm that uses public key encryption is the *Rivest-Shamir-Adelman* (*RSA*) algorithm. Introduced in 1978 and named after its three inventors (Rivest, Shamir, and Adelman), RSA remains secure to date with no serious flaws yet found. To understand how RSA works, see the "Rivest-Shamir-Adelman (RSA) Encryption" sidebar.

RIVEST-SHAMIR-ADELMAN (RSA) ENCRYPTION

The RSA encryption algorithm combines results from number theory with the degree of difficulty in determining the prime factors of a given number. The RSA algorithm operates with arithmetic mod n; mod n for a number P is the remainder when you divide P by n.

The two keys used in RSA for decryption and encryption are interchangeable; either can be chosen as the public key and the other can be used as private key. Any plain text block P is encrypted as P^e mod n. Because the exponentiation is performed, mod n and e as well as n are very large numbers (e is typically 100 digits and n typically 200), and factoring P^e to decrypt the encrypted plain text is almost impossible. The decrypting key d is so chosen that $(P^e)d$ mod $n = P$. Therefore, the legitimate receiver who knows d can simply determine $(P^e)^d$ mod $n = P$ and thus recover P without the need to factor P^e. The encryption algorithm is based on the underlying problem of factoring large numbers, which has no easy or fast solution.

How are keys determined for encryption? If your plain text is P and you are computing P^e mod n, then the encryption keys will be the numbers e and n, and the decryption keys will be d and n. A product of the two prime numbers p and q, the value of n should be very large, typically almost 100 digits or approximately 200 decimal digits (or 512 bits) long. If needed, n can be 768 bits or even 1024 bits. Larger the value of n, larger the degree of difficulty in factoring n to determine p and q.

As a next step, a number e is chosen such that e has no factors in common with $(p - 1) \times (q - 1)$. One way of ensuring this is to choose e as a prime number larger than $(p - 1)$ as well as $(q - 1)$.

Last, select such a number d that mathematically:

$e \times d = 1 \bmod (p - 1) \times (q - 1)$

As you can see, even though n is known to be the product of two primes, if they are large, it is not feasible to determine the primes p and q or the private key d from e. Therefore, this scheme provides adequate security for d. That is also the reason RSA is secure and used commercially. It is important to note, though, that due to improved algorithms and increased computing power RSA keys up to 1024 bits have been broken (though not trivially by any means). Therefore, the key size considered secure enough for most applications is 2048 bits; for more sensitive data, you should use 4096 bits.

Digital Signature Algorithm Encryption (DSA)

Another popular algorithm using public key encryption is *DSA* (*Digital Signature Algorithm*). Although the original purpose of this algorithm was signing, it can be used for encrypting, too. DSA security has a theoretical mathematical basis based on the discrete logarithm problem and is designed using the assumption that a discrete logarithm problem has no quick or efficient solution. Table 8-1 compares DSA with RSA.

Table 8-1. *DSA vs. RSA*

Attribute	DSA	RSA
Key generation	Faster	
Encryption		Faster
Decryption	Faster**	
Digital signature generation	Faster	
Digital signature verification		Faster
Slower client		Preferable
Slower server	Preferable	

**Please note that "Faster" also implies less usage of computational resources*

To summarize, DSA and RSA have almost the same cryptographic strengths, although each has its own performance advantages. In case of performance issues, it might be a good idea to evaluate where the problem lies (at the client or server) and base your choice of key algorithm on that.

Applications of Encryption

In many cases, one type of encryption is more suited for your needs than another, or you may need a combination of encryption methods to satisfy your needs. Four common applications of encryption algorithms that you'll encounter are cryptographic hash functions, key exchange, digital signatures, and certificates. For HDFS, client data access uses TCP/IP protocol, which in turn uses SASL as well as data encryption keys. Hadoop web consoles and MapReduce shuffle use secure HTTP that uses public key certificates. Intel's Hadoop distribution (now Project Rhino) uses symmetric keys for encryption at rest and certificates for encrypted data processing through MapReduce jobs. To better appreciate how Hadoop and others use these applications, you need to understand how each works.

Hash Functions

In some situations, integrity is a bigger concern than secrecy. For example, in a document management system that stores legal documents or manages loans, knowing that a document has not been altered is important. So, encryption can be used to provide integrity as well.

In most files, components of the content are not bound together in any way. In other words, each character is independent in a file, and even though changing one value affects the integrity of the file, it can easily go undetected. Encryption can be used to "seal" a file so that any change can be easily detected. One way of providing this seal is to compute a cryptographic function, called a *hash* or *checksum*, or a *message digest*, of the file. Because the hash function depends on all bits of the file being sealed, altering one bit will alter the checksum result. Each time the file is accessed or used, the hash function recomputes the checksum, and as long as the computed checksum matches the stored value, you know the file has not been changed.

DES and AES work well for sealing values, because a key is needed to modify the stored value (to match modified data). Block ciphers also use a technique called *chaining*: a block is linked to the previous block's value and hence to all previous blocks in a file like a chain by using an exclusive OR to combine the encrypted previous block with the encryption of the current one. Subsequently, a file's cryptographic checksum could be the last block of the chained encryption of a file because that block depends on all other blocks. Popular hash functions are *MD4*, *MD5* (MD meaning Message Digest), and *SHA/SHS* (Secure Hash Algorithm or Standard). In fact, Hadoop uses the SASL MD5-DIGEST mechanism for authentication when a Hadoop client with Hadoop token credentials connects to a Hadoop daemon (e.g., a MapReduce task reading/writing to HDFS).

Key Exchange

Suppose you need to exchange information with an unknown person (who does not know you either), while making sure that no one else has access to the information. The solution is public key cryptography. Because asymmetric keys come in pairs, one half of the pair can be exposed without compromising the other half. A private key can be used to encrypt, and the recipient just needs to have access to the public key to decrypt it. To understand the significance of this, consider an example key exchange.

Suppose Sam and Roy need to exchange a shared symmetric key, and both have public keys for a common encryption algorithm (call these K_{PUB-S} and K_{PUB-R}) as well as private keys (call these K_{PRIV-S} and K_{PRIV-R}). The simplest solution is for Sam to choose any symmetric key K, and encrypt it using his private key (K_{PRIV-S}) and send to Roy, who can use Sam's public key to remove the encryption and obtain K. Unfortunately, anyone with access to Sam's public key can also obtain the symmetric key K that is only meant for Roy. So, a more secure solution is for Sam to first encrypt the symmetric key K using his own private key and then encrypt it again using Roy's public key. Then, Roy can use his private key to decrypt the first level of encryption (outer encryption)—something only he can do—and then use Sam's public key to decrypt the "inner encryption" (proving that communication came from Sam). So, in conclusion, the symmetric key can be exchanged without compromising security.

Digital Signatures and Certificates

Today, most of our daily transactions are conducted in the digital world, so the concept of a signature for approval has evolved to a model that relies on mutual authentication of digital signatures. A *digital signature* is a protocol that works like a real signature: it can provide a unique mark for a sender, and enable others to identify a sender from that mark and thereby confirm an agreement. Digital signatures need the following properties:

- Unreproducible

- Uniquely traceable source authenticity (from expected source only)

- Inseparable from message

- Immutable after being transmitted

- Have recent one-time use and should not allow duplicate usage

Public key encryption systems are ideally suited to digital signatures. For example, a publishing company can first encrypt a contract using their own private key and then encrypt it again using the author's public key. The author can use his private key to decrypt the first level of encryption, and then use publisher's public key to decrypt the inner encryption to get to the contract. After that, the author can "sign" it by creating a hash value of the contract and then encrypting the contract and the hash with his own private key. Finally, he can add one more layer of encryption by encrypting again using the publisher's public key and then e-mail the encrypted contract back to the publisher. Because only the author and publisher have access to their private keys, the exchange clearly is unforgeable and uniquely authentic. The hash function and checksum confirm immutability (assuming an initial checksum of the contract was computed and saved for comparison), while the frequency and timestamps of the e-mails ensure one-time recent usage. Figure 8-3 summarizes the process.

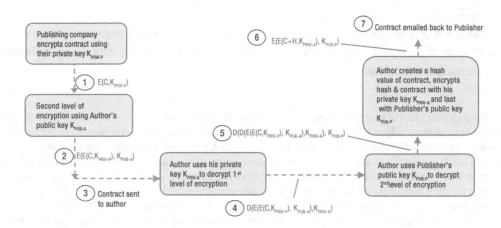

Figure 8-3. *Using Digital signatures for encrypted communication*

In Figure 8-3, $E(C,K_{PRIV-P})$ means contract C was encrypted using K_{PRIV-P}. Similarly, $D(E(E(C,K_{PRIV-P}), K_{PUB-A}), K_{PRIV-A})$ means the first level of the doubly encrypted contract sent to the author was decrypted using K_{PRIV-A}.

Founded on trust between parties through a common respected individual, a digital certificate serves a similar role among multiple parties that a digital signature does for two individuals. A public key and user's identity are associated in a *certificate*, which is then "signed" by a *certificate authority*, certifying the accuracy of the association and authenticating identity.

For example, a publishing company might set up a certificate scheme to authenticate authors, their agents, and company editors in the following way. First, the publisher selects a public key pair, posts the public key where everyone in the company has access to it, and retains the private key. Then, each editor creates a public key pair, puts the public key in a message together with his or her identity, and passes the message securely to the publisher. The publisher signs it by creating a hash value of the message and then encrypting the message and the hash with his or her private key. By signing the message, the publisher affirms that the public key (the editor's) and the identity (also the editor's) in the message are for the same person. This message is called the editor's certificate. The author can create a message with his public key, and the author's agent can sign, hash, and return it. That will be the author's certificate. So, the author and editor's certificates can thus be set up and used for verifying their identities. Anyone can verify the editor's certificate by starting with the publisher's public key and decrypting the editor's certificate to retrieve his or her public key and identity. The author's certificate can be verified by starting with the public key the agent obtained from the publisher and using that to decrypt the certificate to retrieve the author's public key and identity.

Because Hadoop uses different types of encryption for its various components, I will briefly discuss where each of these encryptions is used in the next section.

Hadoop Encryption Options Overview

When considering encryption of sensitive data in Hadoop, you need to consider data "at rest" stored on disks within your cluster nodes, and also data in transit, which is moved during communication among the various nodes and also between nodes and clients. Chapter 4 explained the details of securing data in transit between nodes and applications; you can configure individual Hadoop ecosystem components for encryption (using the component's configuration file) just as you would configure Hadoop's RPC communication for encryption. For example, to configure SSL encryption for Hive, you would need to change configuration within `hive-site.xml` (the property `hive.server2.use.SSL` in `hive-site.xml` needs to be set to `true` and the KeyStore needs to be specified using properties `hive.server2.keystore.path` and `hive.server2.keystore.password`). This chapter, therefore, focuses on configuring Hadoop data at rest.

■ **Note** Encryption is a CPU-intensive activity that can tax your hardware and slow its processing. Weigh the decision to use encryption carefully. If you determine encryption is necessary, implement it for all the data stored within your cluster as well as for processing related to that data.

For a Hadoop cluster, data at rest is the data distributed on all the DataNodes. Need for encryption may be because the data is sensitive and the information needs to be protected, or perhaps encryption is necessary for compliance with legal regulations like the insurance industry's HIPAA or the financial industry's SOX.

Although no Hadoop distribution currently provides encryption at rest, such major vendors as Cloudera and Hortonworks offer third-party solutions. For example, Cloudera works with zNcrypt from Gazzang to provide encryption at rest for data blocks as well as files. For additional protection, zNcrypt uses process-based ACLs and keys. In addition, Amazon Web Services (AWS) offers encryption at rest with its Elastic MapReduce web service and S3 storage (you'll learn more about this shortly), and Intel's distribution of Hadoop also offers encryption at rest. But all these solutions are either proprietary or limit you to a particular distribution of Hadoop.

For an open source solution to encrypt Hadoop data at rest, you can use Project Rhino. In 2013, Intel started an open source project to improve the security capabilities of Hadoop and the Hadoop ecosystem by contributing code to Apache. This code is not yet implemented in Apache Foundation's Hadoop distribution, but it contains enhancements that include distributed key management and the capability to do encryption at rest. The overall goals for this open source project are as follows:

- Support for encryption and key management
- A common authorization framework (beyond ACLs)
- A common token-based authentication framework
- Security improvements to HBase
- Improved security auditing

You can check the progress of Project Rhino at `https://github.com/intel-hadoop/project-rhino`, and learn more about it in the next section.

Encryption Using Intel's Hadoop Distro

In 2013, Intel announced its own Hadoop distribution—a strange decision for a hardware manufacturing company, entering the Big Data arena belatedly with a Hadoop distribution. Intel, however, assured the Hadoop world that its intentions were only to contribute to the Hadoop ecosystem (Apache Foundation) and help out with Hadoop security concerns. Intel claimed its Hadoop distribution worked in perfect harmony with specific Intel chips (used as the CPU) to perform encryption and decryption about 10 to 15 times faster than current alternatives.

Around the same time, I had a chance to work with an Intel team on a pilot project for a client who needed data stored within HDFS to be encrypted, and I got to know how Intel's encryption worked. The client used Hive for queries and reports and Intel offered encryption that covered HDFS as well as Hive. Although the distribution I used (which forms the basis of the information presented in this section), is not available commercially, most of the functionality it offered will be available through Project Rhino and Cloudera's Hadoop distribution (now that Intel has invested in it).

Specifically, the Intel distribution used codecs to implement encryption (more on these in a moment) and offered file-level encryption that could be used with Hive or HBase. It used symmetric as well as asymmetric keys in conjunction with Java KeyStores (see the sidebar "KeyStores and TrustStores" for more information). The details of the implementation I used will give you some insight into the potential of Project Rhino.

KEYSTORES AND TRUSTSTORES

A *KeyStore* is a database or repository of keys or trusted certificates that are used for a variety of purposes, including authentication, encryption, and data integrity. A key entry contains the owner's identity and private key, whereas a trusted certificate entry contains only a public key in addition to the entity's identity. For better management and security, you can use two KeyStores: one containing your key entries and the other containing your trusted certificate entries (including Certificate Authorities' certificates). Access can be restricted to the KeyStore with your private keys, while trusted certificates reside in a more publicly accessible TrustStore.

Used when making decisions about what to trust, a *TrustStore* contains certificates from someone you expect to communicate with or from Certificate Authorities that you trust to identify other parties. Add an entry to a TrustStore only if you trust the entity from which the potential entry originated.

Various types of KeyStores are available, such as PKCS12 or JKS. JKS is most commonly used in the Java world. PKCS12 isn't Java specific but is convenient to use with certificates that have private keys backed up from a browser or the ones coming from OpenSSL-based tools. PKCS12 is mainly useful as a KeyStore but less so for a TrustStore, because it needs to have a private key associated with certificates. JKS doesn't require each entry to be a private key entry, so you can use it as a TrustStore for certificates you trust but for which you don't need private keys.

Step-by-Step Implementation

The client's requirement was encryption at rest for sensitive financial data stored within HDFS and accessed using Hive. So, I had to make sure that the data file, which was pushed from SQL Server as a text file, was encrypted while it was stored within HDFS and also was accessible normally (with decryption applied) through Hive, to authorized users only. Figure 8-4 provides an overview of the encryption process.

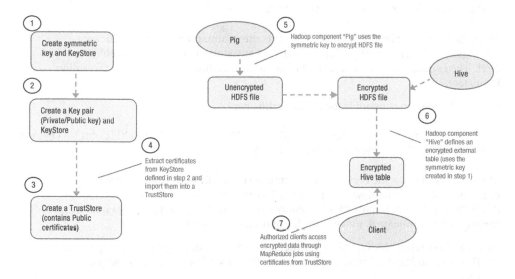

Figure 8-4. Data encryption at Intel Hadoop distribution

The first step to achieve my goal was to create a secret (symmetric) key and KeyStore with the command (I created a directory/keys under my home directory and created all encryption related files there):

```
> keytool -genseckey -alias BCLKey -keypass bcl2601 -storepass bcl2601 -keyalg AES -keysize 256
-KeyStore BCLKeyStore.keystore -storetype JCEKS
```

This keytool command generates the secret key BCLKey and stores it in a newly created KeyStore called BCLKeyStore. The keyalg parameter specifies the algorithm AES to be used to generate the secret key, and keysize 256 specifies the size of the key to be generated. Last, keypass is the password used to protect the secret key, and storepass does the same for the KeyStore. You can adjust permissions for the KeyStore with:

```
> chmod 600 BCLKeyStore.keystore
```

Next, I created a key pair (private/public key) and KeyStore with the command:

```
> keytool -genkey -alias KEYCLUSTERPRIVATEASYM -keyalg RSA -keystore clusterprivate.keystore
-storepass 123456 -keypass 123456 -dname "CN= JohnDoe, OU=Development, O=Intel, L=Chicago, S=IL,
C=US" -storetype JKS -keysize 1024
```

This generates a key pair (a public key and associated private key) and single-element certificate chain stored as entry KEYCLUSTERPRIVATEASYM in the KeyStore clusterprivate.keystore. Notice the use of algorithm RSA for public key encryption and the key length of 1024. The parameter dname specifies the name to be associated with alias, and is used as the issuer and subject in the self-signed certificate.

I distributed the created KeyStore clusterprivate.keystore across the cluster using Intel Manager (admin) ➤ configuration ➤ security ➤ Key Management.

To create a TrustStore, I next took the following steps:

1. Extract the certificate from the newly created KeyStore with the command:

    ```
    > keytool -export -alias KEYCLUSTERPRIVATEASYM -keystore clusterprivate.keystore -rfc
    -file hivepublic.cert -storepass 123456
    ```

    From the KeyStore clusterprivate.keystore, the command reads the certificate associated with alias KEYCLUSTERPRIVATEASYM and stores it in the file hivepublic. cert. The certificate will be output in the printable encoding format (as the -rfc option indicates).

2. Create a TrustStore containing the public certificate:

    ```
    > keytool -import -alias HIVEKEYCLUSTERPUBLICASYM -file hivepublic.cert -keystore
    clusterpublic.TrustStore -storepass 123456
    ```

    This command reads the certificate (or certificate chain) from the file hivepublic. cert and stores it in the KeyStore (used as a TrustStore) entry identified by HIVEKEYCLUSTERPUBLICASYM. The TrustStore clusterpublic.TrustStore is created and the imported certificate is added to the list of trusted certificates.

3. Change clusterpublic.TrustStore ownership to root, group to hadoop, and permissions "644" (read/write for root and read for members of all groups) with the commands:

    ```
    > chmod 644 clusterpublic.TrustStore
    > chown root:hadoop clusterpublic.TrustStore
    ```

4. Create a file TrustStore.passwords, set its permission to "644", and add the following contents to the file: keystore.password=123456.

5. Copy the /keys directory and all of its files to all the other nodes in the cluster. On each node, the KeyStore directory must be in /usr/lib/hadoop/.

With the TrustStore ready, I subsequently created a text file (bcl.txt) to use for testing encryption and copied it to HDFS:

```
> hadoop fs -mkdir /tmp/bcl.....
> hadoop fs -put bcl.txt /tmp/bcl
```

I started Pig (> pig) and was taken to the grunt> prompt. I executed the following commands within Pig to set all the required environment variables:

```
set KEY_PROVIDER_PARAMETERS 'keyStoreUrl=file:////root/bcl/BCLKeyStore.keystore&keyStoreType-
JCEKS&password=bcl2601';
set AGENT_SECRETS_PROTECTOR 'com.intel.hadoop.mapreduce.crypto.KeyStoreKeyProvider';

set AGENT_PUBLIC_KEY_PROVIDER 'org.apache.hadoop.io.crypto.KeyStoreKeyProvider';

set AGENT_PUBLIC_KEY_PROVIDER_PARAMETERS 'keyStoreUrl=file:////keys/clusterpublic.TrustStore&keyStor
eType=JKS&password=123456';
set AGENT_PUBLIC_KEY_NAME 'HIVEKEYCLUSTERPUBLICASYM';
set pig.encrypt.keyProviderParameters 'keyStoreUrl=file:////root/bcl/BCLKeyStore.
keystore&keyStoreType-JCEKS&password=bcl2601';
```

Next, to read the bcl.txt file from HDFS, encrypt it, and store it into the same location in a directory named bcl_encrypted, I issued the commands:

```
raw = LOAD '/tmp/bcl/bcl.txt' AS (name:chararray,age:int,country:chararray);
STORE raw INTO '/tmp/bcl/bcl_encrypted' USING PigStorage('\t','-keyName BCLKey');
```

After exiting Pig, I checked contents of the encrypted file by issuing the command:

```
> hadoop fs -cat /tmp/bcl/bcl_encrypted/part-m-00000.aes
```

The control characters appeared to confirm the encryption. I created a Hive external table and pointed it to the encrypted file using the following steps:

1. Start Hive.

2. Set the environment variables:

```
set hive.encrypt.master.keyName=BCLKey;
set hive.encrypt.master.keyProviderParameters=keyStoreUrl=file:////root/bcl/BCLKeyStore.k
eystore&keyStoreType=JCEKS&password=bcl2601;
set hive.encrypt.keyProviderParameters=keyStoreUrl=file:////root/bcl/BCLKeyStore.keystore
&keyStoreType=JCEKS&password=bcl2601;
set mapred.crypto.secrets.protector.class=com.intel.hadoop.mapreduce.cryptocontext.
provider.AgentSecretsProtector;
set mapred.agent.encryption.key.provider=org.apache.hadoop.io.crypto.KeyStoreKeyProvider;
set mapred.agent.encryption.key.provider.parameters=keyStoreUrl=file:////keys/
clusterpublic.TrustStore&keyStoreType=JKS&password=123456;
set mapred.agent.encryption.keyname=HIVEKEYCLUSTERPUBLICASYM;
```

3. Create an encrypted external table pointing to the encrypted data file created by Pig:

```
create external table bcl_encrypted_pig_data(name STRING, age INT, country STRING) ROW
FORMAT DELIMITED FIELDS TERMINATED BY ',' STORED AS TEXTFILE LOCATION '/tmp/bcl/bcl_
encrypted/' TBLPROPERTIES("hive.encrypt.enable"="true", "hive.encrypt.keyName"="BCLKey");
```

4. Once the table is created, decrypted data can be viewed by any authorized client (having appropriate key and certificate files within /usr/lib/hadoop/keys directory) using the select query (in Hive syntax) at the Hive prompt:

```
> select * from bcl_encrypted_pig_data;
```

To summarize, to implement the Intel distribution for use with Hive, I set up the keys, KeyStores, and certificates that were used for encryption. Then I extracted the certificate from the KeyStore and imported it into a TrustStore. Note that although I created the key pair and certificate for a user JohnDoe in the example, for a multiuser environment you will need to create a key pair and certificates for all authorized users.

A symmetric key was used to encrypt data within HDFS (and with Hive). MapReduce used a public key and certificate, because client communication within Hive uses MapReduce. That's also the reason a key pair and certificate will be necessary for authorized users for Hive (who are authorized to access the encrypted data).

Special Classes Used by Intel Distro

The desired functionality of encryption at rest needs special codecs, classes, and logic implemented. Although many classes and codecs were available, they didn't work in harmony backed by a common logic to provide the encryption functionality. Intel has added the underlying logic in its distribution.

For example, org.apache.hadoop.io.crypto.KeyStoreKeyProvider is an implementation of the class org.apache.hadoop.io.crypto.KeyProvider. The corresponding Apache class for HBase is org.apache.hadoop.hbase.io.crypto.KeyStoreKeyProvider, which is an implementation of org.apache.hadoop.hbase.io.crypto.KeyProvider. This class is used to resolve keys from a protected KeyStore file on the local file system. Intel has used this class to manage keys stored in KeyStore (and TrustStore) files. The other Hbase classes used are:

```
org.apache.hadoop.hbase.io.crypto.Cipher
org.apache.hadoop.hbase.io.crypto.Decryptor
org.apache.hadoop.hbase.io.crypto.Encryptor
```

How are these classes used? For example, in Java terms, the method Encryption.decryptWithSubjectKey for class org.apache.hadoop.hbase.io.crypto.Cipher decrypts a block of encrypted data using the symmetric key provided; whereas the method Encryption.encryptWithSubjectKey encrypts a block of data using the provided symmetric key. So, to summarize, this class provides encryption/decryption using the symmetric key.

The Intel custom class com.intel.hadoop.mapreduce.crypto.KeyStoreKeyProvider was designed for encrypted MapReduce processing and works similar to the Apache Hadoop crypto class mapred.crypto.KeyStoreKeyProvider. It is adapted for use with MapReduce jobs and is capable of processing certificates as well as keys.

Most of these classes are developed and used by the Apache Foundation. The only difference is that the Apache Foundation's Hadoop distribution doesn't use these classes to provide cumulative functionality of encryption at rest, nor do any of the other distributions available commercially. Project Rhino is trying to remedy that situation, and since even the Intel custom classes and codecs are available for their use, you can expect the encryption-at-rest functionality to be available through Project Rhino very soon.

Using Amazon Web Services to Encrypt Your Data

As you have seen, installing and using encryption can be a tough task, but Amazon has consciously endeavored to make it simple. AWS offers easy options that eliminate most of the work and time needed to install, configure, manage, and use encryption with Hadoop. With AWS, you have the option of doing none, some or all of the work depending on the configured service you rent. For example, if you need to focus on other parts of your project (such as design of ETL for bulk load of data from RDBMS (relational database management system) to HDFS or Analytics), you can have AWS take care of fully implementing encryption at rest for your data.

Deciding on a Model for Data Encryption and Storage

AWS provides several configurations or *models* for encryption usage. The first model, model A, lets you control the encryption method as well as KMI (key management infrastructure). It offers you the utmost flexibility and control, but you do all the work. Model B lets you control the encryption method while AWS stores the keys.; you still get to manage your keys. The most rigid choice, model C, gives you no control over KMI or encryption method, although it is the easiest to implement because AWS does it all for you. To implement model C, you need to use an AWS service that supports server-side encryption, such as Amazon S3, Amazon EMR, Amazon Redshift, or Amazon Glacier.

To demonstrate, I will implement encryption at rest using Amazon's model C. Why C? The basic steps are easy to understand, and you can use the understanding you gain to implement model A, for which you need to implement all the tasks (I have provided steps for implementing model A as a download on the Apress web site). I will use Amazon EMR (or Elastic MapReduce, which provides an easy-to-use Hadoop implementation running on *Amazon Elastic Compute Cloud,* or *EC2*) along with Amazon S3 for storage. Please note: One caveat of renting the EMR service is that AWS charges by the "normalized" hour, not actual hours, because the plan uses multiple AWS "appliances" and at least two EC2 instances.

If you are unfamiliar with AWS's offerings, EC2 is the focal point of AWS. EC2 allows you to rent a virtual server (or virtual machine) that is a preconfigured Amazon Machine Image with desired operating system and choice of virtual hardware resources (CPU, RAM, disk storage, etc.). You can boot (or start) this virtual machine or *instance* and run your own applications as desired. The term *elastic* refers to the flexible, pay-by-hour model for any instances that you create and use. Figure 8-5 displays AWS management console. This is where you need to start for "renting" various AWS components (assuming you have created an AWS account first): `http://aws.amazon.com`.

Figure 8-5. *AWS Management console*

Getting back to the implementation using model C, if you specify server-side encryption while procuring the EMR cluster (choose the Elastic MapReduce option in the AWS console as shown in Figure 8-5), the EMR model provides server-side encryption of your data and manages the encryption method as well as keys transparently for you. Figure 8-6 depicts the "Envelope encryption" method AWS uses for server-side encryption. The basic steps are as follows:

1. The AWS service generates a data key when you request that your data be encrypted.

2. AWS uses the data key for encrypting your data.

3. The encrypted data key and the encrypted data are stored using S3 storage

4. AWS uses the key-encrypting key (unique to S3 in this case) to encrypt the data key and store it separately from the data key and encrypted data.

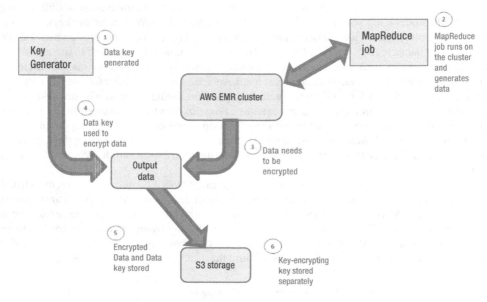

Figure 8-6. *Envelope encryption by AWS*

For data retrieval and decryption, this process is reversed. First, the encrypted data key is decrypted using the key-encrypting key, and then it is used to decrypt your data.

As you can see from Figure 8-6, the S3 storage service supports server-side encryption. Amazon S3 server-side encryption uses 256-bit AES symmetric keys for data keys as well as master (key-encrypting) keys.

Encrypting a Data File Using Selected Model

In this section, I will discuss step-by-step implementation for the EMR-based model C, in which AWS manages your encryption method and keys transparently. As mentioned earlier, you can find the steps to implement model A on the Apress web site.

Create S3 Storage Through AWS

You need to create the storage first, because you will need it for your EMR cluster. Simply log in to the AWS management console, select service S3, and create a bucket named htestbucket and a folder test within (Figure 8-7).

Figure 8-7. *Create an S3 bucket and folder*

Specify server-side encryption for folder test that you created (Figure 8-8).

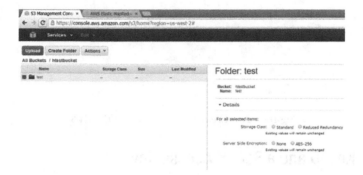

Figure 8-8. *Activate server-side encryption for a folder*

Adjust the permissions for the bucket htestbucket created earlier, as necessary (Figure 8-9).

Figure 8-9. *Adjust permissions for an S3 bucket*

Create a Key Pair (`bclkey`) to Be Used for Authentication

Save the `.pem` file to your client. Use PuTTYgen to create a `.ppk` (private key file) that can be used for authentication with PuTTY to connect to the EMR cluster (Master node). For details on using PuTTY and PuTTYgen, please see Chapter 4 and Appendix B. Figure 8-10 shows the AWS screen for key pair creation. To reach it, choose service EC2 on the AWS management console, and then the option Key Pairs.

Figure 8-10. *Creating a key pair within AWS*

Create an Access Key ID and a Secret Access Key

These keys are used as credentials for encryption and are associated with a user. If you don't have any users created and are using the `root` account for AWS, then you need to create these keys for `root`. From the Identity and Access Management (IAM) Management console (Figure 8-11), select Dashboard, and then click the first option, Delete your root access keys. (If you don't have these keys created for `root`, you won't see this warning). To reach IAM console, choose service "Identity & Access Management" on the AWS management console.

Figure 8-11. *IAM console for AWS*

Click the Manage Security Credentials button, and ignore the warning to "Continue to Security credentials" (Figure 8-12).

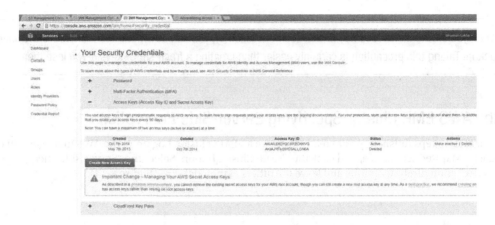

Figure 8-12. *Creation of security credentials*

Your AWS root account is like a UNIX root account, and AWS doesn't recommend using that. Instead, create user accounts with roles, permissions, and access keys as needed. If you do so, you can more easily customize permissions without compromising security. Another thing to remember about using the root account is that you can't retrieve the access key ID or secret access key if you lose it! So, I created a user Bhushan for use with my EMR cluster (Figure 8-13). I used the "Users" option and "Create New Users" button from the Identity and Access Management (IAM) Management console (Figure 8-11) to create this new user.

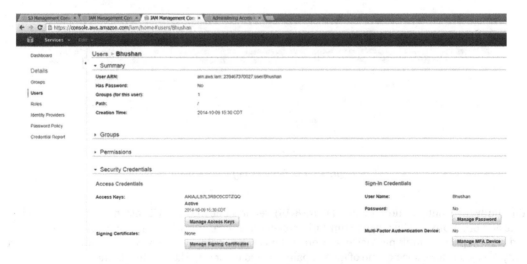

Figure 8-13. *Creation of a user for use with EMR cluster*

To set your keys for a user, again begin on the IAM Management Console, and select the Users option, then a specific user (or create a user). Next, open the Security Credentials area and create an access key ID and a secret access key for the selected user (Figure 8-13).

■ **Note** When you create the access key ID and secret access key, you can download them and save them somewhere safe as a backup. Taking this precaution is certainly easier than creating a fresh set of keys if you lose them.

Create the AWS EMR Cluster Specifying Server-Side Encryption

With the preparatory steps finished, you're ready to create an EMR cluster. Log on to the AWS management console, select the Elastic MapReduce service, and click the Create Cluster button. Select the "Server-side encryption" and "Consistent view" configuration options and leave the others at their defaults (Figure 8-14).

Figure 8-14. *Creation of EMR cluster*

In the Hardware Configuration section (Figure 8-15), request one Master EC2 instance to run JobTracker and NameNode and one Core EC2 instance to run TaskTrackers and DataNodes. (This is just for testing; in the real world, you would need to procure multiple Master or Core instances depending on the processing power you require.) In the Security Access section, specify one of the key pairs created earlier (bclkey), while in the IAM Roles section, set EMR_DefaultRole and EMR_EC2_DefaultRole for the EMR roles. Make sure that these roles have permissions to access the S3 storage (bucket and folders) and any other resources you need to use.

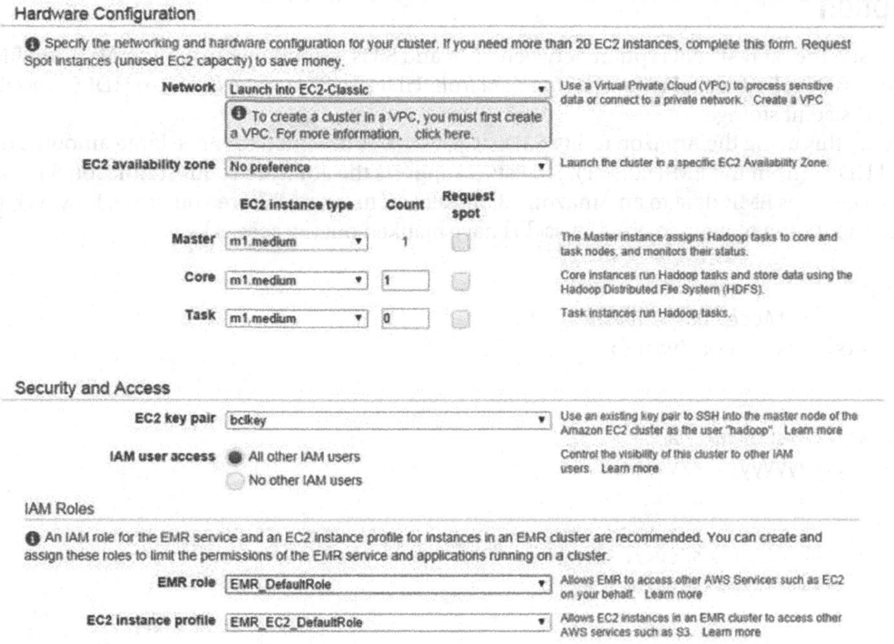

Figure 8-15. *Hardware configuration for EMR cluster*

After you check all the requested configuration options, click on the "Create Cluster" button at the bottom of the screen to create an EMR cluster as per your requirements.

In a couple of minutes, you will receive a confirmation of cluster creation similar to Figure 8-16.

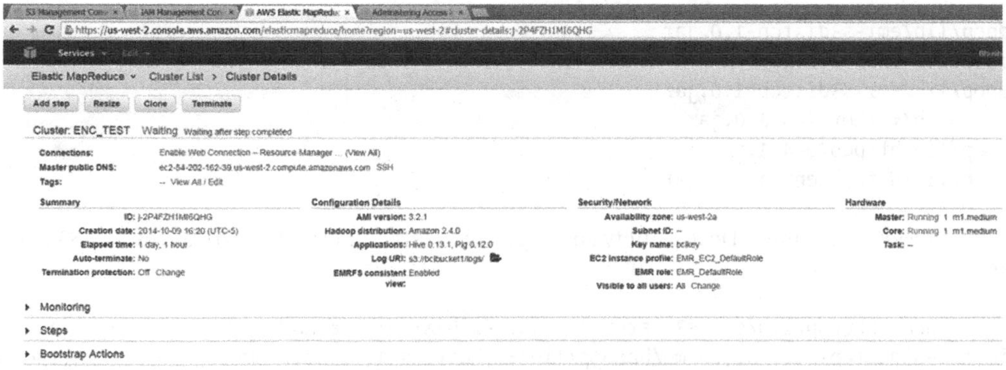

Figure 8-16. *EMR cluster created*

Test Encryption

As a final step, test if the "at rest" encryption between EMR and S3 is functional. As per the AWS and EMR documentation, any MapReduce jobs transferring data from HDFS to S3 storage (or S3 to HDFS) should encrypt the data written to persistent storage.

You can verify this using the Amazon utility S3DistCp, which is designed to move large amounts of data between Amazon S3 and HDFS (from the EMR cluster). S3DistCp supports the ability to request Amazon S3 to use server-side encryption when it writes EMR data to an Amazon S3 bucket you manage. Before you use it, however, you need to add the following configuration to your `core-site.xml` (I have blanked out my access keys):

```
<property>
 <name>fs.s3.awsSecretAccessKey</name>
 <value>xxxxxxxxxxxxxxxxxxxx</value>
</property>
<property>
 <name>fs.s3.awsAccessKeyId</name>
 <value>yyyyyyyyyyyyyyyyyyyy</value>
</property>
<property>
 <name>fs.s3n.awsSecretAccessKey</name>
 <value>xxxxxxxxxxxxxxxxxxxx</value>
</property>
<property>
 <name>fs.s3n.awsAccessKeyId</name>
 <value>yyyyyyyyyyyyyyyyyyyy</value>
</property>
```

Remember to substitute values for your own access key ID and secret access key. There is no need to restart any Hadoop daemons.

Next, make sure that the following jars exist in your /home/hadoop/lib (/lib under my Hadoop install directory). If not, find and copy them there:

```
/home/hadoop/lib/emr-s3distcp-1.0.jar
/home/hadoop/lib/gson-2.1.jar
/home/hadoop/lib/emr-s3distcp-1.0.jar
/home/hadoop/lib/EmrMetrics-1.0.jar
/home/hadoop/lib/httpcore-4.1.jar
/home/hadoop/lib/httpclient-4.1.1.jar
```

Now, you're ready to run the S3DistCp utility and copy a file test1 from HDFS to folder test for S3 bucket htestbucket:

```
> hadoop jar /home/hadoop/lib/emr-s3distcp-1.0.jar -libjars /home/hadoop/lib/gson-2.1.jar,/home/
hadoop/lib/emr-s3distcp-1.0.jar,/home/hadoop/lib/EmrMetrics-1.0.jar,/home/hadoop/lib/httpcore-
4.1.jar,/home/hadoop/lib/httpclient-4.1.1.jar --src /tmp/test1 --dest s3://htestbucket/test/
--disableMultipartUpload --s3ServerSideEncryption
```

My example produced the following response in a few seconds:

```
14/10/10 03:27:47 INFO s3distcp.S3DistCp: Running with args: -libjars /home/hadoop/lib/gson-
2.1.jar,/home/hadoop/lib/emr-s3distcp-1.0.jar,/home/hadoop/lib/EmrMetrics-1.0.jar,/home/hadoop/lib/
httpcore-4.1.jar,/home/hadoop/lib/httpclient-4.1.1.jar --src /tmp/test1 --dest s3://htestbucket/
test/ --disableMultipartUpload --s3ServerSideEncryption
....
....
14/10/10 03:27:51 INFO client.RMProxy: Connecting to ResourceManager at
14/10/10 03:27:54 INFO mapreduce.Job: The url to track the job: http://10.232.45.82:9046/proxy/
application_1412889867251_0001/
14/10/10 03:27:54 INFO mapreduce.Job: Running job: job_1412889867251_0001
14/10/10 03:28:12 INFO mapreduce.Job:  map 0% reduce 0%
....
....
14/10/10 03:30:17 INFO mapreduce.Job:  map 100% reduce 100%
14/10/10 03:30:18 INFO mapreduce.Job: Job job_1412889867251_0001 completed successfully
```

Clearly, the MapReduce job copied the file successfully to S3 storage. Now, you need to verify if the file is stored encrypted within S3. To do so, use the S3 management console and check properties of file test1 within folder test in bucket htestbucket (Figure 8-17).

Figure 8-17. *Verifying server-side encryption for MapReduce job*

As you can see, the property Server Side Encryption is set to AES-256, meaning the MapReduce job from the EMR cluster successfully copied data to S3 storage with server-side encryption!

You can try other ways of invoking MapReduce jobs (e.g., Hive queries or Pig scripts) and write to S3 storage to verify that the stored data is indeed encrypted. You can also use S3DistCp to transfer data from your own local Hadoop cluster to Amazon S3 storage. Just make sure that you copy the AWS credentials in core-site.xml on all nodes within your local cluster and that the previously listed six .jar files are in the /lib subdirectory of your Hadoop install directory.

If you'd like to compare this implementation of encryption using AWS EMR with implementation of the more hands-on model A (in which you manage encryption and keys, plus you need to install specific software on EC2 instances for implementing encryption), remember you can download and review those steps from the Apress web site.

You've now seen both alternatives for providing encryption at rest with Hadoop (using Intel's Hadoop distribution and using AWS). If you review carefully, you will realize that they do have commonalities in implementing encryption. Figure 8-18 summarizes the generic steps.

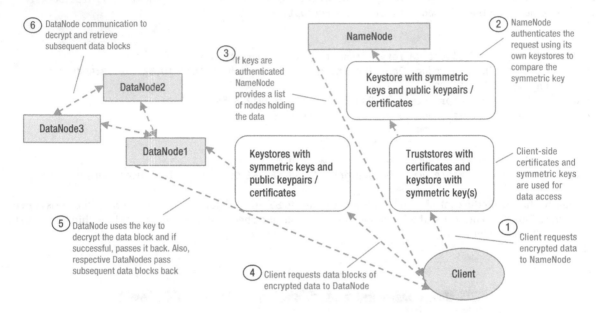

Figure 8-18. *DataNode uses symmetric key (from client) to decrypt the data block and if successful, retrieves the data block. Respective DataNodes retrieve and pass subsequent data blocks back*

Summary

Encryption at rest with Hadoop is still a work in progress, especially for the open source world. Perhaps when Hadoop is used more extensively in the corporate world, our options will improve. For now, you must turn to paid third-party solutions. The downside to these third-party solutions is that even though they claim to work with specific distributions, their claims are difficult to verify. Also, it is not clear how much custom code they add to your Hadoop install and what kind of performance you actually get for encryption/decryption. Last, these solutions are not developed or tested by trained cryptographers or cryptanalysts. So, there is no reliability or guarantee that they are (and will be) "unbreakable."

Intel entered the Hadoop and encryption-at-rest arena with lot of publicity and hype, but quickly backed off and invested in Cloudera instead. Now the future of Project Rhino and possible integration of that code with Cloudera's distribution doesn't seem very clear. There are open source applications in bits and pieces, but a robust, integrated solution that can satisfy the practical encryption needs of a serious Hadoop practitioner doesn't exist yet.

For now, let's hope that this Hadoop area generates enough interest among users to drive more options in the future for implementing encryption using open source solutions.

Whatever the future holds, for the present, this is the last chapter. I sincerely hope this book has facilitated your understanding of Hadoop security options and helps you make your environment secure!

PART V

Appendices

APPENDIX A

■ ■ ■

Pageant Use and Implementation

Pageant is an SSH authentication agent that can be used with PuTTY or WinSCP for holding your decrypted keys in memory, so that you don't need to enter your passphrase to decrypt your key every time you are authenticating to a server using a key pair (Chapter 4 discusses key-based authentication in detail). If you are using multiple key pairs to authenticate to multiple servers, Pageant is even more useful. You can use Pageant to hold all your decrypted keys in memory, meaning you need to enter the respective passphrases only once when you start your Windows session. When you log off your Windows session, Pageant exits without saving the decrypted keys on disk, which is the reason you need to enter your passphrase again when you start your Windows session.

Because Pageant is part of PuTTY installation package, you can download it from the same URL (http://www.chiark.greenend.org.uk/~sgtatham/putty/download.html). When you run the executable file Pageant.exe to start Pageant, an icon that looks like a computer wearing a hat will appear in your system tray. Right-click the icon to invoke the Pageant menu, and then select the menu option you need: New Session, Saved Sessions, View Keys, Add Key, About, or Exit. If you select View Keys before adding keys, however, you will just see an empty list box.

Using Pageant

To use Pageant, you need first to generate a key pair and copy the public key to the server to which you need to connect. For example, I generated a key pair and saved the keys as keytest.ppk (private key) and keytest.pub (public key). I then encrypted the private key using a passphrase. Because I wanted to connect to the host pract_hdp_sec, I pasted my public key in the authorized_keys file in .ssh directory (as discussed in Chapter 4). Next, I will store the decrypted private key in Pageant. Figure A-1 illustrates selecting and adding the key.

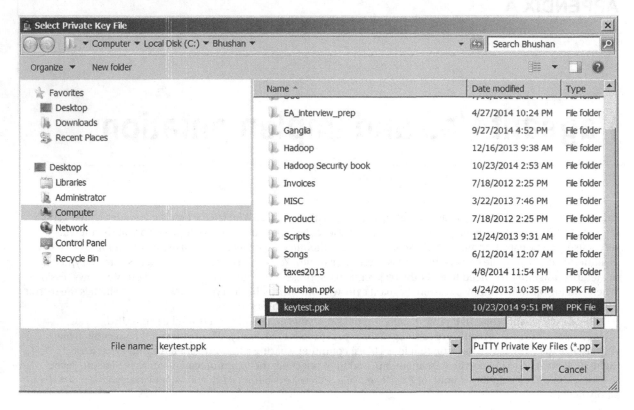

Figure A-1. *Adding a key to Pageant*

When you select a key (here, `testkey.ppk`), you are prompted for the passphrase (Figure A-2).

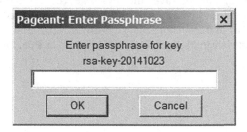

Figure A-2. *Using Pageant to store passphrase for a key*

After you enter the right passphrase, Pageant decrypts your private key and holds it in memory until you log off your Windows session. You can see your key listed within Pageant, as shown in Figure A-3.

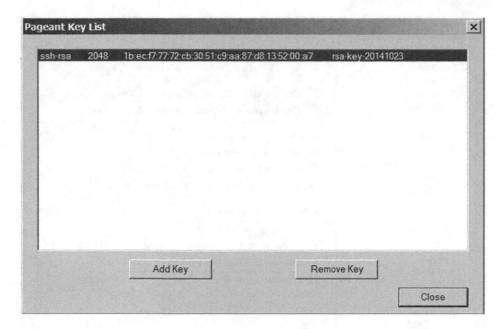

Figure A-3. *Listing a stored key within Pageant*

Now, you just need to specify your private key as means of authorization within PuTTY (Figure A-4).

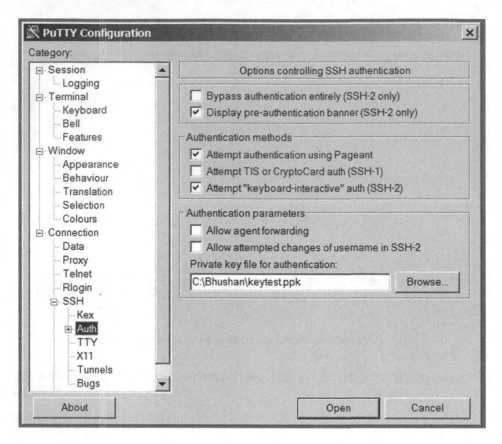

Figure A-4. *Specifying key-based authentication within PuTTY*

Next time you want to connect to the server `pract_hdp_sec`, just open a PuTTY session, and it will prompt you for login name. Once you enter the login name, PuTTY directly connects you to the server, as you can see in Figure A-5.

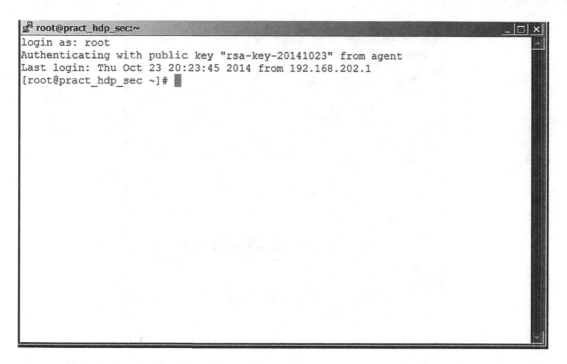

```
root@pract_hdp_sec:~                                              _ □ ×
login as: root
Authenticating with public key "rsa-key-20141023" from agent
Last login: Thu Oct 23 20:23:45 2014 from 192.168.202.1
[root@pract_hdp_sec ~]#
```

Figure A-5. *Key-based authentication performed using decrypted key from Pageant*

PuTTY recognizes that Pageant is running, retrieves the decrypted key automatically, and uses it to authenticate. You can open as many PuTTY sessions for the same server as you need without typing your passphrase again.

In addition, Pageant can load multiple private keys automatically when it starts up. For example, suppose you need to connect to ten servers on a daily basis. Manually adding the keys every day to Pageant is difficult as well as error-prone. To automatically load multiple keys, use a Pageant command line similar to the following; the directory path, of course, depends on where your Pageant.exe or your private key file (.ppk file) is located:

```
C:\Users\Administrator\Desktop>pageant.exe c:\bhushan\keytest.ppk c:\bhushan\bhushan.ppk
```

You can add multiple keys separated by space. If the keys are encrypted, Pageant will prompt for passphrases at startup. If Pageant is already running and you execute this command, it will load keys into the existing Pageant.

You can also create a shortcut and specify the command line there, as shown in Figure A-6.

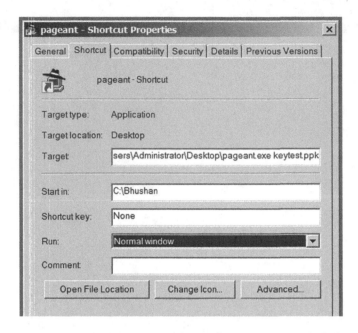

Figure A-6. *Specifying a starting (default) directory for multiple keys*

If you have just one private key, specify its full path within the **Target** field:

```
C:\Users\Administrator\Desktop>pageant.exe c:\bhushan\keytest.ppk
```

If you have multiple keys and the path is long, instead of specifying path for each key, you can just specify a starting directory. For example, to specify a starting point for my previous multi-key example, in the **Target** field enter C:\Users\Administrator\Desktop>pageant.exe keytest.ppk and in the **Start in** field enter C:\Bhushan.

After Pageant initializes and loads the keys specified on its command line, you can direct Pageant to start another program. This program (for e.g. WinSCP or PuTTY etc.) can then use the keys that Pageant loaded. The syntax is as follows:

```
C:\Users\Administrator\Desktop>pageant.exe c:\bhushan\keytest.ppk -c C:\PuTTY\putty.exe
```

Security Considerations

Holding your decrypted private keys in Pageant is more secure than storing key files on your local disk drive, but still has some known security issues.

For example, Windows doesn't protect "swapped" data (memory data written to a system swap file) in any way. So, if you using Pageant for a long time, the decrypted key data could likely be swapped and written to disk. A malicious attacker who gains access to your hard disk could also gain access to your keys. This is, of course, much more secure than storing an unencrypted file on your local disk drive, but still has vulnerabilities.

Windows only has safeguards to prevent excutable code writing into another excutable program's memory space; but still provides Read access to it. In other words, programs can access each other's memory space, which is intended as a way to assist in debugging. Unfortunately, malicious programs can exploit this feature and can access Pageant's memory to extract the decrypted keys and use them for unlawful purposes.

These risks can easily be mitigated, however, by making sure that your network infrastructure is secure and firewalls in place.

APPENDIX B

■ ■ ■

PuTTY and SSH Implementation for Linux-Based Clients

In the section "Key-Based Authentication Using PuTTY" in Chapter 4, you reviewed how PuTTY can effectively be used for key-based authentication for a Windows-based client. What about key-based authentication for Linux-based clients? The answer is PuTTY again.

You can download the Linux-based version of PuTTY from various sources. I used rpm (Red Hat Package Manager, a package management system used for software distribution in Linux domain) for the latest PuTTY version (0.63) for CentOS 6.2; the file is putty-0.63-1.el6.rf.x86_64.rpm. You can download the rpm from various sources; you just need to search for your operating system. After you download the file, install the rpm:

```
rpm -Uvh putty-0.63-1.el6.rf.x86_64.rpm
```

To generate a pair of private and public keys in the Linux version of PuTTY, you use a command line utility called PuTTYgen, which is installed automatically when you install PuTTY via rpm. To generate the key pair, use the following command:

```
puttygen -t rsa -C "my key pair" -o bcl.ppk
```

PuTTYgen then prompts you to enter a passphrase. Make a note of it, because you will need to specify the same passphrase every time you use the key pair to connect to a host.

You can save the key in your home directory (easy to remember the location) and then export the public key to the authorized_keys file using the following command:

```
puttygen -L bcl.ppk >> $HOME/.ssh/authorized_keys
```

Next, copy the authorized_keys file to hosts you need to connect to (using PuTTY). Note that if your host already has an authorized_keys file in the $HOME/.ssh directory, then copy your newly created file using a different name and append its contents to the existing authorized_keys file.

Next, invoke PuTTY at the command prompt by typing **putty**. The interface looks identical to its Windows-based counterpart (Figure B-1).

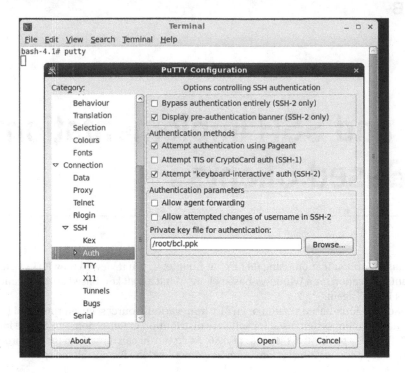

Figure B-1. *Linux PuTTY with key-based authentication*

For connecting to a server, click the option SSH to open the drop-down and then click the option Auth (authorization) under that. On the right side of the PuTTY interface, click Browse and select the private key file you saved earlier (/root/bcl.ppk in this example). Click Open to open a new session.

That's it! You are now ready to use PuTTY with key-based authentication! Figure B-2 shows the login prompt and the prompt for a passphrase.

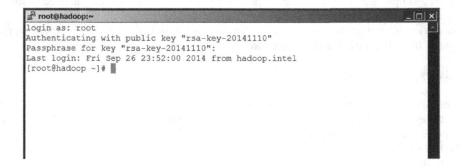

Figure B-2. *Using Linux PuTTY with passphrase*

Using SSH for Remote Access

You can also use SSH to connect remotely to a host. If you want to use a key pair for authentication with SSH, you first need to use a utility called ssh-keygen to generate the keys. By default, the keys are saved in the $HOME/.ssh directory as files id_rsa (private key) and id_rsa.pub (public key). Figure B-3 shows a key pair generated in the default location without a passphrase (you can specify a passphrase for additional security).

```
root@Master:~                                         _ □ ×

File  Edit  View  Search  Terminal  Help

[root@Master ~]# ssh-keygen
Generating public/private rsa key pair.
Enter file in which to save the key (/root/.ssh/id_rsa):
Created directory '/root/.ssh'.
Enter passphrase (empty for no passphrase):
Enter same passphrase again:
Your identification has been saved in /root/.ssh/id_rsa.
Your public key has been saved in /root/.ssh/id_rsa.pub.
The key fingerprint is:
c2:92:4b:e4:b0:6f:ad:75:f1:a1:de:e0:40:30:6c:ed root@Master
The key's randomart image is:
+--[ RSA 2048]----+
|                 |
|   . .           |
|  . * .          |
|   * *           |
|  . = E S .      |
|   o = . + .     |
|    + + + .      |
|   . o = o       |
|    .   o .      |
+-----------------+
[root@Master ~]# 
```

Figure B-3. *Using ssh-keygen to generate a key pair for remote access*

The public key can be copied to appropriate hosts and appended to the existing authorized_keys file in $HOME/.ssh directory. To use the private key file to connect to a host, use the syntax:

```
ssh -i ~/.ssh/id_rsa root@Master
```

Here, root is the user and Master is the server to which you are trying to connect.

In case you have multiple hosts and you want to organize the process of connecting to them, you can create host entries in a file called config in directory $HOME/.ssh. The entries are created using the following format:

```
Host Master
User root
HostName Master
IdentityFile ~/.ssh/id_rsa
```

Then, you can simply connect as:

```
ssh -f -N Master
```

■ ■ ■

Setting Up a KeyStore and TrustStore for HTTP Encryption

A *KeyStore* is a database or repository of keys and certificates that are used for a variety of purposes, including authentication, encryption, or data integrity. In general, a *KeyStore* contains information of two types: key entries and trusted certificates.

I have already discussed how to configure your Hadoop cluster with network encryption in Chapter 4's "Encrypting HTTP Communication" section. As a part of that set up, you need to create HTTPS certificates and KeyStores.

Create HTTPS Certificates and KeyStore/TrustStore Files

To create HTTPS certificates and KeyStores, you need to perform the following steps:

1. For each host, create a directory for storing the KeyStore and TrustStore at $KEYLOC (you can substitute the directory name of your liking).

2. For each host, create a key pair and a separate KeyStore. If your operating system command prompt is $, you have set the $KEYLOC directory parameter, and assuming an example of a two-node cluster with hosts pract_hdp_sec and pract_hdp_sec2, the necessary code would look like the following:

```
$ cd $KEYLOC

$ keytool -genkey -alias pract_hdp_sec -keyalg RSA -keysize 1024 –dname "CN=pract_hdp_sec,OU=IT,
O=Ipsos,L=Chicago,ST=IL,C=us" -keypass 12345678    -keystore phsKeyStore1 -storepass 87654321

$ keytool -genkey -alias pract_hdp_sec2 -keyalg RSA -keysize 1024 -dname "CN=pract_hdp_sec2,OU=IT,
O=Ipsos,L=Chicago,ST=IL,C=us" -keypass 56781234    -keystore phsKeyStore2 –storepass 43218765
```

This code generates two key pairs (a public key and associated private key for each) and single-element certificate chain, stored as entry pract_hdp_sec in KeyStore phsKeyStore1 and entry pract_hdp_sec2 in KeyStore phsKeyStore2, respectively. Notice the use of the RSA algorithm for public key encryption and the key length of 1024.

3. For each host, export the certificate's public key to a separate certificate file:

```
$cd $SKEYLOC;
$keytool -export -alias pract_hdp_sec -keystore phsKeyStore1 -rfc -file pract_hdp_sec_cert
-storepass 87654321
$keytool -export -alias pract_hdp_sec2 -keystore phsKeyStore2 -rfc -file pract_hdp_sec2_cert
-storepass 43218765
```

4. For all the hosts, import the certificates into TrustStore file:

```
$cd $SKEYLOC;
$keytool -import -noprompt -alias pract_hdp_sec -file pract_hdp_sec_cert -keystore phsTrustStore1
-storepass 4324324
$keytool -import -noprompt -alias pract_hdp_sec2 -file pract_hdp_sec2_cert -keystore phsTrustStore1
-storepass 4324324
```

Note that the TrustStore file is newly created in case it doesn't exist.

5. Copy the KeyStore and TrustStore files to the corresponding nodes:

```
$scp phsKeyStore1 phsTrustStore1 root@pract_hdp_sec:/etc/hadoop/conf/
$scp phsKeyStore2 phsTrustStore2 root@pract_hdp_sec2:/etc/hadoop/conf/
```

6. Validate the common TrustStore file:

```
$keytool -list -v -keystore phsTrustStore1 -storepass 4324324
```

Adjust Permissions for KeyStore/TrustStore Files

The Keystore files need to have read permissions for owner and group only, and the group should be set to hadoop. The Truststore files should have read permissions for every one (owner, group, and others). The following commands set this up:

```
$ssh root@pract_hdp_sec "cd /etc/hadoop/conf;chgrp hadoop phsKeyStore1;
chmod 0440 phsKeyStore1;chmod 0444 phsTrustStore1

$ssh root@pract_hdp_sec2 "cd /etc/hadoop/conf;chgrp hadoop phsKeyStore2;
chmod 0440 phsKeyStore2;chmod 0444 phsTrustStore2
```

If need be, you can generate public key certificates to install in your browser. This completes the setup of a KeyStore and TrustStore for HTTP encryption.

APPENDIX D

■ ■ ■

Hadoop Metrics and Their Relevance to Security

In Chapter 7's "Hadoop Metrics" section, you reviewed what Hadoop metrics are, how you can apply filters to metrics, and how you can direct them to a file or monitoring software such as Ganglia. As you will soon learn, you can use these metrics for security, as well.

As you will remember, you can use Hadoop metrics to set alerts to capture sudden changes in system resources. In addition, you can set up your Hadoop cluster to monitor NameNode resources and generate alerts when any specified resources deviate from desired parameters. For example, I will show you how to generate alerts when deviation for the following resources exceed the monthly average by 50% or more:

```
FilesCreated
FilesDeleted
Transactions_avg_time
GcCount
GcTimeMillis
LogFatal
MemHeapUsedM
ThreadsWaiting
```

First, I direct output of the NameNode metrics to a file. To do so, I add the following lines to the file hadoop-metrics2.properties in the directory $HADOOP_INSTALL/hadoop/conf:

```
*.sink.tfile.class=org.apache.hadoop.metrics2.sink.FileSink
namenode.sink.tfile.filename = namenode-metrics.log
```

Next, I set filters to include only the necessary metrics:

```
*.source.filter.class=org.apache.hadoop.metrics2.filter.GlobFilter
*.record.filter.class=${*.source.filter.class}
*.metric.filter.class=${*.source.filter.class}
namenode.sink.file.metric.filter.include=FilesCreated
namenode.sink.file.metric.filter.include=FilesDeleted
namenode.sink.file.metric.filter.include=Transactions_avg_time
namenode.sink.file.metric.filter.include=GcCount
namenode.sink.file.metric.filter.include=GcTimeMillis
namenode.sink.file.metric.filter.include=LogFatal
namenode.sink.file.metric.filter.include=MemHeapUsedM
namenode.sink.file.metric.filter.include=ThreadsWaiting
```

My filtered list of metrics is now being written to the output file `namenode-metrics.log`.

Next, I develop a script to load this file daily to HDFS and add it to a Hive table as a new partition. I then recompute the 30-day average, taking into account the new values as well, and compare the average values with the newly loaded daily values.

If the deviation is more than 50% for any of these values, I can send a message to my Hadoop system administrator with the name of the node and the metric that deviated. The system administrator can then check appropriate logs to determine if there are any security breaches. For example, if the `ThreadsWaiting` metric is deviating more than 50%, then the system administrator will need to check the audit logs to see who was accessing the cluster and who was executing jobs at that time, and then check relevant jobs as indicated by the audit logs. For example, a suspicious job may require a check of the JobTracker and appropriate TaskTracker logs.

Alternately, you can direct the outputs of these jobs to Ganglia and then use Nagios to generate alerts if any of the metric values deviate.

Tables D-1 through D-4 list some commonly used Hadoop metrics. The JVM and RPC context metrics are listed first, because they are generated by all Hadoop daemons.

Table D-1. *JVM and RPC Context Metrics*

Metric Group	Metric Name	Description
JVM	GcCount	Number of garbage collections of the enterprise console JVM
	GcTimeMillis	Calculates the total time all garbage collections have taken in milliseconds
	LogError	Number of log lines with Log4j level ERROR
	LogFatal	Number of log lines with Log4j level FATAL
	LogWarn	Number of log lines with Log4j level WARN
	LogInfo	Number of log lines with Log4j level INFO
	MemHeapCommittedM	Calculates the heap memory committed by the enterprise console JVM
	MemHeapUsedM	Calculates the heap memory committed by the enterprise console JVM
	ThreadsBlocked	Number of threads in a BLOCKED state, which means they are waiting for a lock
	ThreadsWaiting	Number of threads in a WAITING state, which means they are waiting for another thread to perform an action
	ThreadsRunnable	Number of threads in a RUNNABLE state that are executing in the JVM but may be waiting for system resources like CPU
	ThreadsTerminated	Number of threads in a TERMINATED state, which means they finished executing. This value should be around zero since the metric only collects information over live threads.
	ThreadsNew	Number of threads in a NEW state, which means they have not been started

(continued)

Table D-1. (*continued*)

Metric Group	Metric Name	Description
RPC	ReceivedBytes	Number of RPC received bytes
	SentBytes	Number of RPC sent bytes
	RpcProcessingTimeAvgTime	Average time for processing RPC requests
	RpcProcessingTimeNumOps	Number of processed RPC requests
	RpcQueueTimeAvgTime	Average time spent by an RPC request in the queue
	RpcQueueTimeNumOps	Number of RPC requests that were queued
	RpcAuthorizationSuccesses	Number of successful RPC authorization calls
	RpcAuthorizationFailures	Number of failed RPC authorization calls
	RpcAuthenticationSuccesses	Number of successful RPC authentication calls
	RpcAuthenticationFailures	Number of failed RPC authentication calls

Table D-2. *NameNode and DataNode Metrics*

Metric Group	Metric Name	Description
Hadoop.HDFS.NameNode	AddBlockOps	Number of add block operations for a cluster
	CapacityRemaining	Total capacity remaining in HDFS
	CapacityTotal	Total capacity remaining in HDFS and other distributed file systems
	CapacityUsed	Total capacity used in HDFS
	CreateFileOps	Number of create file operations for a cluster
	DeadNodes	Number of dead nodes that exist in a cluster
	DecomNodes	Number of decommissioned nodes that exist in a cluster
	DeleteFileOps	Number of "delete" file operations occurring in HDFS
	FSState	State of the NameNode, which can be in safe mode or operational mode
	FileInfoOps	Number of file access operations occurring in the cluster
	FilesAppended	Number of files appended in a cluster
	FilesCreated	Number of files created in a cluster
	FilesDeleted	Number of files deleted in a cluster
	FilesInGetListingOps	Number of get listing operations occurring in a cluster
	FilesRenamed	Number of files renamed in a cluster
	LiveNodes	Number of live nodes in a cluster
	NonDfsUsedSpace	Calculates the non-HDFS space used in the cluster
	PercentRemaining	Percentage of remaining HDFS capacity

(*continued*)

Table D-2. (*continued*)

Metric Group	Metric Name	Description
	PercentUsed	Percentage of used HDFS capacity
	Safemode	Calculates the safe mode state: 1 indicates safe mode is on; 0 indicates safe mode is off
	SafemodeTime	Displays the time spent by NameNode in safe mode
	Syncs_avg_time	Average time for the sync operation
	Syncs_num_ops	Number of sync operations
	TotalBlocks	Total number of blocks in a cluster
	TotalFiles	Total number of files in a cluster
	Transactions_avg_time	Average time for a transaction
	Transactions_num_ops	Number of transaction operations
	UpgradeFinalized	Indicates if the upgrade is finalized as true or false
	addBlock_avg_time	Average time to create a new block in a cluster
	addBlock_num_ops	Number of operations to add data blocks in a cluster
	blockReceived_avg_time	Average time to receive a block operation
	blockReceived_num_ops	Number of block received operations
	blockReport_num_ops	Number of block report operations
	blockReport_avg_time	Average time for block report operation
	TimeSinceLastCheckpoint	Calculates the amount of time since the last checkpoint
Hadoop.HDFS.DataNode	BlocksRead	Number of times that a block is read from the hard disk, including copying a block
	BlocksRemoved	Number of removed or invalidated blocks on the DataNode
	BlocksReplicated	Number of blocks transferred or replicated from one DataNode to another
	BlocksVerified	Number of block verifications, including successful or failed attempts
	BlocksWritten	Number of blocks written to disk
	BytesRead	Number of bytes read when reading and copying a block
	BytesWritten	Number of bytes written to disk in response to a received block
	HeartbeatsAvgTime	Average time to send a heartbeat from DataNode to NameNode
	BlocksRemoved	Number of removed or invalidated blocks on the DataNode
	BlocksReplicated	Number of blocks transferred or replicated from one DataNode to another
	HeartbeatsNumOps	Number of heartbeat operations occurring in a cluster

Table D-3. *MapReduce Metrics Generated by JobTracker*

Metric Group	Metric Name	Description
Hadoop.Mapreduce.Jobtracker	blacklisted_maps	Number of blacklisted map slots in each TaskTracker
	Heartbeats	Total Number of JobTracker heartbeats
	blacklisted_reduces	Number of blacklisted reduce slots in each TaskTracker
	callQueueLen	Calculates the RPC call queue length
	HeartbeatAvgTime	Average time for a heartbeat
	jobs_completed	Number of completed job
	jobs_failed	Number of failed jobs
	jobs_killed	Number of killed jobs
	jobs_running	Number of running jobs
	jobs_submitted	Number of submitted jobs
	maps_completed	Number of completed maps
	maps_failed	Number of failed maps
	maps_killed	Number of killed maps
	maps_launched	Number of launched maps
	memNonHeapCommittedM	Non-heap committed memory (MB)
	memNonHeapUsedM	Non-heap used memory (MB)
	occupied_map_slots	Number of occupied map slots
	map_slots	Number of map slots
	occupied_reduce_slots	Number of occupied reduce slots
	reduce_slots	Number of reduce slots
	reduces_completed	Number of reducers completed
	reduces_failed	Number of failed reducers
	reduces_killed	Number of killed reduces
	reduces_launched	Number of launched reducers
	reserved_map_slots	Number of reserved map slots
	reserved_reduce_slots	Number of reserved reduce slots
	running_0	Number of running jobs
	running_1440	Number of jobs running for more than 24 hours
	running_300	Number of jobs running for more than five hours
	running_60	Number of jobs running for more than one hour
	running_maps	Number of running maps

(*continued*)

Table D-3. (*continued*)

Metric Group	Metric Name	Description
	running_reduces	Number of running reduces
	Trackers	Number of TaskTrackers
	trackers_blacklisted	Number of blacklisted TaskTrackers
	trackers_decommissioned	Number of decommissioned TaskTrackers
	trackers_graylisted	Number of gray-listed TaskTrackers
	waiting_reduces	Number of waiting reduces
	waiting_maps	Number of waiting maps

Table D-4. *HBase Metrics*

Metric Group	Metric Name	Description
hbase.master	MemHeapUsedM	Heap memory used in MB
	MemHeapCommittedM	Heap memory committed in MB
	averageLoad	Average number of regions served by each region server
	numDeadRegionServers	Number of dead region servers
	numRegionServers	Number of online region servers
	ritCount	Number of regions in transition
	ritCountOverThreshold	Number of regions in transition that exceed the threshold as defined by the property rit.metrics.threshold.time
	clusterRequests	Total number of requests from all region servers to a cluster
	HlogSplitTime_mean	Average time to split the total size of a write-ahead log file
	HlogSplitTime_min	Minimum time to split the total size of a write-ahead log file
	HlogSplitTime_max	Maximum time to split the write-ahead log file after a restart
	HlogSplitTime_num_ops	Time to split write-ahead log files
	HlogSplitSize_mean	Average time to split the total size of an Hlog file
	HlogSplitSize_min	Minimum time to split the total size of an Hlog file
	HlogSplitSize_max	Maximum time to split the total size of an Hlog file
	HlogSplitSize_num_ops	Size of write-ahead log files that were split
hbase.regionserver	appendCount	Number of WAL appends
	blockCacheCount	Number of StoreFiles cached in the block cache
	blockCacheEvictionCount	Total Number of blocks that have been evicted from the block cache
	blockCacheFreeSize	Number of bytes that are free in the block cache

(*continued*)

Table D-4. (*continued*)

Metric Group	Metric Name	Description
	blockCacheExpressHitPercent	Calculates the block cache hit percent for requests where caching was turned on
	blockCacheHitCount	Total number of block cache hits for requests, regardless of caching setting
	blockCountHitPercent	Block cache hit percent for all requests regardless of the caching setting
	blockCacheMissCount	Total Number of block cache misses for requests, regardless of caching setting
	blockCacheSize	Number of bytes used by cached blocks
	compactionQueueLength	Number of HRegions on the CompactionQueue. These regions call compact on all stores, and then find out if a compaction is needed along with the type of compaction.
	MemMaxM	Calculates the total heap memory used in MB
	MemHeapUsedM	Calculates the heap memory used in MB
	MemHeapCommittedM	Calculates the heap memory committed in MB
	GcCount	Number of total garbage collections
	updatesBlockedTime	Number of memstore updates that have been blocked so that memstore can be flushed
	memstoreSize	Calculates the size of all memstores in all regions in MB
	readRequestCount	Number of region server read requests
	regionCount	Number of online regions served by a region server
	slowAppendCount	Number of appends that took more than 1000 ms to complete
	slowGetCount	Number of gets that took more than 1000 ms to complete
	slowPutCount	Number of puts that took more than 1000 ms to complete
	slowIncrementCount	Number of increments that took more than 1000 ms to complete
	slowDeleteCount	Number of deletes that took more than 1000 ms to complete
	storeFileIndexSize	Calculates the size of all StoreFile indexes in MB. These are not necessarily in memory because they are stored in the block cache as well and might have been evicted.
	storeFileCount	Number of StoreFiles in all stores and regions
	storeCount	Number of stores in all Regions
	staticBloomSize	Calculates the total size of all bloom filters, which are not necessarily loaded in memory
	writeRequestCount	Number of write requests to a region server
	staticIndexSize	Calculates the total static index size for all region server entities

Index

Get the eBook for only $10!

Now you can take the weightless companion with you anywhere, anytime. Your purchase of this book entitles you to 3 electronic versions for only $10.

This Apress title will prove so indispensible that you'll want to carry it with you everywhere, which is why we are offering the eBook in **3 formats** for only $10 if you have already purchased the print book.

Convenient and fully searchable, the PDF version enables you to easily find and copy code—or perform examples by quickly toggling between instructions and applications. The MOBI format is ideal for your Kindle, while the ePUB can be utilized on a variety of mobile devices.

Go to www.apress.com/promo/tendollars to purchase your companion eBook.

Apress®
THE EXPERT'S VOICE™